Political Agency and the Medicalisation of Negative Emotions

I0061513

Series Editors: Alex Thomson, Benjamin Arditi, Andrew Schaap
International Advisory Editors: Michael Dillon, Michael J. Shapiro, Jeremy Valentine

Offering new perspectives on contemporary Political Theory, books in this series 'take on' the political in accordance with the ambivalent colloquial sense of the phrase – as both an acceptance and a challenge. They interrogate received accounts of the relationship between political thought and political practice, criticise and engage with the contemporary political imagination, and reflect on the ongoing transformations of politics. Concise and polemical, the texts are oriented towards critique, developments in Continental thought, and the crossing of disciplinary borders.

https://edinburghuniversitypress.com/series-taking-on-the-political.html

Political Agency and the Medicalisation of Negative Emotions

Dan Degerman

EDINBURGH
University Press

Edinburgh University Press is one of the leading university presses in the UK. We publish academic books and journals in our selected subject areas across the humanities and social sciences, combining cutting-edge scholarship with high editorial and production values to produce academic works of lasting importance. For more information visit our website: edinburghuniversitypress.com

© Dan Degerman, 2022

Edinburgh University Press Ltd
The Tun – Holyrood Road
12(2f) Jackson's Entry
Edinburgh EH8 8PJ

First published in hardback by Edinburgh University Press 2022

Typeset in 11/13 Sabon by
IDSUK (DataConnection) Ltd, and
printed and bound by CPI Group (UK) Ltd,
Croydon, CR0 4YY

A CIP record for this book is available from the British Library

ISBN 978 1 3995 0439 3 (hardback)
ISBN 978 1 3995 0440 9 (paperback)
ISBN 978 1 3995 0441 6 (webready PDF)
ISBN 978 1 3995 0442 3 (epub)

The right of Dan Degerman to be identified as the author of this work has been asserted in accordance with the Copyright, Designs and Patents Act 1988, and the Copyright and Related Rights Regulations 2003 (SI No. 2498).

Contents

Acknowledgements

This book started as a Wellcome Trust-funded PhD project in philosophy (108539/Z/15/Z) completed at Lancaster University under the supervision of Rachel Cooper and Garrath Williams in 2019. I am immensely grateful for their advice, helpful guidance and support. My PhD examiners, Keith Breen and Christopher MacLeod, also deserve a big thanks. The dissertation evolved into a book with the invaluable help and hard work of Andrew Schaap, the series co-editor of *Taking on the Political* at Edinburgh University Press, as well as the efforts of staff and reviewers of the Press. I extensively revised the manuscript during my Leverhulme Early Career Fellowship (ECF-2020-583), which I began in 2020 at the University of Bristol. My mentor Havi Carel's encouragement ensured this happened despite the COVID-19 pandemic raging at the time. I am also very grateful to Mohammed Rashed and Stacy Clifford Simplican, who provided feedback on an earlier version of this book as part of a 2021 manuscript roundtable sponsored by CRITIQUE and the Association for Political Thought. Others have generously taken the time to read and comment on parts of the book as well. They include Jonathan Beazer, Kevin Blackwell, Todd Cain, Sam Fellowes, Ari-Elmeri Hyvönen, Matthew Johnson, Hane Maung, Moujan Mirdamadi, Faye Tucker and Anne-Katrin Weber. Aristea Grivakou deserves a special thanks for using her rare expertise in politics, emotions and art to find the perfect cover art for this book.

This book draws on some of my recently published articles. Parts of Chapter 1 are based on Degerman (2019a) and Degerman (2019b). Chapter 3 and Chapter 6 are expanded and revised versions of Degerman (2019b) and Degerman (2020c) respectively. Parts of the conclusion are adapted from Degerman (2020b). I greatly appreciate the feedback provided by the editors and reviewers for the journals in which these articles appeared. Due thanks as well are participants and organisers at the conferences and workshops where I have presented my work, including several Joint Annual Conferences of the Society for European Philosophy and the Forum for European Philosophy, the 'Unpacking Political Agency' conference at San Raffaele University, the Philosophy of Psychiatry Work in Progress Workshop at Lancaster University, and the 'Ethics of Disordering' workshop at Keele University.

The Department of Philosophy at the University of Bristol and the Department of Philosophy, Politics and Religion at Lancaster University have afforded me with supportive environments and exceptional colleagues. I also want to recognise the mentors who have shaped me professionally and personally. I am particularly grateful to James 'G' Giordano. He showed me how to be a philosopher – and how to drink whiskey. Thanks also to Michael Soupios, Roger Goldstein and Abby Dress for moulding a young Swedish student in the United States into a writer and a thinker.

Words cannot express the gratitude I feel towards my friends for putting up with endless talk about Hannah Arendt, emotions and medicalisation, reading draft upon draft, and providing me with oases during the storms of the past few years. I especially want to thank Fredrik Hammarbäck, Jack Simpson, Matthew Winder, James 'Alby' Earley, Rudolph Struck and Paul Jones. Each, in their own way, helped me to complete what sometimes seemed an impossible task. Last, but certainly not least, I want to thank my parents and siblings, and, of course, Nagymama, for their love and support, and for teaching me – at their own peril – to question everything.

This book has been completed with the support of a Leverhulme Trust Early Career Fellowship (ECF-2020-583) and a Wellcome Trust Society and Ethics Studentship (ref.: 108539/Z/15/Z).

Introduction:
The Politics of Medicalisation

Imagine you are on the losing side of a referendum that will profoundly shape the future of your country. You have been deeply invested in the campaign leading up to the vote, getting angry about the inaccurate claims of the opposing side and afraid of what a loss would mean. When you learn of the loss, an overwhelming sense of grief strikes you. Over the next few weeks, you keep thinking about how this could have happened, what it means, what more you could have done, and what you should do now. Though you mostly carry on with life as usual, you get into a few heated arguments, some at work. One day, your boss tells you your attitude has been poor lately. When you explain yourself, they say that politics and work are separate, pointing out that your colleagues have no problem leaving politics at the office door. You mention the conversation to your partner, who says that you have been different lately and that it is not healthy to think so much about the referendum. Maybe they are right, you think. Maybe there is something wrong with you. A little googling confirms your worries. An article on a mental health charity website warns that your feelings might be early symptoms of mental disorder. Getting help through the public healthcare system would take months, but you have some money to spare, so you book a therapist. In your first meeting, the therapist explains that what you are feeling actually is not about the outcome of the referendum and no amount of getting out on the street, writing your MP or community organizing will help to address it. Your feelings are about you and you alone. You are not immediately convinced, but do not dismiss it. The therapist is the expert, after all; they know what they are talking about. You start going to weekly therapy sessions. And, sometime later, you realise that the grief is gone, and you decide that the therapist was right. After all, you cannot really do much about the referendum result. It is what it is. You just had to accept it, let it go and move on with your life.

Has this ever happened to you? Probably not. Based on this story alone, I doubt you are ready to buy whatever I am looking to sell you. But something you probably have experienced is the suspicion that some emotion you are experiencing could be a symptom of mental disorder. Indeed, evidence suggests that we, as a society, are increasingly understanding negative emotions as mental health problems. The UK Adult Psychiatric Morbidity Survey found that, between 1993 and 2014, the proportion of people judged to have recently experienced symptoms of depression had increased by more than 70 per cent and symptoms of anxiety by about a third (McManus et al. 2016). Over roughly the same period, prescriptions for antidepressants rose dramatically too, from 61 prescriptions per 1,000 people in 1995 to 129.9 in 2011 (Mars et al. 2017). Also remarkable is the number of people who self-report experiences of mental disorder. A recent survey found that two in five people said they 'had experienced depression' and 65 per cent said they had experienced some mental disorder (Mental Health Foundation 2017). One explanation of these statistics is that the prevalence of mental disorder is increasing because more people are getting sick than before. Another explanation, propagated by a large and growing body of critical literature, is that people have come to understand an increasing range of negative emotions – like certain forms of sadness, fear and anger – as medical problems, or, more specifically, as symptoms of mental disorder. Differently put, negative emotions are being medicalised.

Our understanding of what negative emotions can count towards a diagnosis of mental disorder has changed. Consider the recent history of the *Diagnostic and Statistical Manual of Mental Disorders* (DSM), sometimes called 'the bible of psychiatry'. The DSM lists and provides diagnostic criteria for recognised mental disorders used in mental health care in the United States and in research across the world. Along with the World Health Organisation's *International Classification of Diseases* (ICD), the DSM is the dominant classification of mental disorders internationally (Tyrer 2014).[1] Though the DSM has been around since 1952, the third edition of the manual, published in 1980, broke drastically from the previous two editions. *DSM-III* introduced a symptom-orientated diagnostic approach to mental disorder, which is still used today in the latest editions of the DSM and the ICD. So, if we compare diagnoses in *DSM-5* to their rough equivalents in *DSM-I*, radical differences are in no short supply. However, we need not go for such low-hanging fruit for evidence of the medicalisation of negative emotions. Even between the publication of *DSM-III* and the publication of the latest of edition, *DSM-5*, in 2013, the diagnostic criteria for some disorders have changed considerably. Take the mental disorder that we colloquially call depression, or what in *DSM-III* corresponded to Major Depression. To be diagnosed with this disorder, an individual had to show five or more of the following symptoms: 'depressed mood'; 'significant weight gain or loss, or change in appetite'; 'observable psychomotor agitation or retardation'; 'loss of interest or pleasure in activities'; 'loss of energy or fatigue'; 'feelings of worthlessness, or excessive or inappropriate guilt'; 'diminished ability to think or concentrate or indecisiveness'; and 'recurrent thoughts of death, suicidal ideation or suicide attempt'. In addition to depressed mood, at least four of the other criteria needed to be present most days over a two-week period. Unless symptoms were attributable to bereavement or better described by another diagnosis, a person presenting could be diagnosed with Major Depression (APA 1980). Critics argue that the *DSM-III* definition of depression was already general enough to encompass many forms of sadness that had until then been considered reasonable responses to adverse events, something that is reflected in the sharp increase in the prevalence of depression after 1980 (Horwitz and Wakefield 2007; Horwitz 2015). The next edition went further still. DSM-IV renamed Major Depression to Major Depressive Disorder (MDD) and modified associated criteria. In the revised diagnosis, loss of interest could substitute for depressed mood as the compulsory criterion along with any four of the other symptoms. It also limited the bereavement exclusion to two months, after which symptoms apparently triggered by the loss of a spouse or family member could count towards a diagnosis of MDD (APA 1994). With the 2013 publication of *DSM-5*, the latest edition of the handbook, the bereavement exclusion was pared back to a footnote (APA 2013).[2] Hence, what some perceived as an overly inclusive diagnosis to begin with has continued to expand, making it possible to diagnose a growing range of sadness as mental disorder.

Why does this matter? Thinking about an experience as a medical disease has numerous implications. Some are beneficial. Having a disease entitles a person to understanding and support from their peers, time off from work to recover, and – in most liberal democracies – to free healthcare. Mental disorder specifically can also grant a person accused of a crime leniency in the eyes of the law, because they are deemed to have been unable to act as a normal, reasonable person. Relatedly, but more negatively, having one's experiences or behaviour judged as symptoms of mental disorder can lead to forced care. The laws regulating this in England and Wales are the Mental Health Acts 1983 and 2007 and the Mental Capacity Act 2005.[3] They empower authorities, subject to the judgement of certified mental health professionals, to detain and impose care on anyone who has been deemed a danger to themselves or others and is unwilling or unable to consent. The practice of assigning diminished legal responsibility to and permitting the forced commitment of some individuals with mental disorder highlights a common and deep-seated feature of our understanding of mental disorder and its symptoms: they are signs that the afflicted person lacks reason in an instance or in general. A diagnosis of mental disorder can undermine a person's credibility across a range of social contexts. The presumption seems to be that diseased thoughts and experiences are irrational and that words spoken or actions taken on their basis cannot be judged the way we would judge a normal person's words or actions, for example, morally, legally or politically. Instead, they must be understood and treated medically.

The ongoing transformation of negative emotions into symptoms of mental disorder is concerning from a political perspective. Recent philosophical, historical and psychological research has underlined the importance of emotion in political life. Indeed, many of us probably recognise intuitively that negative emotions are central drivers of political action. When we decide to act politically, it is often because we perceive some wrong in the world that evokes negative emotions in us. The more powerful these emotions are, the more likely we are to act on them. Medicalisation potentially threatens our ability to use negative emotions this way. Labelling some emotion as a mental disorder signals to the subject and others that it is a medical rather than a political problem. The medicalisation of negative emotions may thereby foreclose the possibility of comprehending this experience as an understandable reaction to something that could – and perhaps should – be understood and addressed politically. It is especially concerning since historically disadvantaged groups like women, minorities and working-class people, who are more likely to suffer from structural injustices, also appear more likely to receive diagnoses of and pharmaceutical treatments for mental disorder. Consequently, where disadvantaged and suffering people may previously have found the impetus and resources for political action against injustice, they may now find reason to visit the doctor or take a pill. In other words, the medicalisation of negative emotions threatens to depoliticise critical political issues and to disempower citizens of liberal democracies, rendering it more challenging to identify and address injustices. It is therefore vital to ask: how does the medicalisation of negative emotions impact political agency?

This book explores this question through case studies of political action by people whose emotional and mental fitness for public life has been called into question. I argue that the medicalisation of negative emotions profoundly affects the factors that empower us to channel our emotions into political action. Medicalisation can turn concepts that previously granted you credibility into marks of ignorance, exclude you from spaces in which you had a voice, open you up to intervention from laws that previously protected you, and lead friends and family to urge you to change yourself rather than the world. Crucially, however, medicalisation can sometimes also have the opposite effect. That is, it can help us to access the resources we need to channel negative emotions into political action.

Political Abuses of Psychiatry

Psychiatric diagnoses have, in some notorious instances, been used systematically to silence political dissent. While some would argue that 'all madmen are political dissidents' (Cooper 1980: 23) and claim that psychiatry is intrinsically oppressive, I am thinking here specifically of the silencing of people who more obviously speak out and against a political order or regime. Dissidents in the Soviet Union, for instance, were notoriously diagnosed with 'sluggish schizophrenia', a diagnosis that involved symptoms like 'reform delusions', 'struggle for the truth' and 'perseverance' (Bloch 1989; cited in van Voren and Keukens 2015). Political abuses of psychiatry in the USSR were potent fuel for the anti-psychiatry movement in the 1960s and 1970s. As early as 1965, the libertarian anti-psychiatrist Thomas Szasz ([1965] 1984: 233–8) used it as part of his indictment of the profession in the West. According to him, it was simply the latest and most obvious instance of 'the psychiatric suppression of dissent', which is an 'integral part of all Western societies'. Indeed, apparently, unbeknownst to Szasz, the Soviet abuse of the schizophrenia diagnosis against dissident had its parallels in the United States of the 1960s, where some psychiatrists claimed that the focus on civil rights and Black nationalism was causing 'protest psychosis' among some Black people, a specific form of schizophrenia that involved symptoms such as 'a repudiation of "white civilization"' (Metzl 2009: 100).

The psychiatric profession took concerns about political abuses of psychiatry seriously. In the following decades, the two main diagnostic handbooks of psychiatry – the DSM and the ICD, Chapter V – along with international professional and legal frameworks were revised to safeguard against such abuses (Busfield 2011: 27–8; Perlin 2006; van Voren and Keukens 2015). Since its fourth edition, the DSM has stated that political behaviour should not be regarded as a mental disorder, although it is a qualified exclusion (APA 1994: xxii).[4] For example, the *DSM-5* (APA 2013: 20) definition of mental disorder stipulates: 'Socially deviant behavior (e.g. political, religious, or sexual) and conflicts are not mental disorders unless the deviance or conflict results from a dysfunction in the individual.' Several diagnoses also expressly exclude politically motivated actions.

That the DSM explicitly calls on psychiatrists to disregard political actions in diagnostic practice is significant. Such provisions offer some protection against state abuses of psychiatry and, presumably, a check on psychiatrists, who might think twice if they are asked to assess people involved in protests or other political actions. But despite the efforts of the DSM's authors to deal with this complex issue, the results do not safeguard against the medicalisation of dissent today. Even if psychiatrists and other mental health professionals managed to avoid diagnosing anyone who could motivate their behaviour politically – and it is far from clear that this is desirable, since severely distressed people who could benefit from diagnosis and healthcare may justify their actions in political terms (see Grossman-Kahn 2021) – it would not stop others from using psychiatric concepts and aetiologies to medicalise the words and actions of 'deviants', whether evidently political or not. Moreover, the qualification that political behaviour can be classified as mental disorder if the behaviour can be attributed to an individual dysfunction does water down the protection. With a few exceptions, there are no separate tests to determine whether the symptoms of mental disorder are caused by an individual dysfunction. Indeed, in clinical practice, the presence of symptoms is what is taken to indicate the presence of individual dysfunction.[5] There are, thus, still important reasons to worry about political abuses of psychiatry and the medicalisation of emotions.

Foucault, Psychiatry and Political Agency

The disempowering effects of psychiatry need not be so blatant as in the USSR or other historical instances where individuals or groups have been diagnosed with a mental disorder because of their political affiliations, beliefs or actions. Even if psychiatry is not wielded by a totalitarian regime, repressive state officials, or, for that matter, by politicians and pundits seeking to delegitimise their opponents, it can profoundly impact the political agency of a polity's citizens. Psychiatric diagnoses, treatments, clinics and hospitals, psychiatrists and mental health experts are all factors that shape our understanding of what and who is normal or abnormal, healthy or sick, safe or dangerous, desirable or undesirable, and, potentially, political or apolitical. These factors form part of a web of relationships that influences how we judge and act on ourselves and others, from family and friends to celebrities and strangers.

The pre-eminent figure in the study of the subtler, regulative impact of psychiatry is of course Michel Foucault. His *Madness and Civilization* (1988) has been tremendously influential.[6] Notwithstanding well-grounded challenges to its historical accuracy (e.g., Scull 1992), the book was a path-breaking study in the marginalisation of individuals deemed insane and the factors that facilitated this. In subsequent work, Foucault developed his ideas about the subtle ways in which psychiatry and other disciplines shape individuals and collectives, sometimes with insidious effects. Through studies of prisons (1977) and hospitals (2003a), he explored how scientific truths, technologies and spaces produce particular kinds of power relations and individuals.

Foucault (2003b) famously distinguished between three forms of power: sovereign power, disciplinary power and biopower. The latter two are most relevant to us here. Disciplinary power takes the individual body as its object to get hold of the soul, placing it in a hierarchical relationship to specific experts and expertise to correct troublesome idiosyncrasies (243). The relationship between the psychiatrist and the insane within the asylum in the 1800s is a historical exemplar here (2006b). However, according to Foucault, psychiatry's disciplinary power extends beyond the asylum, penetrating families, communities and other institutions (85). These have long served as extensions of the 'psychiatric gaze', searching for and identifying the symptoms of madness or mental disorder in individuals and urging them to seek expert treatment (124). By contrast, biopower takes the population – a statistically defined collective body – as its object to regularise it (2003: 248). By measuring and analysing the characteristics of the population, biopower creates norms that can be used to split recalcitrant parts into more predictable and manageable pieces (255), which can then be subjected to normalising measures. Along these lines, psychiatry has enabled the creation of mentally disordered populations that are subject to the kinds of special laws, surveillance and attitudes I discussed above. Psychiatry can, in effect, function both as disciplinary power and biopower (252; see also Havis and Mosko 2019). Its norms and technologies both discipline individuals – for example, through diagnoses and treatments – and regularise populations – for example, through mental health norms, statistics and government policies.

Foucauldian critics of medicalisation have often focused on his claims about the coercive and constraining effects of power (e.g., Armstrong 1983; Taylor 2010; Wheatley 2005), despite Foucault's insistence that power can also be productive and enabling. Accordingly, these critics have often conceived medicine and psychiatry as handmaids of the neoliberal order, whose primary function is to produce 'docile bodies' (Lupton 1997) – that is, obedient and productive members of society (Foucault 1977: 138). While Foucault did not develop a concept of political agency, he once stated that an imperative of disciplinary power was to 'neutralize the effects of counter-power . . . which form a resistance to the power that wishes to dominate it: [for example,] agitations, revolts, spontaneous organizations, coalitions – anything that may establish horizontal conjunctions' (1977: 219; see also 2006a: 69). Notably, this notion of 'counter-power' gestures at something resembling the Arendtian idea of political agency that I develop and apply in this book. But, of course, one of Foucault's most significant contributions to political theory was his elaboration of the productive features of power, 'the fact that it doesn't only weigh on us as a force that says no' (2000: 120); it also says yes. A particular configuration of power relations can enable individuals to become certain types of people with abilities or disabilities they would not otherwise have had; it 'makes up people', to use Ian Hacking's (1986) phrase. With its specific relationships, spaces, technologies, policies and concepts, psychiatry also produces these kind of effects. What I shall consider in this book is how these effects impact one specific capacity, namely, political agency.

Foucault's theoretical and methodological insights have influenced the conception of this project. However, my direct engagement with him beyond this point will be limited for two reasons. The first is that many ambitious studies have already explored medicalisation and psychiatry from a Foucauldian perspective (see Lupton 1997). Most notable here is the work of Nikolas Rose (e.g., 1999a, 1999b, 2006, 2013, 2019), who has examined the political impact of psychiatry and other so-called 'psy-professions' in a series of remarkable studies. His work has yielded rich insights into how psychiatry functions within historical and contemporary structures of governance – 'the conduct of conduct' – and the kind of people it makes.

Yet Rose and other Foucauldian scholars have had little to say about how the development of psychiatry has impacted political agency. This is probably because Foucault himself seemingly does not leave much room for political agency (see Fraser 1981), which is my second reason for not focusing on his theory of power. Although Foucault's later works develop an idea of the individual's capacity to resist the effects of power, this idea of resistance seems, on the one hand, too negative and narrow a concept to be capable of explaining the productive effects of certain forms of political action (Allen 1999; Hyvönen 2016), and, on the other, too preoccupied with the individual to register significant obstacles to effective political action (Myers 2008; though cf. McNay 2009). So, to shine new light on the political impact of psychiatry, I assume a different theoretical perspective and focus, drawing upon Hannah Arendt's theory of political action.[7] This approach emphasises collective and public forms of political action over the individual, sometimes hidden, occasionally unintentional and frequently ingenious forms of resistance that come to the fore in Foucauldian scholarship (e.g., Leeb 2020). Some of these subtle 'power effects' shaping the political possibilities of individuals – which Foucault and his followers have so skilfully excavated – will not come into focus in this book. Some will be reconceptualised within the theoretical framework I outline in the first two chapters, but others will fall out of view. Nevertheless, I believe the strengths of my Arendtian framework outweigh its limitations. By bringing to the fore the capacity of individuals to not just resist, but to actively shape the world together, this approach enables a deeper and more politically grounded analysis of how political agency can be constrained by medicalisation and other processes shaping public life in the twenty-first century.

Medicalisation & Co.

A few definitions will be helpful at this point. Two concepts loom-
ing over the discussion so far are political agency and negative emotions. I will defer an extended discussion of these until Chapter 1,
but, very briefly, inspired by Arendt, I understand political agency as
the individual's capacity to act in concert with other people to shape
or respond to public issues, while I take a negative emotion to be a
kind of emotion that feels bad. In this section, however, I want to
unpack another key concept, namely, medicalisation.

Medicalisation names the 'process by which medical definitions
and practices are applied to behaviors, psychological phenomena,
and somatic experiences not previously within the conceptual or
therapeutic scope of medicine' (Davis 2010; see also Conrad 1992).
Medicalisation is a dynamic process; it does not always occur top-
down, although its critics have sometimes depicted it that way (e.g.,
Zola 1972). As Peter Conrad (2007: ch. 7), the pre-eminent scholar
of medicalisation, has emphasised in recent work, several 'engines'
drive medicalisation, including medical experts, pharmaceutical companies, grassroots groups and public figures. These sometimes work
in different directions – one pushing for medicalisation while another
is resisting it. Consequently, it can be difficult to say conclusively
whether a phenomenon has been medicalised. One strong indicator is
if a problem has been defined as a disorder or a symptom in a major
diagnostic manual, like the American Psychiatric Association's (APA)
DSM. Even that need not be conclusive, however. After all, that an
authoritative medical organisation has defined some experience as a
mental disorder does not mean everyone accepts or is even aware of
it. Few, for example, have been diagnosed with or heard of 'Caffeine-
Related Disorders', even though the category has been included in the
DSM since its fourth edition (APA 1994: 212; APA 2013: 503).

Throughout this book, I will use 'medicalisation' to describe
the transformation of negative emotions and apparently emotional
actions into psychiatric disorders. In so doing, I am eschewing related
terms, such as biomedicalisation, psychiatrisation and pathologisation. Each of these concepts has merits and demerits, which I can only
explore in passing here. Biomedicalisation, which has been proposed
as a term for describing contemporary forms of technoscientific and
individualistic medicalisation (Clarke et al. 2003), seems too broad,
cumbersome and negatively loaded (Busfield 2017; Conrad 2007: 14).
Psychiatrisation apparently differs from medicalisation only in that

it focuses on the transformation of non-medical problems into psychiatric problems (Rimke 2016). However, it is too narrow, partly because mental disorders are often diagnosed and treated by non-psychiatrist medical professionals, such as general practitioners. Lastly, pathologisation is closely connected to medicalisation. Some of the uses of psychiatric concepts examined in the forthcoming case studies could perhaps be described as instances of pathologisation (see Sholl 2017). It is apparently the preferred term among political theorists, who sometimes use it to name what I call medicalisation or medicalising attacks.[8] However, they tend to apply pathologisation to a much broader range of phenomena, ranging from dissenters being diagnosed with mental disorder to labour strikes being characterised as out of the ordinary to the machinations of diffuse anti-political forces.[9] The term is seldom defined, and when political theorists say that something has been pathologised they seem to mean simply that it has come to be regarded as very bad. The conceptual muddle surrounding pathologisation in political theory is further exacerbated by the use of pathology as a term of art within certain subfields. For example, critical theorists use the term 'social pathology' in political theory to describe structural issues unrelated to medicine (e.g., Honneth 1996). Yet even if pathologisation were defined and used more carefully, medicalisation would still be a preferable concept.[10] That is because medicalisation directs our attention to the fact that to describe some experience using a psychiatric concept is to imply that this experience fits into a web of specifically *medical* relationships, spaces, technologies, institutions and regulations. Finally, by using the term medicalisation to describe the process by which some negative emotions have been transformed into psychiatric diagnoses, I am highlighting that many people have come to believe that these negative emotions are problems demanding medical attention and treatment. I am also following an interdisciplinary convention – extending across philosophy, sociology and psychiatry, if not political theory – which will hopefully make my argument easier to follow.

The medicalisation concept does have its own problems. Much work on medicalisation has been explicitly or implicitly critical of the process it describes. This has led some to understand the concept itself as inherently critical and implying over-medicalisation (Rose 2007). However, Conrad (2007) and others have emphasised that medicalisation is not inherently detrimental but can have both socially positive and negative effects (see also Parens 2011). Its effects are, in other words, bivalent. For example, the medicalisation of certain aspects of human reproduction, which has enabled women to control their bodies in ways that have opened up new career paths and undermined gender stereotypes, seems positive – even politically empowering (Parens 2011). On the other hand, the medicalisation of homosexual love was negative – and politically disempowering. Notably, the effects of medicalisation are also differentiated. They are shaped by factors such as age, gender, ethnicity, and socioeconomic status (Davis 2010; Lock 2004). For example, women's anger appears more likely to be medicalised than men's (Potter 2004).[11]

Given these bivalent and differentiated potentialities, the primary worry should not be about the medicalisation of problems as such. Rather, as Alistair Wardrope (2017: 606) has argued, we should concern ourselves with 'what society does' with medicalised descriptions of problems. Such descriptions can, for instance, be used to exclude non-medical understandings and approaches to individual suffering or enhance the salience of a group's suffering and demands in public discourse. Wardrope's observation hence implies the need to investigate the uses and effects of medicalised definitions of problems. This book aims to do just that.

I will trace one way that society uses medicalisation, or, perhaps more accurately, one way that medicalisation is used in society. I will focus primarily on what I call medicalising attacks. By this, I mean instances in which psychiatric concepts are deployed to characterise some aspect of a person's mind or behaviour as a medical problem. These are attacks as far as they strike at the political agency of the targeted person or people. They often do so by challenging the connection that this person has made between their emotions and politics. Though people may sometimes deliberately use medicalising attacks to disempower their political opponents, it need not be the intended effect. Medicalising attacks may be no less disempowering just because those who deploy them have no ill intentions.

Focusing on medicalising attacks can also help us avoid pitfalls that other studies of the political impact of medicalisation in politics have fallen into. That a negative emotion has been medicalised in the sense of being included among the criteria of a mental disorder tells us that it may be possible for psychiatrists and non-experts to convincingly label the emotions of political actors as a mental disorder. But it does not show us that psychiatric diagnoses are being used to this end. That much should be obvious since people are not usually accused of being mentally ill when they express grief, anger, or fear, or, for that matter, when they protest or act in concert to shape public issues in some other way.

Medicalisation in the broader sense is still crucial in the context of this book: it creates the conditions that make medicalising attacks possible, plausible and, sometimes, incredibly powerful.[12] Once again, I grant that focusing on medicalising attacks in this sense means that some of the subtler power effects of medicalisation will pass out of view. However, it will allow us to understand some crucial and powerful ways in which the medicalisation of negative emotions shapes political agency.

One might evaluate the uses and effects of medicalisation along several possible dimensions. I am concerned with its *political* uses and effects. Sociologists, philosophers and psychiatrists have long warned that medicalisation may depoliticise problems by individualising and disconnecting them from the contexts in which they have arisen and are maintained (e.g., Conrad 1992; Horwitz and Wakefield 2007; Moncrieff 2010). In saying that medicalisation is or can be depoliticising, these scholars usually mean that designating suffering as a medical problem diminishes the ability of an individual or group to describe and act on it politically. Thereby, medicalisation arguably undermines individuals' ability to politicise their suffering.

But if this is the case, why am I not speaking of depoliticisation instead of political agency? I do not think that the concept of depoliticisation is very useful in understanding the political impact of medicalisation. As I mentioned earlier, it can be difficult to determine when a problem has been medicalised, even though there are official diagnostic handbooks of mental disorders and other diseases. No equivalent lists exist for political issues. Some issues are widely regarded as political in a polity; others are regarded so by relatively few. When we say that some issue has been depoliticised, we generally mean that it is not widely treated as a political issue. Yet some people might still be acting on it politically. I do not just mean that an issue might be treated as political by a fringe group whose actions have little effect on others. Governments act on certain issues that affect millions, issues that most people perceive as unamenable to the political actions of ordinary citizens (Foster et al. 2014). For the individuals who constitute the government, this is empowering. It enables them to act with less resistance and more support. For activists, on the other hand, circumstances under which their concerns are widely considered apolitical may be profoundly disempowering because others are more likely to see their actions as irrelevant, irrational or even dangerous.

Medicalisation can produce and result from similar dynamics as depoliticisation. Critics of psychiatry have observed that psychiatric diagnoses are constituted politically (e.g., Mayes and Horwitz 2005). Indeed, this is a fairly accurate designation for the DSM revision process, which involves influential mental health professionals gathering to review evidence, debate and decide what counts as mental disorder and what does not. While most psychiatrists may not like to call this activity political, it fits the operant definition of political action in this book: action in concert to shape a public issue. As we shall see, increasing numbers of citizens without expert credentials have tried to influence the revision process in recent decades. Despite this, psychiatric diagnoses are generally regarded as apolitical concepts that describe medical problems. Again, this is empowering to some and disempowering to others. For example, the apolitical status of diagnoses grants psychiatrists significant authority over issues labelled as psychiatric problems in medical and public discourse, but may diminish the political agency of people who dispute the legitimacy and authority of conventional psychiatry.

So, simply taking psychiatric diagnoses and the experiences they are used to describe as depoliticised or apolitical obscures the variegated political effects of medicalisation. Unless we specify when, where and to whom psychiatric diagnoses are depoliticised, the term is misleading. It elides the struggle of those who resist these concepts and the authority of those who use them. Depoliticisation and medicalisation of issues and experiences affect individuals and groups differently depending on, for example, their body, gender, class, ethnicity, culture and profession (see Dean 2014: 459). Therefore, the effects of these processes do not align with simplistic dichotomies about the 'elite' and the 'masses' or 'capital' and 'proletariat' (*pace,* e.g,. Cohen 2016; Zola 1972).

By focusing instead on political agency, this book will provide a more fruitful and original analysis of the political effects of medicalisation, which considers their complexity and unevenness. Drawing our attention to the kind of dynamics of dis/empowerment touched on above, it will permit us to recognise that the process of medicalisation, even when depoliticising in one instance, may be simultaneously empowering and disempowering. Not only does the medicalisation of experiences affect individuals differently depending on the factors just mentioned. It can also be politically empowering for an individual with regard to one issue while disempowering with regard to another.

Looking beyond the DSM

The approach of this book differs from other studies of the political impact of medicalisation not just conceptually but also in terms of the phenomena it explores. Many contemporary scholars have warned that psychiatry is being used to suppress political dissent and action in liberal democracies. These warnings tend to be based on detailed analysis of and extrapolation from psychiatric diagnostic criteria, aetiologies and treatments, while failing to consider whether and how psychiatry is actually deployed in political contexts. Unsurprisingly, this can yield conceptually and evidentially shaky claims about the political impact of psychiatry.

For an example of this, we can look at the social theorist Bruce Cohen's book *Psychiatric Hegemony* (2016), which constitutes one of the most comprehensive recent attempts to understand the political impact of psychiatry. Among Cohen's core arguments is that 'psychiatry and allied disciplines ha[ve] been a useful tool for pathologising collective action and political dissent' (170), including recent social movements like Occupy (193). Besides pointing to the kind of historical examples I mentioned earlier, Cohen draws evidence for this claim from the DSM itself by analysing the frequency of what he calls 'protest-related' terms and phrases in each DSM edition since 1952, which is when the first edition was published. This permits him to detect marked shifts in language, which he claims demonstrate that psychiatry is increasingly being used to suppress dissent. For instance, Cohen observes that the terms 'political', 'sociopolitical' and 'politics' were not used in *DSM-I*, while they appeared thirteen times in *DSM-5*. However, as mentioned, *DSM-5*, unlike *DSM-I*, explicitly excludes behaviours that are politically motivated or that may be regarded as deviant for political reasons. Cohen fails to note that in nine of the thirteen instances in which 'political' and 'sociopolitical' are used, it is to rule out political behaviours. Some of the remaining four uses are possibly more problematic – such as the inclusion of 'changes . . . in political beliefs' as a symptom of major or mild frontotemporal neurocognitive disorder. Still, it is difficult to see how the statement that the highest rates of post-traumatic stress disorder 'are found among survivors of . . . politically motivated internment or genocide' (APA 2013: 276) threatens dissent. Cohen's approach not only ignores the wider medical, legal and social context in which these words are used, but even the literal con-*text* in which they appear in the DSM. Therefore, it reveals little about the political impact of psychiatry.

Another approach that Cohen uses more fruitfully is conceptual analysis. For instance, examining the criteria for antisocial personality disorder (ASPD), he contends that the diagnosis is 'the perfect catch-all' for medicalising dissent, including paradigmatic forms of protest (Cohen 2016: 196). Cohen is right that the ASPD criteria are politically problematic. They include features like 'failure to conform to social norms with respect to lawful behaviours', 'irritability and aggressiveness' and 'a pattern of disregard for, and violation of, the rights of others' (APA 2013: 645). Many powerful and important instances of political action have involved disadvantaged people claiming rights by calling into question the exclusive rights of the privileged through campaigns of civil disobedience and other actions that the privileged perceive as obnoxious (see Rancière 1999). It *could* therefore be used to medicalise some forms of political action. This is all that a conceptual analysis of this kind allows us to say. It does not support the implication that ASPD or psychiatry more broadly *has been* used to medicalise dissent. Furthermore, the instances in which ASPD can be used to medicalise political action are limited by the DSM stipulation that political behaviour cannot be used to diagnose mental disorder, unless it is due to an individual dysfunction.[13] Endeavours to extract the political implications of psychiatry from close readings of diagnostic handbooks are hence also limited.

Similar problems arise in political critiques of psychiatric aetiologies. A common concern is that contemporary aetiologies of mental disorder appear to locate the causes of disease within the individual's body alone. The neurochemical imbalance theory is one example of this. Originally conceived as an explanation for depression but later extended to other mental disorders, the theory underpins the popular metaphor that depression is like diabetes and that like people with diabetes need insulin to restore normal levels of the hormone, people with depression need antidepressants to restore normal levels of serotonin in the brain. Though prominent psychiatrists consider the neurochemical imbalance theory discredited (e.g., Pies 2019; though cf. Vatel et al. 2019), it still circulates widely in popular and medical discourse. Furthermore, even if the neurochemical imbalance theory has fallen out of fashion within psychiatry, newer neuroscientific aetiologies are picking up the slack of translating human problems into the language of brains and genes (Rose 2019; Rose and Abi-Rached 2013). The reason critics regard such aetiologies as politically problematic is straightforward; by attributing deep sadness and other negative emotions to an error in the individual's brain, it apparently rules out consideration of external causes and solutions, including political ones. Mark Fisher (2009) has argued that this has contributed to 'reflexive impotence', whereby individuals 'know things are bad' but also 'know that they can't do anything about it' – at least politically. Many individuals may well be in the grips of such reflexive impotence. However, other commentators have reached grander conclusions from the same premises, premises that cannot bear the weight of these conclusions. For instance, Joanna Moncrieff (2008: 249) says that neuroscientific aetiologies of mental disorder are making 'society as a whole increasingly deaf to social and political critique'. This is different from theorising the styles of thinking that neuroscience or psychiatry might engender. Like Cohen, Moncrieff is making assertions about the political, and she is doing so based on her reading of a particular element on the medical. Yet if we want to understand how medicalisation affects political dissent, we must surely pay at least some attention to the experiences of political dissenters and the events in which they are engaged.

I am not claiming that we cannot reach interesting insights about the potential dangers of medicalisation through careful analysis of diagnostic handbooks, models of disease or other medical resources and technologies. Implicitly at least, Moncrieff, Cohen and others appear to be following Foucault's injunction to focus on the capillaries of power, an approach that has yielded important insights about the perils of medicalisation. Significantly, it has helped us to understand the weight of social experience, the calcified power relations that disempower individuals. As Lois McNay (2014) has observed, such an understanding is absent in much radical democratic political theory, leading theorists in the field to either over- or underpredict the political agency of the marginalised. However, critics of medicalisation and psychiatry have mistakenly assumed that operations in capillaries reflect those in the arteries. Despite their preoccupation with the political dangers of psychiatry, they have paid little attention to the events and actions that we conventionally understand as politics. In order to provide a better understanding of how the medicalisation of negative emotions affects political agency, it is to the arteries of liberal democratic public life – elections, referenda, party politics, protests and community organising – that this book turns.

Specifically, I will explore the role of negative emotions and medicalisation in the context of the Brexit referendum, the Occupy movement, the rise of the UK Independence Party and the psychiatric service user/survivor movement. I have chosen to look at these four expressions of political agency for several reasons. They encompass the diverse and important forms of political action I mentioned above. They also represent a broad range of political perspectives – left and right, populists and technocrats, internationalists and nationalists. Finally, they allow us to have a closer look at grief, anger and fear, three emotions that have not only occasioned considerable interest among political scholars precisely because of their relationship to political agency, but which philosophers and sociologists of psychiatry have identified as targets of medicalisation.

There are many other social movements and political events I could have focused on as well or instead. The election and presidency of Donald Trump, the Black Lives Matter (BLM) movement, Me Too, Extinction Rebellion, and collective mobilisations during the COVID-19 pandemic. Any of these might have been suitable case studies. Take Donald Trump's rise to the presidency. Not only did many journalists and academics attribute his election to the irrational anger of his supporters (Lozada 2020: 22–6), but the man himself was publicly accused of being mentally ill by psychiatrists and mental health experts (e.g., Lee 2017). The role of emotions and medicalisation in the context of the pandemic, I have explored at length elsewhere (see Degerman 2020b; Degerman et al. 2020; Johnson et al. 2021). I have not examined the other four because they overlap with the other movements and events covered in this book. Donald Trump's political rise, BLM, Me Too and Extinction Rebellion all involve forms of political action – party politics, elections and protests – and negative emotions – anger, grief and fear – that figure in my chosen cases. There is also some similarity in political perspectives, with all the protest movements being broadly aligned with the political left. That said, covering BLM and Me Too could have brought into view racial and gendered dimensions of the medicalisation of negative emotions and its impact on political agency. These are important dimensions that warrant investigation.[14] Statistics from the United Kingdom suggest that Black people are four times more likely than average to be sectioned under the Mental Health Act (NHS Digital 2021). Moreover, prominent examples of gendered and racialised diagnoses can be found both in our past – for example, hysteria (see Scull 2009) and schizophrenia (see Metzl 2009) – and present – for example, borderline personality disorder (see Potter 2009) and oppositional defiant disorder (see Potter 2016). There were only so many cases I could examine within the scope of this book, however. While a chapter about BLM or Me Too could have replaced another, I decided against doing so because it would have meant trading away insights that the current set of cases bring into view. Furthermore, and relatedly, I do not consider *why* some people might be more vulnerable to medicalising attacks in public life than others. A satisfactory answer to this question would require a book in itself. So, this book does leave some critical gaps. I hope that the analysis and tools developed in this book may help others fill them in the future.

The Structure of the Book

My core argument is that the medicalisation of negative emotions profoundly affects the factors that empower us to channel our emotions into political action. More specifically, I contend that negative emotions can motivate and sustain political action if they are transformed into a public shape that we can share, discuss and act on with other people, that is, into a public issue. Such transformations can be facilitated or undermined by what I call dis/empowering factors, which include affiliations, public spaces, laws and institutions, and concepts. However, even after an emotion has been transformed into a public issue, it is fragile, vulnerable to attacks that dispute its relevance to public life. Medicalisation has given rise to psychiatric diagnoses and other factors that can be mobilised in medicalising attacks to individualise and delegitimise negative emotions, effectively destroying their public shape. However, the medicalisation of negative emotions is not necessarily disempowering; it has also resulted in factors that individuals can use to articulate and act on their negative emotions in new and politically effective ways.

The book will proceed as follows. Chapters 1 and 2 set out the theoretical framework of the book. For this task, I draw primarily on Hannah Arendt, but also engage with the philosophy and political theory of emotion. Defining political agency as the capacity to act in concert with other people to shape or respond to public issues, I suggest that negative emotions can support political agency in this sense in four ways: they can motivate us to reflect on the causes of our experiences; drive us to act to address them; communicate our authentic concern with a particular issue; and help to constitute and sustain social cohesion between political actors. I then evaluate Arendt's understanding of emotions, suggesting that we can find two key insights about the relationships between emotions and political agency in her work. First, emotions are not inherently political; to support political agency, they must be transformed into something political that we can share, talk about and act on with other people, namely, a public issue. Secondly, the public shape resulting from such transformations is 'fragile' in the sense that it is easily undermined by doubts about what people *really* feel and the *real* reasons they do so. I identify four types of empowering factors that help individuals to transform their emotions into public issues and maintain this transformation: affiliations, spaces, laws and institutions, and, finally, concepts. These factors do not just facilitate the transformation of emotions into public issues; they support political agency in general. However, each factor also comes in disempowering forms, which inhibit political action and reflection on emotion. The medicalisation of negative emotions can create and mobilise such disempowering factors, but, as we shall see, it does not necessarily do so.

In the following chapters, I use this framework to explore four case studies of political action in which people's emotional and mental fitness for public life has been called into question. The cases are grounded in primary research and analysis of news coverage, as well as psychiatric professional publications, mental health blogs and websites, administrative documents, court records and scholarly sources. The order in which they are presented correlates broadly to the prominence of medicalising attacks. Chapters 3–5 each focus on the role of one negative emotion in the context of each case: grief in Brexit, anger in Occupy and fear in UKIP. Each chapter opens with an analysis of the emotion in question, which highlights the emotion's political potential and its vulnerability to medicalising attacks by engaging with recent philosophical and political debates.

The chapters on Brexit and Occupy document the use and theorise the impact of medicalising attacks on negative emotions. In Chapter 3, I show how in the aftermath of a campaign suffused with emotion, many Remainers were left with deep grief at the loss, grief with a clear political potential. This grief soon became subject to medicalising attacks. These attacks created imperatives for people to disconnect themselves from empowering factors, connect to disempowering ones and, ultimately, give up on any idea that their grief and other negative emotions about Brexit were politically relevant, all in order to preserve their health.

In Chapter 4, I argue that medicalising attacks were a factor in the failure of the Occupy movement, in which psychiatric concepts were deployed to disempower angry protesters. The medicalising attacks on Occupy were more circumspect than those in the aftermath of the Brexit referendum. Rather than accusing protesters generally of being mentally ill, commentators claimed that the movement was contaminated by people with mental disorder, people who were too irrational, vulnerable or dangerous to participate in the protests. Strikingly, no one appeared to consider that individuals with mental disorder might have been trying to express the same anger about inequality that animated others in the movement. Besides striking at the credibility and affiliations of the protesters, these attacks contributed towards undermining their access to public space and mobilising the law against them.

Chapter 5 focuses on fear and the rise of UKIP. UKIP seems a likely target of medicalising attacks. The driving emotion of the party was widely considered to be fear. This emotion is not only among the most vilified emotions in contemporary political thought, but it is also a symptom of several increasingly common mental disorders. Yet UKIP surprisingly avoided medicalising attacks. Instead, opponents targeted the fear that ostensibly animated the party with what I call hyper-emotionalising attacks, which frame the emotion as primitive and dangerous. I warn that while efforts to delegitimise fear in public life may seem justified when aimed at the far right, these efforts also risk disempowering others.

Unlike the subjects of the other chapters, the user/survivor movement, which I discuss in Chapter 6, involves people who were diagnosed with a mental disorder before they started acting politically. Therefore, this case does not tell us about how particular negative emotions can be medicalised in public life, but about how people may be able to channel their emotions into public life *after* they have been medicalised. Users/survivors face several disempowering factors related to their medical status, including prejudices about mental disorder. Another problem they face is the appropriation of user/survivor concepts in policy and mental healthcare, as this may undermine their ability to articulate their suffering as public issues. However, I argue that appropriation can also empower these activists by enabling them to make collective and effective demands on private corporations and public institutions.

I conclude the book with some reflections on its political implications. I warn that while psychiatric concepts (and by extension the medicalisation of negative emotions) can be empowering in some contexts, we should not be too blithe about the disempowering potential of medicalisation. For, even though psychiatric concepts and other medical factors can facilitate the transformation of negative emotions into public issues, it seems that they put private understandings of those experiences closer to hand. I also stress the need for political theorists to attend more closely to medicalisation, suggesting that this might complicate stories of democratic decay and help us to conceive of new ways to empower people politically.

Notes

1. The most recent editions of the ICD and the DSM have been, in the words of the *DSM-5* authors, 'harmonized' (APA 2013: xii; see also Tyrer 2014: 283).
2. Some social theorists critical of psychiatry mistakenly claim that the bereavement exclusion has been removed in *DSM-5* (e.g., Davies 2015: 167). For a measured discussion of how and why the bereavement exclusion was changed, and a survey of the arguments for and against it, see Zachar (2014: ch. 10).
3. In Scotland, the equivalent – though not identical (Mackay 2011) – law is the Mental Health (Care and Treatment) (Scotland) Act 2003.
4. *DSM-III* also stated that 'social deviance . . . by itself [is not] a mental disorder', but did not give political behaviour as an example (APA 1980: 6).
5. However, since clinicians also use their own judgement and take the individual's history and context into account, the qualified prohibition against diagnosing political behaviours is not as circular in practice as it may seem in theory.
6. *Madness and Civilization* is an abridged version of a longer work, *Folie et Déraison*, first published in French in 1961. An unabridged version was recently published in English as *History of Madness* (2006a).
7. Others have tried to reconcile Arendtian and Foucauldian concepts, particularly Arendt's idea of the social and Foucault's idea of biopolitics (e.g., Allen 1999, 2002; Blencowe 2010; Dolan 2005). These efforts have been fruitful. But apart from noting that the social/biopolitics *does* shape the conditions for political action/agency, they have little to say about *what* these conditions are and *how* they are affected by specific social/biopolitical processes, such as medicalisation. Relegating to the

background the idea of biopolitics and the controversial concept of the social (see Pitkin 1998), I show in the next chapter that other aspects of Arendt's own work can provide resources for understanding how medicalisation impacts political agency.

8. See, e.g., Brudholm (2008) and Luxon (2016) on the pathologisation of anger; Eng and Kazanjian (2003b) and McIvor (2016) on grief; and Pupavac (2002) and Moon (2009) for mental suffering more generally. However, I have found no corresponding concerns about the pathologisation fear. Note, too, that Pupavac and Moon focus on cases of transitional justice and make few claims about the existence or effects of the pathologisation of emotion beyond such cases.

9. For an illustrative range of examples, see contributions in Staiger et al. (2010); Demertzis (2013); Eng and Kazanjian (2003a).

10. Claire Moon (2009) defines and deploys the term pathologisation with considerably greater precision than most political theorists. It is probably no coincidence that Moon also demonstrates an awareness of the history of psychiatry and psychiatric diagnosis that is unusual within political theory.

11. For a convincing defence of the medicalisation concept, see Busfield (2017).

12. Medicalising attacks might contribute to medicalisation in the broader sense. For instance, if people frequently deploy psychiatric concepts to describe political actors and issues, this likely fuels the general readiness to understand behaviours and experiences in medical terms.

13. That said, it is noteworthy that unlike the criteria for some other diagnoses, like pyromania, the ASPD criteria do not include a specific exclusion for behaviours that are politically motivated.

14. For analyses that touch on some political causes and consequences of the medicalisation of negative emotions in relation to race and gender, see, for example, Cohen (2016); Metzl (2009); Potter (2009, 2016).

Chapter 1
Hannah Arendt, Political Agency and Negative Emotions

In this chapter and the next, I set out the theoretical framework of the book, a framework grounded in the political thought of Hannah Arendt. The present chapter focuses on the relationship between political agency and negative emotions. After outlining an Arendt-inspired definition of political agency and identifying it as a non-sovereign understanding of agency, I show that negative emotions have four benefits that can support political agency. They can motivate us to reflect on the causes of our experiences, drive us to act to address them, communicate our authentic concern with a particular issue, and help to constitute and sustain social cohesion between political actors. But this does not mean that negative emotions are inherently politically empowering, and Arendt can help us to see why. On standard interpretations, Arendt denounces negative emotions as apolitical or even anti-political. I challenge these interpretations, beginning with the idea that Arendt is committed to a reason–emotion dichotomy that idealises the human capacity for reason. In fact, she warns against efforts to use either reason or emotion as a basis for political participation. Still, Arendt is troubled by what she perceives as the potentially harmful effects of emotions in politics. To explore whether her concerns are warranted, I proceed to unpack her understanding of emotions. Though this understanding is flawed, it contains two crucial insights. The first is that negative emotions must be transformed into public issues to support political agency. The second, which I consider in the next chapter, is that the product of such transformations is fragile.

A Definition of Political Agency

Political agency is a concept frequently invoked but seldom defined. There might be good reasons for this. For one, any effort to separate political agency from other types of agency risks ignoring the political significance of some actions while overemphasising that of others. Yet if we provisionally take agency to refer to an individual's capacity to influence some matter or category of matters, it seems worth distinguishing between the capacity to influence matters that seemingly concern only me as an individual – like what I have for dinner or whether I sleep in tomorrow – from the capacity to influence matters that concern some public – like the threatened closure of a local factory or the election of a political representative. While more needs to be said, influencing the latter kind of matters involves what I call political agency.

There are both instrumental and intrinsic reasons to care about political agency (Honohan 2002: 216–18). Perhaps the most evident and important instrumental reason is that people need political agency to protect against and address injustices affecting themselves and others. A more abstract, though theoretically crucial, instrumental reason is that the legitimacy of liberal democratic governments rests on the effective participation of citizens, the *demos*. Under circumstances in which many citizens lack sufficient political agency, the legitimacy of governments and other institutions may deteriorate, with potential consequences for their functioning and stability. Among the intrinsic reasons to care about political agency is that participation in, as opposed to mere subjection to, politics is, arguably, an essential component of the dignity of citizens (Breen 2019: 75; Nussbaum 2001a: 79).

While discussions of agency seldom define *political* agency, they often delineate a fault line between two influential ideas of agency, which applies equally to political agency. The view that has long dominated Western political thought is sometimes termed sovereign agency. In this view, agency is the capacity of an individual to determine their own actions. The political version of sovereign agency is the individual's capacity to determine the actions of others, corresponding to Robert Dahl's (1957) influential definition of power as the capacity to make other people do something they would otherwise not have done. Accordingly, an individual has more or less political agency depending on the efficacy and scope of their commands.

Though sovereign agency remains the dominant conception, it has been subject to sustained critique, especially by feminist theorists. Feminists have pointed out that this conception rests upon an ideal of an 'actor as an autonomous, unencumbered, and fully rational being' (McNay 2016), an ideal closely associated with the white, property-owning male. This has several negative implications. The idea of sovereign agency has, for instance, facilitated the disempowerment of disadvantaged individuals and groups by leading others to underestimate or deny their ability to effect change in the world (Clifford Simplican 2015). Historically, women, working-class men and some ethnic minorities were denied voting rights partly because they were regarded as lacking the capacities necessary for agency, especially those required for political agency. Today, the denial of voting rights to children and, in some countries, to people with mental disabilities or disorders is justified on similar grounds. Furthermore, histories of social movements furnish many examples of people who seemingly fail to live up to the ideals entailed by sovereign agency, but whose actions, nevertheless, affected their community, polity and even the world profoundly. Although an important critical ideal, sovereign agency can, thus, distort our understanding of how people's actions come to shape the world with varying efficacy.

The power of social movements is better captured by non-sovereign or relational accounts of agency. In this view, agency is not something one has only by virtue of personal capacities and the absence of external constraints; it is a socially and materially distributed capacity that emerges through an individual's ongoing relationships (McNay 2016). This perspective does not render individual capacity irrelevant. But it obliges us to pay more attention to how an individual's relationships to other people and things structure the possibilities for and effectiveness of action (Krause 2016).

The idea of non-sovereign political agency has become increasingly popular in recent years. For example, prominent analytical political theorists like Will Kymlicka now espouse the importance of thinking about political agency in relational terms and revising theories and laws of citizenship accordingly. Kymlicka rightly observes that one implication of non-sovereign political agency is that it can enable us to more easily recognise a capacity for political action among people who apparently fall below conventional standards of independence and rationality, like children or individuals with disabilities (Kymlicka and Donaldson 2017) and, I would add, individuals diagnosed with mental disorders. Such recognition is crucial to this project, because it is partly by influencing our understanding of who does and does not reach those standards that medicalisation shapes political agency.

In this book, I, therefore, develop and deploy an idea of non-sovereign political agency. I do so by engaging with the work of

Hannah Arendt, a thinker whose ideas have exercised a strong influence on non-sovereign accounts of agency. Arendt's central claim is that when individuals act in concert for a shared purpose, they generate power, the power to constitute, maintain, change or destroy human relationships and anything that rests upon them, including laws, institutions, governments and meanings. Much of Arendt's political thought is dedicated to exploring the conditions for and obstacles to political action. Therefore, her political theory of action provides a promising framework for my own project to understand how the medicalisation of negative emotions impacts the political agency of liberal democratic citizens. However, since Arendt herself did not use the term political agency, the task of defining it falls on us.[1]

Drawing on Arendt's understanding of political action, I propose to define political agency as the capacity of an individual to act in concert with others to shape or respond to a public issue. The term public issue, which I borrow from C. Wright Mills (1959: 8–9), refers to a problem that an individual shares with others and they perceive as requiring structural change on a group, community or societal level. Though this is, again, not a term that Arendt herself used, it fits well with and clarifies her claim that political action always concerns 'men in the plural', never 'man in the singular' (Arendt 1998: 4; see also Pitkin 2006).

This definition encompasses a wide range of activities. Women attending a secret consciousness-raising session to articulate collectively the problems they face; individuals protesting the medicalisation of their lives outside a psychiatry conference; a politician standing for public office and the people backing her are all acting politically according to this definition. However, a useful definition of political agency must also be able to exclude some behaviours, even if they are concerted in some sense, such as playing team sports or walking to work. Some theorists may want to categorise these behaviours as incipiently political because they reproduce power relations. Walking to work, for example, can be said to sustain the political order since it involves people conforming to and performing norms in view of others. Although these and many other behaviours might have political ramifications, there are good analytical and practical reasons to define political action narrowly enough to exclude them. Analytically, a useful concept of political agency should allow us to recognise when it is being exercised and, relatedly, who is more or less able to exercise it in different contexts. If we take any collective behaviour that conforms to a prevailing order as an expression of political agency simply because this behaviour sustains that order, we might reach some perverse conclusions about both relative and absolute political agency. It might lead us to conclude, for example, that the political agency of slaves in the United States may have been greater than that of slaveholders because slavery depended on the mass obedience of the enslaved and because mass *dis*obedience could perhaps have overthrown it. But, obviously, slaves' conformity to the norms of slavery despite extreme suffering and the systematic deprivation of factors that could have enabled mass disobedience testifies to a profound lack of political agency (Patterson 1982). Practically, moreover, it seems desirable to have a definition of political agency that permits individuals to recognise opportunities for and challenges to effective political action. An excessively broad conception of political agency, wherein everything pertaining to power relations is political, can have the opposite effect, leaving individuals less able or unable to perceive any opportunity for meaningful political action (see also Rancière 1999: 32). The definition I have proposed here constrains the scope of political agency to apply to the capacity to act together with others specifically with regard to public issues. This implies that to act politically an individual must not only perceive some matter as political, but be able to act with other people who perceive this matter as political and are willing to join her or let her join in action as well. Moreover, the implication is also that although an activity like walking to work is not a political action by default, it can, like most matters, become a public issue and the object of political action (see Honig 1995).

Despite these limits, this definition implies that political agency is a common capacity, which most people exercise in some form, at certain times, and with widely varying potency. Considering this, the critical question is not *if* an individual has *any* political agency – political agency is not an all-or-nothing phenomenon. Rather, the question is *how much* political agency an individual has. This, we shall see later, depends on several different conditions and factors. But first, let us consider the relationship between political agency and negative emotions.

Negative Emotions in Politics

The emotions have enjoyed a renaissance of interest in the study of politics and particularly political theory in recent decades.[2] Negative emotions, including anger, fear and grief – which I take to be a particular form of sadness – have been widely recognised as drivers of political action generally and protests movements especially (e.g., Goodwin et al. 2001; Gould 2001, 2012; Holmes 2004, 2012).[3] Of the three, anger has received the most attention among political theorists, many of whom recognise that this emotion can play a constructive political role by alerting us to acts of injustice and motivating us to redress them (e.g., Adkins 2020; Aristotle 2004; Hall 2005; Krause 2008; Srinivasan 2018). However, an influential strain of thought warns about the destructive political influence of anger, advocating careful control and avoidance of the emotion whenever possible (e.g., Nussbaum 2016; Pettigrove 2012; Seneca 2010). Fear is similarly capable of driving political action by alerting individuals to threats. The political reputation of fear is also poor (e.g., Furedi 2018; Nussbaum 2018; Robin 2004). Think, for example, of how fear of terrorism after the 9/11 and 7/7 attacks facilitated infringements of civil rights in the United States, Britain and across Europe. But fear can also, as Rebecca Kingston (2011: 181) points out, 'reinforce a deeper sense of humanity and build new solidarities as well as cultivate a sense of political humility' (see also Fisher 2002: 250; Marcus 2002: ch. 6). Grief might seem like the odd one out in this trio. We tend to consider grief as a passive emotion that leaves us unable or less able to respond to events. And grief certainly can leave us apathetic to the world around us and incapable of acting with others or even seeing the possibilities for it; people with depression often report such experiences (Ratcliffe 2015). Yet that this would be intrinsic to grief is belied by the fact that we quite often express it publicly, through elaborate, collective action, especially when our loss is related to explicitly political issues (Butler 2003; Cvetkovich 2012; McIvor et al. 2020). Consider, for example, the words that the then-presidential candidate Joe Biden spoke at the televised funeral of George Floyd in the summer of 2020, the Black man whose killing at the hands of police sparked protests across the United States and the world. In the opening lines of the eulogy, directed at Floyd's family and friends, Biden (2020) said: 'Unlike most, you must grieve in public. It's a burden. A burden that is now your purpose to change the world for the better in the name of George Floyd.' The killing of Floyd was seen across the world and interpreted as a gruesome exemplar of police violence and racism against Black and Brown people. Consequently, his family's grief was transformed, regardless of whether they wanted it to be or not, into a political issue and action, forcing upon them the burden but also the purpose and possibilities of public life.[4]

Anger, fear and grief can, like all emotions, be overwhelming. This relates to why I am referring to them as *negative* emotions – a beleaguered (Solomon 2003a), though commonly used label in philosophy (e.g., Tappolet et al. 2018), political theory (e.g., Mihai 2016) and psychiatry (e.g., APA 2013). The label connotes the moral, cognitive, and affective attributes associated with such experiences. First, some emotions, including the three just mentioned, are often labelled negative because they are perceived as bad for the subject who experiences them and other people (see Tappolet 2018: 23–5). This perception is partly based on social and political norms that serve the aims of the privileged (Stephens 2016). If we already know that anger is bad, it is all the easier to dismiss the words and deeds of women, minorities, lower-income people and other marginalised individuals who might be unable or unwilling to conceal their ire about the injustices they face. Yet negative emotions do sometimes fuel rash and destructive action or, indeed, inaction. Most of us can recall occasions when we have said or done things in anger that we might, even at that moment, have known defied our better judgement. Similarly, many of us have probably in bouts of grief passed on opportunities that we knew might be good for us or others. Secondly, negative emotions seem to involve an evaluation that something bad has or will happen (see Price 2015: ch. 5). In anger and sadness, this evaluation is retrospective, pointing to an offence or a loss that has already occurred. In fear, the evaluation is projective, pointing to an imminent or approaching danger. Finally, these emotions often involve an unpleasant feeling or a negative affect that we want to escape (Brady 2018: 16–31). That fear and sadness involve such affects is patent, and, at least since Aristotle (2004: 1380a), there have been those who take anger to involve painful affect as well. Some scholars might object that anger can feel good, pointing to the fact that individuals sometimes seek out, relish or cling to anger. For that matter, people sometimes also seek out fear and sadness through film, music or art. But that does not mean these emotions do not involve negative affect, only that the affect might be part of a broader, enjoyable experience under certain circumstances. Moreover, people might prefer some negative emotions over other emotions or experiences. Someone grieving the loss of their partner, for example, might prefer their grief over the dull emptiness they expect to face when they begin to rebuild their lives.[5] Hence, while there are some problems with the negative emotions label, it is nevertheless useful in this book because it reflects common understandings and important characteristics of the emotions I discuss.

How Negative Emotions can Support Political Agency

The discussion so far has already indicated some ways in which negative emotions might fuel political agency, but it is worth making these more explicit. Via the work of Michael Brady (2013, 2018, 2019), I will highlight four features of negative emotional experiences that help to engender, increase and maintain political agency: motivational, epistemic, communicative and social cohesive.

The motivational feature of negative emotions is probably the most obvious. When political scientists and sociologists consider negative emotion, they generally focus on the capacity of emotion to drive action. The bad feeling involved in negative emotions is central to this capacity. A negative emotion is a more effective motivator of action than a judgement and probably a positive emotion because we want the negative affect to cease and have the urge to act in ways that might accomplish this (Brady 2018: 78–80). Consider the fact that we can *judge* something as unjust according to some abstract standard of justice without having the inclination to do anything about it. (Those of us who are political theorists and moral philosophers probably know this better than most.) However, when we get angry about an injustice – when we, effectively, *feel* the injustice – the inclination to act might be so strong that it takes considerable effort *not* to act, even if we judge an action to be futile. While it might be clear that fear and anger motivate us to act, it is worth reiterating that some forms of sadness can do so as well. For example, when we have lost someone or something important to us, we may compulsively wish or plead that who or what we have lost be returned to us. The relevance of motivation to political agency is obvious: an effective political agent must be motivated to act and sustain action in the face of obstacles and adversity. We can also discern, provisionally, some ways in which the medicalisation of negative emotions may undermine the capacity of such feelings to motivate political action. For one, understanding our fear as a potential symptom of mental disorder may motivate us to seek medical care rather than act politically. For another, by treating our fear with medication or therapy, we might make our emotion go away along with the motivation to address whatever made us afraid in the first place.

The second relevant feature of emotion is epistemic. Brady observes that there is strong evidence that emotions in general, but negative emotions, in particular, can facilitate understanding of values. They do so 'by focusing our attention onto evaluative situations, and motivating the search for reasons that bear on whether [and why] things are as they are emotionally presented as being' and how we should respond (Brady 2018: 131). The negative affective component of the emotion plays a central role here too. If the evaluation that something is dangerous or unjust did not feel bad, we would be less likely to dwell on it or do something about it (31, 78). After all, there are many things that we know to be unjust that we tend to shrug off because other things take up our attention. We might know that disposable packaging is a threat to the climate, but when we worry about meeting an impending work deadline and feeding our family, we nevertheless opt for the quick and easy frozen meal buried beneath layers of carton and plastic. But when we are afraid of something, ignoring it is often not an option; hence, the incredulity of climate activists, who clearly *feel* the danger of climate change, when other people persist with their climate-destroying behaviours. As Brady suggests, the object of our negative emotion does not simply appear salient to us; it may capture or consume our attention, making it impossible to think about anything unrelated to the emotion.[6]

The epistemic dimensions of emotional experience are crucial to political agency because to act politically, we must, in a broad sense, find some political meaning in our experiences. For related reasons, Arendt is deeply concerned with meaning and the dangers of meaningless in politics. She shows some awareness of the relationship between emotion and meaning, specifically in her reflections on Isak Dinesen: '"All sorrows can be borne if you put them into a story or tell a story about them." The story reveals the meaning of what otherwise would remain an unbearable sequence of sheer happenings' (Arendt 1995: 104). Arendt fails to note here that our sorrows often drive our search for meaning in the first place, although the idea that happenings would be 'unbearable' without manifest meaning gestures to the importance of negative affect (see Brady 2018: 147).[7] A worry that Arendt shares with present-day critics of psychiatry and some political theorists is that the medicalisation can undermine our search for political meanings or even destabilise such meanings after we have found them by guiding us towards medical interpretations of suffering, which is a salient worry in this book too.

The third relevant feature of negative emotions is that they can be communicative. Bodily expressions and acts of emotion can communicate our cares and concerns to others, and are often taken to do so more authentically than mere words (Brady 2018: 156–7). So, for example, we might expect the grieving to cry, the angry to shout and the fearful to tremble. If they fail to do so, we might doubt that they really are experiencing the emotion or care about the matter in question. The communicative feature is obviously important in relationships with romantic partners and friends in which we want to know that the emotions they claim to feel towards us are sincere. But it can also play an important role in social and political contexts. For instance, some groups require applicants to undergo trials that aim to inflict physical or emotional suffering, where such experiences are taken as evidence that the individual possesses some quality, ability or virtue necessary for admission, such as courage, loyalty or pity (Brady 2018: 162–3; see also Brady 2019: 113–15). Sometimes, this involves the individual suppressing the emotion that spectators are already convinced that they must be feeling – like fear in the face of danger. Conversely, the individual might be expected to display the emotion so that others can see that the trial is having the intended effect. The knowledge that all group members have experienced the same painful emotions can then provide the basis for group cohesion, something on which I will elaborate shortly.

Most political organisations do not have such formal trials of admission, of course. Nevertheless, displays of emotion can be crucial for convincing other members that one is genuinely committed to the cause and, hence, for obtaining political agency. This might be unavoidable to an extent, particularly in political groups whose members have good reason to worry about infiltration by those who wish to undermine their cause. Still, as we shall see, Arendt (2006) rightly highlights that demands for emotional authenticity in politics can be dangerous. Such demands can become a way to undermine the political agency of some people, for example, by claiming that their displays of anger about a public issue are actually symptoms of mental disorder. The forthcoming case studies will show that this can drive activists to distance themselves from individuals among them who become targets of such accusations and come to regard these individuals not as passionate allies but as mentally disordered liabilities.

Finally, the fourth relevant feature of negative emotions is that they can facilitate social cohesion. Shared anger, fear or sadness about an issue can help to build trust, solidarity and collective identity between people who may otherwise have little in common (Brady 2019: 122–6; see also Gould 2001). Reactions to the coronavirus pandemic in the United Kingdom provide a powerful example of how fear can work in this way. While public fear partly helped to justify the unprecedented curtailment of private and public rights – bearing out some of Arendt's (2018: 628) concerns about fear in politics – it also gave rise to solidarity and collective acts of courage.[8] In response to warnings about an overstretched healthcare system, more than 750,000 people volunteered to support the National Health Service (NHS). These people were, of course, not engaging in the type of revolutionary political action that Arendt and radical democrats idealise. But they were enacting another aspect of political action that Arendt also emphasised, namely, preservation; that is, they were acting to preserve a political institution (see Arendt 1998: 204).

While the importance of social cohesion for political agency is evident, it is worth spelling out that relying on emotions for social cohesion can be politically dangerous for the same reason that judging authenticity based on emotional displays can be. We do not have direct access to other people's emotions, which, as Arendt's puts it, are hidden in the darkness of the heart. We must, therefore, rely on people's outward shows of emotion to judge that they do share, say, our anger about inequality. Now, as Brady (2018: 157) points out, some experiments suggest that we are pretty good at telling deceptive emotional expressions apart from genuine ones. Nevertheless, such judgements are vulnerable to doubts, particularly when they are challenged by medical experts or others who claim to be able to tell more accurately than us what lies behind mere appearances.

So, despite the potential of negative emotions to lead individuals towards political passivity or danger, their relevance for political agency seems undeniable. After all, when we act politically, it is often because we have perceived some wrong in the world that evokes negative emotions in us, emotions that are strong enough to make us pay sustained attention to this wrong and to move us to act. Worryingly, it is precisely powerful negative emotions that tend to be subject to medicalisation.[9]

Arendt on Emotion and Reason

The theoretical focus and practical importance that I and others accord negative emotions, along with the concern about their medicalisation, might seem to fit awkwardly within an Arendtian framework of political agency. This is because, among political theorists of emotion at least, Arendt is best known for her *critique* of emotion in politics (e.g., Bradshaw 2008; Tevenar 2014; Ure and Frost 2014). Arendt scholars similarly emphasise and frequently criticise her apparent denunciation of the role of emotions in political action (Chakravarti 2014; Heins 2007; Kateb 1984; Newcomb 2007).[10] But Arendt clearly appreciates the political significance of emotions in certain forms. For example, in praising the Hungarian Revolution of 1956, she singles out 'the silent procession of black-clad women in the streets of Russian-occupied Budapest mourning their dead in public' as 'the last political gesture' of the quashed revolution (Arendt 1958a). These women, in effect, transformed their grief into political action – not unlike Floyd's parents. In what follows, I develop this idea of transformation and situate it within Arendt's understanding of emotions. I argue that her core insight about emotions is that they are *not* inherently political, but that they need to be transformed into something political. Such transformations are constitutive of political agency. They are facilitated by the conditions and factors outlined in Chapter 2, perhaps most decisively by the concepts we use to understand them and express them to others.

Arendt has been characterised as a standard-bearer of a philosophical and political tradition that celebrates the coldness of reason over the heat of passion, a tradition stretching back at least as far as the Enlightenment (Heins 2007).[11] Such characterisations construct her views on emotions as a convenient straw man, which incomprehensibly denies the role of emotions and motivations in fomenting political movements particularly and political action generally (e.g., Wilkinson and Kleinman 2016: 190). However, Arendt rejects the reason–emotion dichotomy, as evidenced, for example, by her declaration that the modern glorification of rationality is misguided: 'All that the giant computers prove is that the modern age was wrong to believe with Thomas Hobbes that rationality, in the sense of "reckoning with consequences", is the highest and most human of man's capacities.' This rationality is 'a mere function of the life process itself, or, as David Hume put it, a mere "slave of the passions"' (1998: 172). If anything, the relationship between reason and emotion, in Arendt's understanding, is complementary. 'In order to respond reasonably one must first of all be "moved"', she observes, 'and the opposite of emotional is not "rational", whatever that may mean, but either the inability to be moved, usually a pathological phenomenon, or sentimentality, which is a perversion of feeling' (1972: 161).

Arendt perceives efforts to idealise either the capacity for rationality or feeling as politically dangerous. She had seen first-hand how deadly the idea of a true or superior human nature can be in the hands of ideologues, particularly when their audiences consist of individuals who have lost faith in other people and the world they share (Arendt 1958b: 478). For such people, the idea of an intrinsic nature that unites men of a particular race, nation or class is a seductive replacement for their loss. Whether this idea is based on shared reason or emotion matters little:

> The rationalism and sentimentalism of the eighteenth century are only two aspects of the same thing; both could lead equally to that enthusiastic excess in which individuals feel ties of brotherhood to all men. In any case this rationality and sentimentality were only psychological substitutes, localized in the realm of invisibility, for the loss of the common, visible world. (Arendt 1995: 16)

The danger of these substitutes is that they easily become the basis for exclusion and discrimination. We develop formal and informal assessments and vocabularies that determine whether someone possesses the attribute in question and, hence, whether we should recognise them as full members of our group, ethnicity, nation or polity, or, more radically, if we should consider them non-agents or adversaries.

One of Arendt's (2006) exemplars of this was the French Revolution, during which pity for the poor was elevated to a political virtue. Pity was something that all *true* revolutionaries possessed and which the vicious individuals responsible for the corruption of France's government lacked. The revolution's success thus depended, Robespierre and his followers reasoned, on separating those who truly experienced pity from those who did not. However, they quickly realised that a person's conspicuous show of pity could be an effort to mask the absence of the authentic *feeling* of pity. Although this made the task of distinguishing the virtuous from the vicious virtually impossible, it did not stop the revolutionaries from trying. Their efforts led them down a path on which they saw 'intrigue and calumny, treachery and hypocrisy' everywhere and paved with the corpses of thousands killed in the name of pity (Arendt 2006: 85, 88). For our purposes, what is interesting is not the brutality of the outcome but the technique applied to produce it. Robespierre and his followers deployed an ostensibly superior understanding of human nature to unmask the true feelings of those who were hostile or insufficiently committed to the Revolution and to destroy their ability to shape its course, that is, their political agency.

Although the example of the French Revolution is extreme, it resonates with the medicalising attacks on political actors that we will see in the forthcoming case studies. These attacks also denied that actors' emotions and actions were of the right, authentically political kind by asserting that they were in fact medical problems. For instance, during the Occupy movement, journalists and commentators repeatedly suggested that many protesters were mentally disordered rather than justifiably indignant. Some conservatives went even further. A mental health expert, speaking on a popular right-wing news show in the United States, explained that the protesters were depressed and that their actions were causing further harm to their mental health: 'You see, when we feel out of control in our life, that leads us to depression. What [the Occupy protesters] are actually asking for is to be out of control . . . And that does lead to mental instability' (O'Reilly 2011). Commentators of this ilk cast unwelcome political opinions as symptoms of disease – a deviation from human nature.[12] The implication is that people who express such opinions have no right to be heard; at best, they have a right to be cured.

The Heart's Darkness

Even if Arendt's suspicions also extend to reason, she does appear to be more concerned about the political abuses of emotion, which she identifies in political history and the Western canon of political thought. For example, Arendt denounces Hobbes and Jean-Jacques Rousseau for seeking solutions to political problems within 'the darkness of the heart', thereby subjecting politics to the biological imperatives of the life process (1998: 299–300).

Why then does she consider emotions politically problematic, and are there any merits to her concerns? Arendt locates the emotions within what she calls the darkness of the human heart, a metaphor meant to elucidate the indeterminacy of subjective experience. It is, she explains, 'a darkness which only the light shed over the public realm through the presence of others . . . can dispel' (1998: 237). The darkness of our hearts, according to Arendt, is cause for suspicion in relation to others as well as to ourselves. If we cannot truly know ourselves, we cannot fully trust ourselves either. There is, she says, no continuity or certainty in man's 'ever-changing moods and the radical subjectivism of his emotional life' (39). We alleviate this uncertainty by entering spaces with other people, where we can give our experiences a public shape. The intersubjectivity that grows out of interactions in these spaces permits experiences to assume an 'objective' existence – a permanence and a definite shape lasting beyond subjective perception. These interactions reduce the inherent unreliability of subjectivity by mooring individuals to an intersubjective reality, establishing identities composed of words and deeds rather than hidden emotions and thoughts. However, the light of the public cannot eliminate the darkness of the heart; it only 'dispels' the uncertainty that springs from it (244), meaning that it may re-emerge. This was why French revolutionaries' attempt to base political action on pity was so dangerous. For no matter how hard they cried or how humbly they dressed in front of their peers, such ostentatious shows of pity could only temporarily allay others' doubts about what they truly felt in their heart of hearts (see Reddy 2001: 327).

While the darkness metaphor gestures at the dangers of basing political action on emotion, it tells little of how Arendt understands the relationship between the individual and her emotions. Her last work, *The Life of the Mind* (1978), offers additional clues. In this book, Arendt conceptualises the inner life of humans as two distinct parts: soul and mind. The soul, an innate part of human beings, passively registers bodily sensations – including emotions and desires. By contrast, the mind actively engages in cognition – including thinking, willing and judging. The mind's activities rely on language. The soul, on the other hand, is pure sensational awareness and void of linguistic content. The emotions are, in effect, wordless in their 'unadulterated' form.[13] Emotions may express themselves involuntarily through physical changes and sounds, which serve a communicative function but do not amount to words, much less to dialogue (35). This much seems plausible; after all, visceral emotional reactions lack the formal elements of language, such as grammar and syntax. When Arendt states that emotions 'are no more *meant* to be shown in their unadulterated state than the inner organs by which we live' (32; original emphasis), she is referring to this absence of language and deliberation in emotional reactions. I do not choose to blush when I am embarrassed; that is, I do not *mean* to show my emotions in this 'unadulterated state' any more than I mean for my stomach to rumble when I am hungry. Both the flushing of the cheeks and my stomach rumbling are examples of what Arendt calls 'self-display', which she contrasts against 'self-presentation'. Self-display is the passive exhibition of my qualities as a living creature, while self-presentation is the active and deliberate demonstration of myself as an individual (Arendt 1978: 31). Say that I become angry because of something a friend has done and I unleash a tirade of insults on the friend. When I first experience the anger, I might feel myself turn red and breathe quicker. This is my display of anger – an involuntary effect of my emotion. The tirade, however, is a 'show of anger'; it is how I choose to re-present my subjective experience of anger to those around me. The word 'unleash' highlights the purposive element involved in this act and that I might have kept it 'leashed'. The representation, thus, necessarily 'adulterates' the emotion with a reflection on its meaning and appropriate object; it transforms the radically subjective and involuntary experience of emotion into an intersubjective and deliberate act of communication.[14]

The wordless immediacy of emotional experience helps to explain further the heart's opacity in relation to others and ourselves. A core element of emotion always remains hidden from the view of others, since I cannot point to my emotional experience in the way I can point to a tree to show others what I see. However, the actions, concepts and objects of emotion exist in the intersubjective world (Arendt 1998: 300; Young-Bruehl 1982: 450). Under the right circumstances, we can use them not just to display our emotions but to present them in a public shape.

Arendt's conception of emotion is overly reductive. Even if we take it to encompass both physical and mental feelings, her understanding excludes many other plausible components of emotion, such as evaluations, thoughts and actions (see Scarantino and De Sousa 2018). However, what she gets right is the opacity and indeterminacy of subjective experience and the role that the intersubjective world plays in determining the shape and significance of emotions. I might know that I am experiencing an emotion, but which emotion it is – if it is an emotion at all – and what caused it can be uncertain until I try to express it to others.[15] To illustrate, say I come across a news article about a rich and powerful person running for public office. While reading it, I experience several sensations – a lump in my stomach, hot cheeks and a general feeling of unease – which I associate with various emotions, such as envy, anger and reluctant admiration. Depending on how I represent this experience and to whom I represent it, I may come to different conclusions about what emotion I 'really' had. If I speak to socialists, they might explain that I am angry over the unjust distribution of power suggested by the article. If I speak to libertarians, they may assert that I actually envy or admire the wealthy person. And I may find still another interpretation if I bring these feelings to the attention of a mental health expert.

These insights find support in the psychology and philosophy of emotions. Scholars in these fields have long emphasised the role of social and material factors – including people, spaces and concepts – in shaping interpretations of our own feelings (e.g., Ahmed 2010; Averill 1982; Feldman Barrett 2017; Schachter and Singer 1962). Such interpretations are politically crucial. They influence the kind of causes we look for and might accept, the actions we take, the duration of our emotion, and whether we or others consider my emotion and its associated components to be rational.[16] If I interpret my feelings about the wealthy political candidate as envy caused by my failure to measure up to the candidate's accomplishments, I may decide that I ought to disabuse myself of this emotion and instead find the determination to make something of myself. This does not mean that my emotion will simply dissipate, of course. Something that distinguishes emotions from cognitions, like judgements, is that emotions can be recalcitrant in the face of evidence and other judgements, and we generally accept that this is the case (Döring 2010). So while it seems absurd for someone to hold to two patently conflicting judgements – for example, to judge that I am both right and wrong to lash out at someone who has insulted me – it seems reasonable for someone to have an emotion that conflicts with their judgement – for example, to feel that I should lash out at someone who has insulted me but judge that it is wrong. The recalcitrance of emotions can be problematic – it might lead me, against my better judgement, to strike the person who has insulted me – but it is also part of the political value of emotions. Among other things, it means that individuals can sustain their motivation to pursue political change even when they judge the obstacles to be insurmountable. It also means that even if I judge my envy to be irrational, the emotion may persist. Social critics might consider this a good thing, interpreting it as a sign that the affective effects of inequality cannot easily be reasoned away by ideology. However, emotions are educable (Price 2015: 96–7), meaning that if I and others disapprove of my envy, I might eventually cease to feel this emotion – at least suppress or stop expressing it (see Archer and Mills 2019).

We shall see in the forthcoming chapters that social and material factors can continue to shape interpretations of emotional experiences even after they have been named and their cause has been identified. In some instances, the original categorisation of the emotion may be rejected because subsequent interpretations are regarded as more authoritative. For example, if someone goes to their doctor complaining of persistent grief following the loss of a partner and that this has left them unable to focus on work, they might be diagnosed with depression. So, even if this person and those around them initially thought their grief was a normal emotion, they now understand it as a disease.

Political Transformations

Despite its flaws, Arendt's treatment of emotions thus highlights something that is frequently obscured in contemporary debates about emotions, namely, that emotions and other subjective experiences are *not* inherently political – notwithstanding claims to the contrary (see, e.g., Ahmed 2014; Sokolon 2006; Solomon 2008; Stephens 2016). They must be turned into something political, that is, something that we can share and act on with others. The 'passions of the heart', as Arendt (1998) puts it, 'lead an uncertain shadowy kind of existence unless and until they are transformed, deprivatized and deindividualized, as it were, into a shape to fit them for public appearance' (50). We saw in the previous section that efforts to express our feelings and the contexts in which we do so can greatly influence the shape of our emotions. As Arendt suggests, and we shall now see, the shape our emotion takes has significant consequences for our political agency. The right words at the right moment, with the right people in the right place, can transform our emotion into a public issue and political action. The wrong ones can leave us trapped in the darkness of our hearts or misled about the meaning and significance of our feelings.

Arendt suggests that transformations of subjective experiences into a shape fit for public appearance are facilitated by a common world of speech, relationships, and things (50, 168). She does not pay much attention to how the common world does so – though, as we shall see, there are rich resources in her work for elaborating on this. Instead, she is preoccupied with defining the proper limits of the public contra the private sphere, almost as though their mere existence guaranteed the possibility of political action. This has led critics like Lois McNay (2014) to assert that Arendt and scholars drawing on her political thought presume the existence of ready-made political agents, who are capable of effective action as long as there is a public sphere (104). But obstacles to political action exist within the public sphere as well, and their effects on people vary depending on gender, race, class, and physical and mental capacities. Individuals and groups who face such obstacles in public often end up internalising injustice as negative emotions directed at their individual lives, blaming themselves for their suffering. McNay rightly observes that by 'being incorporated in this manner, the social origins of suffering are obscured and are experienced instead as the fault of the individual' (35).

This criticism of Arendt is partly justified. Yet some of her early work suggests that she also understood how disempowering the inability to transform subjective experiences into a shape 'to fit them for public appearance' could be. Among the texts indicating this is Arendt's (1997) biography of Rahel Varnhagen – a Jewish woman who hosted one of Berlin's most popular salons at the turn of the eighteenth century. Following the rise of Napoleon and anti-Semitism, Varnhagen fell out of favour with high society and spent most of her remaining life trying to regain her standing. Arendt's biography focuses on this latter part of Varnhagen's life. The work can be read as the tragic story of a Jewess who, in her single-minded and self-centred pursuit to improve her status in society, failed to understand the connection between her personal suffering and the political problems of Jews. It illustrates that without the capacity to transform our subjective experiences into a public shape that relates them to matters that we share with other people, political action becomes impossible because it appears that we have nothing in common on which to act together.

The notion that political action entails a transformation of emotion resonates with how other political thinkers and activists have described the experience of acting politically based on emotions. Several have used terms closely related to transformation, such as 'transition', 'transmutation' and 'channelling'. These are often applied to anger, although I think the concept of transformation is applicable to at least all negative emotions. Notably, Mahatma Gandhi and Martin Luther King both spoke in these terms. Gandhi (1999: 155) once said: 'I have learnt through bitter experience the one supreme lesson to conserve my anger and, as heat conserved is transmuted into energy, even so our anger controlled can be transmuted into a power which can move the world.' In a match-ing spirit, King (2005: 444) relayed his experiences of dealing with negative emotions: 'As my sufferings mounted I soon realized that there were two ways that I could respond to my situation: either to react with bitterness or seek to transform the suffering into a cre-ative force.'

Leaders within the second-wave feminist movement also suggested that negative emotions had to be deliberately transformed into some-thing political. The civil rights activist and black feminist writer Audre Lorde (2007: 127) spoke eloquently about this need: 'Every woman has a well-stocked arsenal of anger potentially useful against those oppressions, personal and institutional, which brought that anger into being. Focused with precision it can become a powerful source of energy serving progress and change.' However, Lorde remarked: 'Most women have not developed the tools for facing anger constructively' (130). Consciousness-raising sessions were central to developing these tools (at least among white women), that is, empowering factors that allowed women not just to speak but to be heard and seen where they had previously been silent and invisible. As another activist-scholar put it, these sessions enabled women 'to translate their individual feel-ings of "unfreedom" into a collective consciousness' (Freeman 1973: 800). McNay (2014: 115) also describes how consciousness-raising groups translated 'personal experiences of suffering into an imper-sonal analysis of [women's] subordination'. They provided women with affiliations, space and conceptual resources, which permitted them to transform their subjective experiences into a 'public issue of social structure', to recall Mills' (1959: 8–9) term – as opposed to what he calls a 'personal trouble' in which the source of suffering is located in the individual or her immediate milieu. This transformation imbued their individual experiences with shared meaning, directing their attention and effort towards specific structural problems, such as sexism and workplace discrimination.

The transformation of an emotion into a public issue is not sim-ply an act of communication, whereby one or several people express that their anger or fear about some matter that requires action and change. The features of emotion that I mentioned earlier – the moti-vational, the epistemic, the communicative and the social cohesive – do not have an intrinsic political valence. If I believe that my anger is about my own weakness rather than a social injustice, the emotion will still focus my attention and motivate action, but these will be directed at changing myself. The transformation of an emotion into a public issue turns these features into forces that can help to generate and sustain political action; differently put, it turns emotions into *political* emotions.[17]

Martha Nussbaum (2016) has outlined a comparable but narrower process of moving from anger to political action, which she calls transition. It is worth distinguishing briefly between her idea of emotional *transition* and the idea of emotional *transformation*. Nussbaum's transition implies that the original emotion has been left behind. She demands that anger be purged and replaced by thoughts about the common good, a demanding requirement with few evident benefits but clear downsides since it means giving up the benefits of anger as well. In contrast, my Arendtian conception of transformation presupposes little about the mental life of the actor, except that the actor herself believes that she has experienced an emotion and that her understanding of its basis has shifted into shared terms. Transformation in my rendering, hence, permits the emotion to persist and continue to provide its motivational, epistemic, communicative and socially cohesive benefits.[18]

The kind of factors that allow individuals to transform emotions into public issues – such as a space for speaking, affiliations to other people, analytical concepts – are not unique to political movements. These factors, which I will call empowering factors, are relatively common within liberal democracies, albeit unevenly distributed. Even the more formalised aspects of democracy – such as general elections and referenda – facilitate transformations of emotion by providing empowering factors through which citizens can transform emotions into political views and action. Such factors are not equally accessible or usable for all people. Feminist theorists have pointed to the difficulties women have had historically in expressing their emotions in ways that are taken seriously, especially in public discourse. According to Sue Campbell (1994: 57), this can be explained largely by women's lack of 'access to public institutions that offer sophisticated, expressive resources in the form of both participation within the institution ... and in the powerful metaphorical discourse associated with the institution', that is, a lack of access to empowering factors. Meanwhile, some men, especially wealthy, white men, have long had privileged access to resources that enable them to transform their emotions into public issues and, simultaneously, 'create the appearance of disinterestedness or objectivity' for themselves (Goodwin et al. 2001: 15) – and, we might add, to create the appearance of prejudice and subjectivity in others.

Conclusion

This chapter began by defining political agency as the capacity to act in concert with other people to shape or respond to public issues. It then considered the relationship between political agency and negative emotions. Four features of negative emotions make them vital to political agency. They can motivate us to reflect on the causes of our experiences, drive us to address them, communicate our authentic concern with a particular issue, and help to constitute and sustain social cohesion between political actors. But these features do not have an intrinsically *political* valence. Probably more often than not, we take our emotions to be narrowly *personal*, relating just to ourselves and perhaps our family, friends or colleagues. I argued that one key Arendtian insight about emotions is that emotions must be transformed into public issues to fuel political agency. I then showed that this idea about transforming emotions into public issues finds resonances in political thought and activism of the past century.

Notes

1. In relation to other Arendtian-inspired theories of agency, it is noteworthy that while the account I set out here might run counter to some, like Zerilli's (2005), it seems to complement some general accounts of non-sovereign agency, like Krause's (2011, 2013, 2016).
2. Solomon's *A Passion for Justice* (1995) was path-breaking in the political philosophy of emotion, and Nussbaum's (e.g., 2001b, 2014, 2016, 2018) work on emotions has also been tremendously influential on political thought. But some of the most nuanced and incisive recent political theory perspectives on emotions can be found in the scholarship of Krause (2008); Kingston (2011); and Hall (2005). For edited collections reflecting the breadth of the research on emotions in politics, see Goodwin et al. (2001); Kingston and Ferry (2008); Staiger et al. (2010); and Thompson and Hoggett (2012).
3. I use anger and fear more broadly than they are employed in some philosophical literature. Valuable philosophical work has been done distinguishing between, for example, anger, indignation and resentment; and fear and anxiety. These distinctions, while important in certain contexts, are not central to this project.
4. Scholars have argued that the politicisation of grief has long been a central form of political action for Black Americans (e.g., Pool 2015). Notably, George Schulman has suggested that 'The Black Lives Matter movement can be read as an attempt to keep mourning an open dynamic

in our culture. Unlike earlier Black Power movements, it aligns with the dead, continues the mourning, and refuses the forgetting in front of all of us' (McIvor et al. 2020).

5. See Atkins (2021) for a discussion of a pleasant aspect – the potential 'sweetness' – of grief.

6. For a longer discussion of the epistemic benefits of emotions in general, see Brady (2013).

7. Relatedly, Arendt suggests elsewhere that feeling is integral to understanding (see Degerman 2019: 163–4).

8. For a longer discussion of the role of fear in the coronavirus pandemic, which develops and critiques further Arendt's perspective on fear, see Degerman et al. (2020).

9. Positive emotions – for example, love – are important in political action too (see Nussbaum 2014). They can, for example, help individuals to sustain solidarity, cooperation and trust. Contrary to what Paul Ginsborg and Sergio Labate (2019: 33) have asserted, positive emotions have sometimes been and continue to be subject to medicalisation. The archetypal example of this is homosexual love, which until 1974 was categorised as a mental disorder in the DSM. In the present day, romantic love is arguably being medicalised (Earp et al. 2015) – albeit for very different purposes and with different effects than was homosexual love. The medicalisation of positive emotions may, hence, also affect political agency and calls out for further investigation. However, a quick perusal of *DSM-5* (APA 2013) mental disorders shows that negative emotions are much more likely to be categorised as negative emotions as symptoms of mental disorder than positive ones. This makes, as Gindsborg and Labate rightly observe that the medicalisation of negative emotions a more urgent issue.

10. Some commentators have recently provided more nuanced accounts of Arendt's analysis of emotion (e.g., Nelson 2006; Swift 2011; Samnotra 2020).

11. For an analysis of the reason-emotion dichotomy in liberal political theory, see Hall (2005: ch. 3).

12. Finlay (2010) gives another powerful illustration of this in relation to the idea of 'self-hating Jews'.

13. Arendt emphasises the felt aspects of emotion and seems to reduce emotion to these aspects alone. However, I think it would be a mistake to read her as belonging to the feeling tradition of the philosophy of emotion. This tradition, founded by William James (1884) and carried on by contemporary philosophers like Jesse Prinz (2004), focuses on the physical phenomena associated with emotions. (For an overview of the feeling tradition and the other main traditions in the philosophy of emotion, see Scarantino and De Sousa 2018.) When its proponents talk about feelings of, say, anger, they mean the sensation of an increased

pulse, sweating, tensing muscles and so on. These sensations, which are automatic and passively experienced by their subject, certainly seem to be part of what Arendt has in mind when she describes what emotions are, and they are central aspects of the phenomenology of many emotions. But, especially given the great influence that Martin Heidegger had upon her (Villa 1995) and the centrality of non-physical feelings in his work (see Elpidorou and Freeman 2015; but cf. Loidolt 2018: 209–11), Arendt would surely agree that these are not the only kind of feelings involved in emotion. Many emotions involve non-physical feelings or 'affects' in addition to physical ones (Montague 2009). For example, when we *feel* angry, we may experience a feeling of wrongness, an urge to act and, perhaps, a distinct feeling of anger itself. Such feelings are obviously not reducible to sweating or muscle tension, sensations which I may have, say, after a workout without feeling either angry or motivated to do anything. Nor can these non-physical feelings be reduced to linguistic content, like judgements, for I can judge that I have been mistreated without feeling wronged or moved to do anything about it. But, much like the feeling of my heart beating faster, they are automatic and wordless sensations. Notably, Arendt's idea of unadulterated emotional experience also resembles the idea of affect deployed among affect theorists. A key difference, however, is that affect in Brian Massumi's (1995: 85) influential rendering is understood as a 'nonconscious' experience, whereas I take it that since Arendt speaks of emotional experience as something that is 'registered', she must understand it as a conscious if not conceptualised experience. Indeed, Arendt (1978: 35) was notoriously disdainful of the kind of 'depth psychology' that affect theory seems to imply. When I use the term 'affect' in this book, I refer to the non-physical feelings involved in emotion, rather than in the affect theory sense.

14. This is somewhat controversial given Ekman (1999) and colleagues' influential work on facial expressions and basic emotions. However, as Leys (2017: 233) shows in her critical history of affect, the 'cultural adulteration' of emotional expressions – even apparently involuntary ones – is a pervasive methodological problem for psychological research on emotions.

15. For a relevant discussion, see Campbell (1994).

16. For a similar analysis of the importance of interpretation in emotional experience, see Ahmed (2010). Ahmed also highlights the malleability of certain components of emotion, stressing how our understanding of the causes of emotion is shaped by social factors and practices (27–9). Such understandings can 'stick' to particular objects and experiences, such that we come to expect happiness or sadness from certain things, like marriage, before we have experienced them ourselves (44–5, 230–1 n.1).

17. Henceforth, by 'political emotion' I mean emotions that have been transformed from a merely subjective experience into a public issue. This understanding resembles Jaggar's (1989) concept of 'outlaw emotion', but departs considerably from Szanto and Slaby's (2020) more demanding definition of political emotion. I use the term to describe the outcome of the transformation of emotions into public issues at various points throughout the book; it usefully connotes that when such a transformation has occurred, the emotion exists both as a subjective experience and in a public shape. Generally, however, I opt to talk about emotions being transformed into public issues rather than into political emotions. One reason for this is to emphasise how central the articulation of emotions as public issues is to political agency. Another is to stress that medicalising attacks primarily target the public shape of the emotion rather than the subjective experience, even though they are liable to affect both.

18. In more recent work, Nussbaum (2018) has apparently weakened this requirement, but without explaining or acknowledging the shift.

Chapter 2
The Public Shape of Emotions

Arendt's work contains two key insights about the relationship between emotions and political agency. Chapter 1 focused on one of these: emotions must be transformed into public issues to support political agency. This chapter begins by developing the second insight: the public shape that emotions obtain through such transformations is fragile. With these two insights in place, I draw further on Arendt to argue that people need 'empowering factors' to transform their emotions into public issues and maintain them in this shape. I identify and explore four such factors: affiliations, spaces, institutions and laws, and conceptual resources. Empowering factors do not just facilitate the transformation of emotions into public issues. They also support political agency in general. However, each factor also comes in a disempowering form that inhibits political action and reflection on emotion. Medicalisation can produce and mobilise such disempowering factors, but it does not necessarily do so.

The Fragility of Political Emotions

Women, ethnic minorities, working-class individuals and members of other groups continue to be vulnerable to silencing and exclusion from political discourse based on claims that they are overly emotional and irrational. But resources permitting them to transform their emotions into public issues and action have become more readily available today than they were in the past. A general 'emancipation of emotion' seems to have transpired in recent years (Wouters 2012; see also Han 2017: 41–8; though cf. Scheff 2013). This emancipation is visible not so much in the fact that politicians and other political actors speak and act in ways that appeal to the emotions of their audiences, that is, their use of emotional rhetoric (see Richards 2008). Political actors have been engaging in this at least since Aristotle and undoubtedly for much longer. Instead, I would suggest it is most apparent in the proliferation of *meta*-emotional rhetoric in politics, by which I mean rhetoric *about* emotions, including what emotions people have, what people do with emotions, and what emotions do to people and things. In contemporary politics, voters and media commentators often demand emotional authenticity and ostentatious shows of emotions of politicians and other political actors. For example, in the British snap election of 2017, then-Prime Minister Theresa May was derided for her unemotional style, which earned her the moniker 'Maybot' in the media (Crace 2017).[1] Meanwhile, political actors publicly discuss their intention to act on emotions. British politicians now speak regularly about the need to appeal to 'the hearts and minds' of voters (e.g., McIntosh 2015), and it has become part of a ritual of self-recrimination for political leaders after electoral defeats or policy mistakes to promise that, going forward, they will listen to the (negative) emotions of the voters they lost (e.g., BBC News 2014). Journalistic and academic analyses professing the importance of emotions in determining political events, purportedly based on neuroscientific and psychological research, likely fuel tendencies of this kind (see De Vos 2013, 2016).[2] Such meta-emotional rhetoric reflects and reinforces the idea that emotions and emotional expressions play a necessary and, generally, legitimate part in political discourse. The effects of this emancipation of emotions in politics are not all positive or necessarily empowering. But the emancipation has made resources for transforming subjective emotions into public issues more readily available for many people.

That said, overtly emotional expressions in politics are still problematic. The reason–emotion dichotomy is deeply entrenched in liberal democratic institutions, practices and thought (Hall 2005; Moss et al. 2020). Although recent political events suggest that we expect emotional authenticity of our politicians, they also show that the wrong kind of words or actions, particularly by the wrong people, can quickly be branded as irrationally emotional and, consequently, as lacking credibility; we will see examples of this throughout the forthcoming case studies. The charge of emotionality, thus, remains a potent means for undermining the political agency of some individuals.

Campbell (1994) rightly says of anger that it is 'a politically fragile achievement'. By this, she does not mean that the subjective feelings or cognitions that constitute anger are fragile – though that might be true as well. What she identifies as fragile are the articulations of anger that permit the experiences of certain people in particular spaces to be taken seriously. Even after an individual has transformed her emotion into a public issue, it must be carefully maintained. Many of us will recognise this even from our private lives. After all, we regularly question whether someone's show of emotion is justified, proportionate or genuine, at least if the show fails to comport with our expectations of the emotion, person and context in question.

Arendt also seems conscious of the fragility of the public shape of emotions. Her account of the unmasking of emotions in the French Revolution points to this, for example. But also recall her statement that the heart's darkness can be dispelled only temporarily. The implication is that as time passes and circumstances and people change, the doubts that intersubjectivity allayed tend to re-emerge, embrittling the public shape of the emotion. Someone's recalcitrant grief and anger over Brexit may begin to crumble when everyone around him says that 'we need to just get on with it'. Soon, it may seem to him and others that his persistent negative emotions must be due to some problem with him rather than the political world. Maybe he comes to believe that all the thinking he dedicates to Brexit and all his drive to do something about it are misguided and that people should not listen to what he has to say. Nevertheless, he struggles to get rid of his emotions on his own. So he seeks help from a mental health expert. This example, which draws on one of the accounts forthcoming in Chapter 5, underlines both the fragility and importance of the public shape of emotions. This shape influences not just whether an individual's claims gain uptake by others, but whether the emotion itself can provide the politically-valenced focus, motivation, communication and social cohesion that makes it vital to political agency.

While the public shape of any emotion is politically fragile, that of negative emotions seems to be especially so. As I observed earlier, anger, fear and grief are generally unpleasant both to the person who experiences them, and they can lead her to act against her better judgement. Furthermore, negative emotions are still widely perceived as unconstructive, even destructive, in political as well as ostensibly apolitical contexts (Ehrenreich 2009). The fact that these emotions can be found in the symptom lists of numerous mental disorders is itself a strong indication of this. It is, hence, not surprising that people may want and even *feel* obligated to rid themselves of negative emotions.

In the previous chapter, I suggested that empowering factors facilitate the transformation of negative emotions into public issues and affect the resilience of this shape. There are also disempowering factors, which can destabilise, destroy or prevent such transformations. The conception that negative emotions are always, or almost always, politically destructive is one example of the latter. The remainder of this chapter will explore these factors. Since, as mentioned, one of Arendt's central concerns was to articulate the circumstances that enable political action, her work provides us with a rich resource for this endeavour.

The dis/empowering factors that I will describe do not just enable the transformation of emotions into public issues. They facilitate political agency in general, strengthening it or weakening it, making it or breaking it. While I will indicate how these factors relate to the political transformation of negative emotions, I will present them as the comprehensive political resources they are. This is important in the context of this book for three reasons. First, when medicalising attacks target the emotions of a political actor, they do not just impact the subjective emotional experience of that actor and her ability to draw on this experience for benefits such as focus and motivation. They also, and sometimes primarily, affect her ability to draw on other empowering factors, like affiliations to fellow actors, access to public spaces, and laws protecting her rights to speak and act. They can also subject her to disempowering factors. If an activist is labelled as having a mental disorder, for example, the public shape of her anger about an injustice may be damaged, perhaps even destroyed. Moreover, the activist may also be apprehended by police, disavowed by other activists, and medicated against her will in hospital. Thus, when the emotions of an individual or group have been medicalised, the impact this has on their political agency is not reducible to how dis/empowering factors modulate the public shape of emotion alone.

Secondly, medicalisation can sometimes target an empowering factor rather than an emotion but, nevertheless, undermine the public shape of the emotion. In the context of Occupy, for example, commentators highlighted that the protest camps hosted rudimentary mental health facilities and attracted people with mental disorder. While this did not explicitly target protesters' emotions, the apparent implication of such reporting was that many protesters were there not because they were genuinely angry about inequality but because they were lonely or needed care, or simply because they were 'off their meds'. In such instances, it is difficult to say whether medicalisation has undermined activists' capacity to sustain the public articulation of their emotion or some other aspect of their political agency. It is, therefore, more productive to attend to both simultaneously.

Thirdly, sometimes the medicalisation of emotions constitutes a *strong* background condition for action, as in the case of the user/survivor movement. Recall that I distinguished in the introduction between the medicalisation of negative emotions and medicalising attacks on particular actors and their emotions. In a narrow, technical sense, the negative emotions I focus on have already been medicalised. Anger, fear and grief *can* all be counted as symptoms of certain mental disorders, and this forms a weak background condition for action. However, this does not mean that they always are. For most people, most of the time, their negative emotions are not interpreted as symptoms of mental disorder. In fact, they may have to fight for their emotions to be diagnosed as a disorder. By contrast to medicalisation in that sense, I use the phrase 'medicalising attacks' to signify cases in which someone is directly trying to medicalise the experiences or actions of another individual or group. But, in certain circumstances, medical concepts and other medical factors are very close at hand without being deployed offensively. For instance, during the height of the COVID-19 pandemic, nearly everything seemed open to a medical interpretation, from how we washed our hands to how we walked on the street.[3] Similarly, when people have been diagnosed with a mental disorder, their inner lives have, in a concrete sense, been medicalised. These are instances in which medicalisation forms a strong background condition for political action. In such instances, it may be less interesting to consider whether the emotions of people who face such conditions are subject to medicalising attacks and more interesting to explore the kind of dis/empowering factors they have access to and if these factors can support effective political action. This is what I will do in the final case study, which looks at the psychiatric user/survivor movement.

The Necessary Conditions of Political Agency

When we think about politics, the first things that come to mind are usually states, governments, laws and political parties. This is perhaps to be expected since we have been born into a world where these things precede us. We perceive them around us in, for example, borders, buildings, monuments, titles, documents, procedures. Because of their relative permanence and apparent tangibility, especially compared with our individual lives, it is easy to forget that political institutions depend on ongoing relationships between people. That the political world owes its existence to human plurality, 'the fact that men, not Man live on the earth and inhabit the world', is the premise of Arendt's (1998: 7) political thought. For her, the starting point for political thinking is not the state or the institutions or laws that comprise it. Instead, her theorising begins where these things themselves must have begun, namely, in the concerted actions of individuals seeking to shape their world.

By this definition, plurality is evidently a necessary condition for political action. Arendt herself states that plurality is the *conditio sine qua non* and the *conditio per quam* of political action. That is, it is both a necessary condition for action and the condition through which action occurs. However, in Arendt's work, plurality does not simply refer to a numerical plurality of human beings. According to her, plurality stems from the human condition of natality: the fact that each human that is born is a new individual, separate from others (1998: 9). Separate here does not mean independent from others. It refers to the ontological fact that every individual inhabits a body separate from other bodies and inevitably sees the world from a unique perspective (175–6). This ontological plurality – guaranteed by brute numbers of people – while necessary, does not ensure a capacity for political action. It is possible to be in a crowd of people without having the ability to act with them. Few experiences are as politically paralysing as the appearance of absolute conformity on an issue within a mass of people and the consequent belief that everyone except you holds the same opinion. For political action to be possible, then, there must also be visible differences between people (175, 178) or what can be called actualised plurality (Loidolt 2015).[4] The actualisation of plurality involves the second necessary condition for political action: effective speech. Individuals actualise plurality by disclosing their perspectives to others in words and deeds, which entails both an actor capable of making herself understood – for example, in spoken words, signs or writing – and an audience capable of understanding. This is why both plurality and speech are necessary conditions of political action.

Still, the sense in which plurality is also the medium through which action occurs requires some clarification. When people disclose their perspectives to others who see and listen to them, they establish relationships. The power of individuals acting together for a shared purpose lies in this capacity to constitute and reconstitute relationships between people, as well as between individuals and the spaces and things with which they interact (Arendt 1998: 190–1, 1961: 85). Someone who is alone or incapable of effective communication because they cannot speak or others will not listen cannot have power in this sense. Only when individuals are together with others in word and deed do their actions possess this power to shape the relationships between them, through debate, agreement and disagreement; as Arendt famously puts it, power 'springs up between men when they act together and vanishes the moment they disperse' (1998: 200). The power to shape relationships 'springs up' between political activists, for instance, when they take to the street to protest. It enables them to constitute themselves in relation to one another and others who see and hear them as a group of people with shared concerns. This was what the members of the Occupy movement did, by publicly declaring themselves part of 'the 99%' and denouncing what they perceived as unacceptable levels of socioeconomic inequality. Thereby, they not only formed a movement out of a plurality of individuals; they also generated public debate by prompting spectators to take their own positions on the issue and, perhaps, to act in support or dissent of Occupy.

It can be difficult to tell when power has 'vanished', because power often does not simply vanish. It slowly splinters or deteriorates as people leave the original organisation to create new ones or to retreat into privacy. For instance, while the Occupy camps are long gone, some of the power generated in the occupations is sustained through the actions of groups in the United States and elsewhere, and its effectiveness is visible in the continued political potential of the issues raised by the activists. This indicates that, when it comes to political action, it is indeed, as Rebecca Solnit (2016: 63) has suggested, 'always too soon to go home'; the achievements of social movements are always 'unfinished', both 'in the sense that they continue to spread influence' and 'in the sense that they are not yet fully realized'.

Power is contingent on a kind of togetherness sustained through words and deeds. It does not require physical togetherness – although it may have seemed so to Arendt (Benhabib 2003: 201). After all, the internet and related technologies have enabled individuals to act politically and generate power through online communities, regardless of the distances separating them. Togetherness in this sense does, however, involve timeliness, as Arendt suggests in saying that political action is 'finding the right words at the *right moment*' (1998: 26, my emphasis; see also Markell 2014). Whether considering what to say in a debate or to sign a petition, participation requires us to act before our opportunity to speak is over or the petition closes. If we act too late, our words and deeds become irrelevant. Demands for timeliness unavoidably arise when individuals act in concert because human relationships and the shared issues that arise within them are subject to change. So, although participants in a political action may be spread out in space and form virtual communities, their communications still cannot be spread too thinly across time.

Empowering and Disempowering Factors

Plurality and speech are the only phenomena Arendt mentions that qualify as necessary conditions for political action. One likely and important reason she identifies only these two is that experience convinced her that action could emerge in the most unfriendly and unlikely places. The most recent example of what Arendt (1958a) considered a true political revolution was the Hungarian Revolution of 1956. Before the revolution, the Soviet Union had destroyed what might be considered the pillars of political freedom, or what I call empowering factors. It instated a one-party system, liquidated dissident communist leaders *en masse*, and closed down political debates along with the spaces for them. Its puppet national government took over news media and educational institutions, which spread Soviet ideology and the conviction that the laws of history ordained the victory of communism. Despite these extremely hostile circumstances, the revolution somehow emerged to shake the country, the USSR and, indeed, the world.

Another case in which Arendt believes power 'miraculously' sprang into existence was during the Nazi occupation of France, in which a domestic resistance emerged seemingly against all odds. Here, too, the domination appeared to be total. 'The collapse of France' in the face of the Nazi forces 'had emptied . . . the political scene of [the] country, leaving it to the puppet-like antics of knaves or fools'. But somehow, suddenly, a generation of 'writers and men of letters', lifelong strangers of politics, 'had come to constitute willy-nilly a public realm where – without the paraphernalia of officialdom and hidden from the eyes of friend and foe – all relevant business in the affairs of the country was transacted in deed and word' (1961: 3). Almost by accident, the men and women of the resistance stumbled upon the 'lost treasure' of freedom in action (1961: 5). Thus, even under what Arendt calls 'desert conditions', in which the resources for political action have been destroyed and the loneliness of the 'mass man' seems to have become universal (2005b: 202, 1998: 257), some people have been able to find the ability to act. Of course, neither the French Resistance nor the Hungarian Revolution emerged from nowhere; some conditions must have been present that permitted these people to act despite everything. Yet this is precisely what explains Arendt's refusal to call anything besides plurality and speech necessary conditions for action; not until after political action has taken place can we know what its specific conditions were.[5]

Hence, we are well-advised to avoid over-predicting the power-lessness of individuals or groups. But we can still speak productively about and explore phenomena that generally enhance or diminish political agency, or what we might call *empowering factors* and *disempowering factors*. The previous section touched on some empowering factors, for example, laws protecting free speech, public affiliations, and spaces for debate and action. A disempowering factor could be something that physically isolates an individual or a group from others, such as imprisonment or segregation; it could also be something that deprives an individual or a group of credibility, such as negative stereotypes.

Some factors seem more fundamental to political empowerment than others. The fulfilment of basic needs is one example. When trying to imagine a politically powerless individual, many envision someone poor and miserable – with some good reasons.[6] According to Arendt, poverty is one of the most significant obstacles to political action and power because it 'puts men under the absolute dictates of their bodies' (2006: 50).[7] This is too strong to be sure, but it is easy to see what she is getting at. The need for survival tends to trump other concerns, so someone who is struggling to make ends meet may have less attention and time to dedicate to the community. Indeed, under neoliberal discourses that blame poverty and associated problems on individuals, it may well seem to someone deprived of basic needs that her community has no shared concerns to begin with (McNay 2014: 19–20). Hence, poverty may be disempowering on two levels. First, poverty may make it harder to organise or join an organisation to take political action (see Bohman 1997: 64). Secondly, poverty may make it more difficult to obtain and maintain what Jane Mansbridge (2002) calls 'oppositional consciousness', or what could, in a more phenomenological grammar, be called political 'attunement' (Markell 2012).[8] This is a mental state that involves cognitively and emotionally understanding a problem as shared, urgent and solvable through collective action (Mansbridge 2002: 4–5).

Although poverty's consequences for political agency may be particularly severe, it is not unique in producing these dual effects. All the dis/empowering factors that I explore in this chapter affect the political agency of individuals both externally and internally. The two effects cannot easily be separated. A lack of external or practical resources for effective political action engenders a sense that political action is futile or the prerogative of a select few. And, if this sense is widespread, fewer people will engage in political action, with the likely effect that the empowering factors deteriorate and become fewer and farther between. Conversely, more and better resources for action tend to engender more political action, greater faith in its effectiveness, or at least meaningfulness, and so on.

Below, I explore four broad categories of dis/empowering factors: affiliations, spaces, laws and institutions, and conceptual resources. These categories leave out individual capabilities and attributes that might be empowering or disempowering, such as various types of intelligence, skills, and other physical and mental characteristics. Of course, individual capabilities and attributes affect whether a factor like a public square is empowering or disempowering. However, working with the idea that political agency is the capacity to act in concert with others to shape or respond to a public issue, I focus on how external factors affect the exercise and development of individual capacities rather than the other way around.

Affiliations

Reliable, non-dominating relationships with other people are perhaps the most potent empowering factor. Besides making political action a practical possibility, relationships can also amplify the impact of an individual's words and deeds. Recall that plurality is both the condition for and the medium of power. Political actions traverse and impact the world through the web of relationships that exists between individuals. From this perspective, an elected official is more 'powerful' than regular citizens because the authority of her office puts her into a special relationship with certain people, spaces and other empowering factors. This allows her to participate in parliamentary debates and elite fora, draw on governmental resources, and to direct her staff and advise her constituents. Business leaders may be exceptionally powerful for similar reasons, with the main difference being that their power derives from the resources and organisations that they represent and lead. The configurations of their relationships to people and other empowering factors enable their actions to shape the world profoundly. Most of us do not have direct access to the kind of relationships that politicians and business leaders have, which permit them to mobilise vast resources and large institutions to serve their ends. But the rest of us are not powerless. We too are enmeshed in a web of relationships to family, friends, workplaces, communities, associations, religions and nations. Under the right circumstances, we can mobilise these relationships to discover and shape matters of shared concern.

Arendt emphasises the political potency of 'sober and cool' relationships based on mutual respect and shared interests (1995: 25, 1998: 243). Though she sometimes speaks in terms of civic friendship, a more general term would be affiliations. These are the kind of relationships that exist between members of, for example, neighbourhood associations, professional organizations, trade unions and political parties. It is within and through membership in such groups that many ordinary people find the resources and opportunities for political action. Concretely, they provide us with others with whom we can speak and explore shared issues; more abstractly, they link us into a web of relationships that potentially reaches far beyond any given gathering and amplifies the effects of our actions. An effective union, for instance, is an organisation that not only maintains solidarity among many members but is tied into a network of other unions, business leaders, policymakers and journalists. Such affiliations are empowering because they constitute connections on which the individual can rely for support, but also sever by withdrawing her support from those who rely on her.[9]

Today, many groups in and through which we can find the resources to act politically are single-issue groups – for example, Extinction Rebellion – or interest groups – for example, Disability Rights UK. Arendt (2006: 268–9) spoke of the latter critically, warning that interest groups corrupt politics and crowd out the voices of ordinary citizens (see also Driver et al. 2012). Despite their vices, however, Arendt does not deny that these groups are acting politically, nor does she suggest abolishing them. She considers both interest groups and civil disobedience groups, contemporary forms of 'voluntary associations', organisations formed by individuals pursuing a shared purpose, that is, by individuals acting politically (1972: 56, 96). Quoting Tocqueville, Arendt states that once individuals have combined in a voluntary association, '*they are no longer isolated men but a power seen from afar*, whose actions serve for an example and whose language is listened to' (1972: 95, Arendt's emphasis). Voluntary associations are central to the vitality of a political system, according to Arendt. Not only are they the primary means that citizens have for action, but they also affect individuals' readiness to act. Arendt warns that the contemporary decline in the number and popularity of voluntary associations has been 'paid for by an evident decline in the appetite for action' (1972: 95). Such a decline is ongoing in twenty-first-century Britain, where participation in, for instance, labour unions, religious groups and volunteer organisations has fallen sharply in recent decades (Department for Business, Energy and Strategy 2017; ONS 2017).

Some affiliations are involuntary. We are usually unable to choose whether we belong to a gender, ethnicity or class; even if we manage to change our physical features or economic situation, people may continue to insist that we belong to the group to which our previous appearance or economic status tied us. Arendt herself is ambivalent about the political relevance of such identity-based relationships. At times, she denounces them as anti-political phenomena because they are rooted in sameness or demand conformity (e.g., Arendt 1998: 214–15). At others, however, she seemingly recognises that these connections can and should be acknowledged politically, such as when she notoriously criticised some Jewish leaders in prewar Europe for their inability to see the political problems that they faced as Jews (e.g., 1994: 124–5; see also Feldman 2007: lxviii–lxix). Jewishness is not something that can be escaped through force of will. Jewishness, like womanhood and blackness, whatever biological basis or 'essence' they may have, is intersubjectively constituted through other people's judgements. Even if an individual rejects a label she has received, it may continue to shape her interactions with other people or, for that matter, with spaces, laws, institutions and concepts. The implication is that political action sometimes requires individuals to embrace their own or, indeed, other people's identity-based or 'involuntary' affiliations as a source of solidarity (see Arendt 1995: 18; also Allen 1999: 105–9). In this book, the key example of such an affiliation is that between the members of the psychiatric service user/survivor movement, who have been diagnosed with a mental disorder and share what some activists call 'Mad' identity. Psychiatric diagnoses also impose on their subjects another important involuntary affiliation, namely, with healthcare professionals. At least in some circumstances, this affiliation can be dominating, with the healthcare professional wielding great authority over the diagnosed individual, which many user/survivor activists resist.

I have already touched on some ways that affiliations can both facilitate and undermine the transformation of emotions into public issues. Empirical research indicates that other people might shape our emotions all the way down, so to speak, influencing not just how we explain and act on our emotion but whether we think we are experiencing an emotion at all (Feldman Barrett 2017; Schachter and Singer 1962). Empowering affiliations help to establish and affirm that our emotion is about and explained by some issue that we share with others and should address together. In the process, they may establish that the emotion itself is shared, amplifying the social cohesive function of emotion mentioned earlier.[10] Disempowering affiliations destabilise the public shape we have already given to our emotion or indeed prevent us from giving our emotion such a shape in the first place. Members of a political group may, for example, question whether another member's show of emotion about inequality is authentic, as happened both in the French Revolution and, as we shall see, in the Occupy movement. Sometimes, an individual's empowering and disempowering affiliations compete, pitting political relationships against familial or medical ones. Seeing people protesting a political loss in the street and declaring online their intention to continue to resist the outcome, an individual might be convinced that their grief and anger about the loss is not only justified but politically relevant. However, when confronted by family members and mental health professionals who assert that these emotions are medically disordered, he may come to believe he was mistaken.

Spaces

Town squares, parks, streets and buildings play a central role in gathering, relating and driving individuals to act politically. Shared or sharable spaces are among the empowering factors that Arendt emphasises most strongly: 'Freedom has a space, and only whoever is admitted into it is free; whoever is excluded is not free' (2005a: 170). It is also the factor that political theorists drawing on Arendt have been most concerned with when exploring the conditions of political action.

Liberal democracies have a large, if shrinking, number of designated public spaces, some of which have distinguished histories of political action. One of the most well-known examples of such a space is the National Mall in the United States. For over a century, the Mall has attracted and shaped political action, from presidential inaugurations to protests. These have, in turn, shaped the Mall. Some of the changes have been physical, such as additions of new monuments. But, mainly, it is the shared memories and relationships connected to the Mall that have changed. The political actions of generations have transformed the Mall into the archetypal American space for political consent and dissent. In the process, the Mall and the things within it, like the Lincoln Memorial, have become testimonials to past and present injustices and suffering, as well as to the power and promise of certain kinds of political action.

Governments, including liberal democratic ones, have long used their control of public space to manage and limit protest (Rose 1999b: 250–3). Under the pretext of preventing crime and violence, the British government has permitted private companies to redevelop many seemingly public spaces to render it more difficult for people to gather in large numbers (Minton 2012). A related threat to the availability of public space is the privatisation of spaces like parks, squares and shopping malls. Once these spaces are in private ownership, owners have a legal right to eject and exclude individuals arbitrarily (von Hirsch and Shearing 2001).

Spaces need not be publicly owned to facilitate political action, however. As the Occupy movement demonstrated, some private spaces can be provocations to and sites of political action (Kohn 2013). The spaces where political actions begin can even be hidden from most people; Judith Butler rightly notes: 'Sometimes political action is more effective when launched from the shadows or the margins' (2015: 55). Among Arendt's examples of this was the 'public' space instituted by the members of the French resistance during the Nazi occupation, a realm which 'was hidden from the eyes of friend and foe' (Arendt 1961: 3). Despite Arendt's failure to recognise it, the consciousness-raising groups of the feminist movement of the 1960s appeared within similarly hidden spaces, in community centres and women's homes, away from the eyes of those who sought to suppress the experiences of women before they could be transformed into shared terms and public issues. Such hidden or semi-public spaces, to which admission is restricted to specific individuals, can play and have played a critical role as political incubators from which dissenters can launch into public discourse (Mansbridge 1996: 56–9; see also Fraser 1990: 67–8). Such spaces have also been central in allowing individuals to transform their emotions into a public shape. Within the metaphorical twilight of a more intimate space, attended by sympathetic peers, people can test out and solidify connections between their emotions and the shared world before bringing them into the harsher light of a wider public.

More recently, the internet has become a vital platform for creating and using such hidden or semi-public spaces. For some people, online fora and social media are indispensable for articulating shared issues and organising to address them.[11] The role of social media in the Egyptian revolution is well-known (Tufekci 2017). Less well-known is the political importance of online fora to people diagnosed with mental disorder. Anyone with a psychiatric diagnosis may have difficulties in finding space and people beyond the medical sphere where they can talk about their experiences, especially where they might be able to articulate them as public issues. Although some mental disorders, such as depression, are relatively common, it is possible for an individual with diagnosed depression to never knowingly meet another person with the same diagnosis face-to-face. After all, people's diagnoses are often deliberately hidden from others. Furthermore, mental disorder is an uncomfortable topic for many people due to stigma or a sense that anyone without medical expertise is unqualified to speak on such matters unless it is to offer commiseration or urge medical consultation. Consequent loneliness and isolation can be further compounded by the symptoms associated with an individual's diagnosis, such as difficulties with or aversion to face-to-face communication. The internet has granted people with such problems and symptoms the means to find or form affiliations with others, possibly far away. These communities have proven to be fertile soil for political activism (Charland 2013; Conrad et al. 2016). Though the discussions within such online fora usually focus on personal troubles, they prompt individuals with mental disorder to articulate their subjective experiences in terms that are intelligible to peers. Over time, these articulations can expose public issues, such as inadequacies in healthcare or discrimination, around which people can organise collectively (e.g., Akrich 2010).

The danger, however, is that these spaces become 'self-enclosed ends-in-themselves' (McNay 2014: 122), that is, spaces where suffering people go not to find a way to change the world but to escape it in the company of other sufferers. The insular intimacy and homogeneity that may be found in such spaces, Arendt warns (1995: 12–14), is a strong but dangerous temptation for the pariah, as for anyone at odds with the world. In this form, spaces – and the affiliations formed within them – can become politically disempowering rather than empowering.

Laws and Institutions

As mentioned, political theorising tends to focus on laws, institutions and the distribution of material goods. Though I have until now deferred sustained consideration of the relationship between political agency and the legal and institutional frameworks within and towards which it is usually exercised, these are crucial factors capable of significantly enhancing or diminishing political agency.[12] As I suggested earlier, among the ways they can empower us is by channelling emotions into political action. But they can also disempower, for example, by depriving some medicalised people of the rights afforded to other citizens.

In Arendt's view, the central political function of the law is to constrain the inherent boundlessness of political action and establish and maintain relationships of equality between individuals within which political action is a continuing possibility. Arendt held no illusions that action in concert was inherently good or politically beneficial (*pace* Allen 2002: 142). Power depends on numbers and organisation. A numerically overwhelming majority can use power to tyrannise the minority, and a well-organised minority can generate enough power to dominate a majority (Arendt 1961: 181, 1972: 141).[13] To Arendt, our commitment to some fundamental laws – frequently in the form of a constitution – functions as a promise that our political actions will remain within these boundaries (1958b: 463, 1961: 164). A constitution cannot protect completely against the excesses of political action (1998: 191). Even if actors declare fidelity to a constitution, the outcome when different individuals gather to act at a given place and time remains unpredictable. Nevertheless, it provides a degree of assurance that the political actions of individuals will proceed in such a way as to preserve the possibility for future action: 'laws . . . restrict the power of each that room may remain for the power of his fellow' (2005d: 336). More constructively, a constitution provides a framework within which certain forms of thought and political action become possible (2005a: 109; see also Smith 2010) – and others, such as violent upheavals, less likely. It enables people to, potentially, treat each other as equal citizens despite differences in physical strength or wealth (1998: 215; 2005a: 69, 190).

Positively, a constitution and other laws also help to create and protect spaces for action as well as opportunities and capacities to use them. Though Arendt does not systematically list what constitutional provisions and laws that she thinks are necessary or beneficial for action in concert, we find references to or the outlines of particular kinds of laws in several works, such as protections of citizenship (1958b: 387–8); free speech, public assembly and public space (1972: 88, 2005a: 119); private space and property (1977: 108); and the education and welfare of citizens (1961: 175–6, 1977: 106–7); each of which enhances political agency. At times, she also appeared to advocate strong economic regulations and constraints on the political influence of business (1972: 212–13).

Elections and referenda can also empower, although these were not among Arendt's favoured examples of political action.[14] She famously pronounced: 'The booth in which we deposit our ballots is unquestionably too small, for this booth has room for only one' (1972: 232; see also 2006: 253). But even if elections are fleeting and highly constrained forms of political action for most people, they are still a significant opportunity for citizens to exercise power, which provides these citizens with an impetus to reflect on the relationship between their emotional experiences and public issues. An election does not begin and end with casting a ballot after all (Kateb 1984: 130–3). Before that, an individual decides to stand for public office. Staff, volunteers and audiences then accrue around the candidate, publicly consenting to their ideas and urging others to do the same; without them, there would be no campaign. Thus, even in elections where a candidate might be identified as the initiator of an action – that is, her campaign for office – she is interdependent on those who join her to see through the action (see Arendt 2003b: 47, 1998: 189).

Certain laws and institutions pertain specifically to individuals who have or are suspected of having a mental disorder and directly affect the rights mentioned. Some are empowering – like the UK Equality Act 2010, which prohibits discrimination against individuals with mental disorder and makes it compulsory for employers and service providers to afford such individuals with reasonable accommodations. By contrast, laws facilitating compulsory care and declarations of mental incapacity can obviously be disempowering to the individual whom they target. The status of healthcare systems, like the NHS, is more somewhat more ambiguous. On the one hand, it can be empowering as an institution that safeguards or restores people's welfare. After all, many diseases are incapacitating and undermine our political agency. On the other hand, many user/survivor activists would argue that the NHS has disempowered them in some ways. For example, it has been widely acknowledged that patient voices were silenced within the NHS until recently. In the past couple of decades, the Department of Health committed itself to enhancing user involvement, and patient representatives have been given a seat at the table of NHS boards. However, some activists argue that these are token positions that have done little to increase their influence (e.g., Trivedi 2010). Furthermore, others suggest that the NHS is disempowering individuals in emotional and mental distress in more subtle ways by contributing to the medicalisation of their experiences and subjecting them to medical authority (e.g., Harper and Speed 2012).

Concepts

Finally, I want to highlight how concepts affect political agency. Concepts comprise a crucial part of the resources that individuals within a group, community or polity use to understand their experiences and communicate them to others. Such resources are sometimes referred to as hermeneutical resources, a term popularised by Miranda Fricker (2007) in relation to her idea of epistemic injustice. The concepts and metaphors we use to make sense of the world can be politically empowering. They can help us to perceive a problem as political, provide us with the shared terms we need to act in concert, and enable us to convince others that our concerns matter. They can also be disempowering, obscuring the political meanings of experiences and the possibilities for action, and undermine our credibility in the eyes of others or even ourselves.

How the concepts and metaphors we use to understand the world around us impact our ability to take political action is a central concern of Arendt's. Much of her political thought is devoted to recovering and explicating concepts, metaphors and distinctions that enable individuals to recognise and use power to shape the world in concert with others. Practically, for her, this involves subverting concepts that depoliticise people's relationships with one another and the world they share. To act politically, individuals must first recognise that some problems are not natural or necessary but are a shared issue resulting from and amenable to human action or inaction. As Arendt puts it, they must 'cut loose from the world of fancy and illusion, renounce the comfortable protection of nature, and come to grips with the world of men and women' (2007: 284; see also 1972: 130; Pitkin 1998: 65). The 'protection of nature' is 'comfortable' because it permits us to maintain the 'illusion' that the world and the people in it are the way they are and that ordinary individuals can and should do nothing about it. Nature or necessity, thereby, relinquishes us from responsibility for the things that happen to ourselves and others.

Contemporary culture and public discourse are rife with concepts that obscure the political meanings and possibilities of experiences and events, often to the benefit of some and to the detriment of most. Psychiatric diagnoses and related concepts seem to be prime examples of this. They describe experiences and problems on the individual level, frequently in biological terms, and prescribe courses of action that the individual must follow if he wants to be cured or, at any rate, avoid greater suffering. Arendt rightly calls attention to the depoliticising effects that psychiatric concepts and scientific language generally can have.[15] Unlike many moral and political concepts, which are publicly and essentially contested, psychiatric concepts are not usually open to contestation by non-experts.[16] Stemming from institutional spaces that privilege the words and deeds of scientists, psychiatric concepts carry considerable authority in many contexts, including medical and political discourse.[17] By virtue of this authority, they tend to skew interpretations towards individualised, psychiatric understandings of problems and marginalise alternative ones (e.g., Kidd and Carel 2017; Kurs and Grinshpoon 2017).[18] As Mary Boyle (2011) argues, in a fittingly phenomenological tenor, psychiatric diagnoses can make 'the world go away'. Once they have done so, say, by displacing a non-medical interpretation of a negative emotion, 'bringing the world back' can be onerous, as the political experiences of users/survivors show. This is because, in contrast to political emotions, psychiatric diagnoses constitute a remarkably durable shape for emotional experiences, a shape many people assume only an expert can challenge. The apparent danger, then, when psychiatric concepts are used to describe and explain an increasing range of negative emotions is, in Arendt's words, that 'we begin to think that there is something wrong with us if we cannot live under the conditions of desert life'. In adjusting us to these conditions, psychiatry might be 'taking away our only hope, namely that we, who are not of the desert though we live in it, are able to transform it into a human world' (2005b: 201).[19]

But, crucially, there is a different side to psychiatric concepts, an empowering side, which is also related to the durability of psychiatric diagnosis. Responding to anti-psychiatrists who warned of the disempowering effects of labelling suffering as mental disorder, Peter Sedgwick (1982) argued that they were mistaken about the (anti-)political valence of psychiatric diagnosis. In their efforts to deconstruct and challenge the idea of mental illness, anti-psychiatrists failed to see and indeed obscured the potential for psychiatric concepts to work as focal points for a new kind of political contest, what Sedgwick called 'psycho politics' (see also Cresswell and Spandler 2016). 'Mental illness', Sedgwick insisted, can be a 'critical concept' in the hands of those who are ready to 'make demands upon the health service facilities of the society in which we live'. Contrary to contemporary critics of medicalisation and psychiatry, this suggests that framing an emotional experience in medical terms can enhance political agency. And, as we shall see, sometimes this is indeed the case.

Conclusion

Drawing on Arendt, I have argued that political emotions are fragile. They are dogged by inescapable doubts about whether people really have the emotions they appear to have and whether these emotions are really about the things they appear to be. I proceeded to explore four broad categories of what I have called dis/empowering factors, specifically, affiliations, public spaces, laws and institutions, and concepts. In their empowering form, these factors support political agency in general, but among the main ways they do so is by facilitating the transformation of negative emotions into public issues. Concepts can allow us to establish that our emotions are linked to an actionable issue in the world, affiliations can show that other people share our emotions, public spaces can provide us with the resources to articulate the political dimensions of our emotions to external publics, and so on. But there are also disempowering versions of each kind of factor that have the inverse effect. For example, spaces in which certain expressions of emotion appear dangerous, affiliations that chastise us for feeling strongly about the wrong things, and – crucially, in the context of medicalisation – concepts that lead us to think that our emotions are politically irrelevant.

My aim in this book is to understand how the medicalisation of negative emotions impacts political agency. Differently put, I am asking: what happens to political agency when we increasingly use psychiatric concepts to explain negative emotions in different parts of our lives? In the case studies that follow, I show that these concepts have been deployed against political actors with disempowering effects. However, they are neither as pervasive as some critics of psychiatry would lead us to expect, nor are they necessarily disempowerig.

Notes

1. For a comparable example from the US context, see Berlant (2005). See also Dixon (2015) for a history of sadness suggesting that the ostentatious emotional performances of public figures and their readiness to provide them is a relatively new phenomenon in Britain. For a history with a similar upshot, but focused on fear in the United States, see Stearns (2006). Interestingly, a recent research on the Brexit referendum suggests that many people simultaneously see emotions as 'markers of political authenticity and steadfastness' and 'a dangerously irrational and selfish element in public life' (Moss et al. 2020).
2. Interest in the role of emotions in politics has been growing within political and social studies too in recent years. Scholars involved in this movement have approvingly termed it 'the affective turn' (e.g., Thompson and Hoggett 2012). It is not without its critics. Leys (2017: ch. 7), for example, has convincingly criticised some of the central empirical assumptions of those involved in this turn.
3. For a discussion of the politics of medicalisation in the COVID-19 pandemic, see Degerman (2020b).
4. The distinction between ontological and actualised plurality, developed by Loidolt (2015), is useful in understanding Arendt's idea of political action. After all, the kind of plurality that stems from birth, appears to be intrinsic and – barring some cataclysm – inescapable. Actualised plurality, on the other hand, the kind of plurality we experience through interacting with other people, is, can and has historically been, constrained by various means. When Arendt claims that plurality is threatened by some event or circumstance, it is usually actualised plurality that appears to be at stake, except when human existence itself is under threat, for example, from nuclear weapons (e.g., 1998: 6; 2005a: 107).
5. Exceptions to this might be the kind of total terror and starvation found in the concentration camps, which, according to Arendt (1958b: 464–6), truly destroys the possibilities of acting with others. For a critical discussion of Arendt's analysis of terror, see Robin (2004: ch. 4).

6. Bad reasons for the association between powerlessness and poverty include prejudices against the poor and, relatedly, an attachment to sovereign ideas of agency that deny the political agency of the poor. These can lead us to ignore or dismiss instances in which poor people have engaged in effective political action, perpetuating the presumption that the poor are powerless and limiting their political agency. On this, see Piven and Minnite (2016).

7. Arendt tends to over-predict the powerlessness of the poor (e.g., 1977: 107–8). However, some statements indicate that she recognised that a concern with necessity was compatible with freedom and political action. This seems implied in Arendt's praise of the nineteenth-century labour movement, for example (1998: 212–20; see also Benhabib 2003: 141–6). Arendt also suggests that freedom is possible under relative poverty: '[In ancient Athens] a poor free man preferred the insecurity of a daily-changing labor market to regular assured work, which, because it restricted his freedom to do as he pleased every day, was already felt to be servitude' (1998: 31)._

8. In the German-language version of *The Human Condition*, Arendt repeatedly uses the term *befindlichkeit*, which is often translated as 'attunement' (Elpidorou and Freeman 2015: 661), or, notably, as 'affectivity' (Baugh 1989: 124), or affective disposition (Loidolt 2018: 230, n.1). But Loidolt (2018: 209–11) observes that Arendt seems to use the term without the explicit emotional connotations that we find in, for example, Heidegger.

9. Piven and Minnite (2016) argue that withdrawing from implicit affiliations, like local communities, is often the only path to political action that poor people have, because they lack connections to formal organisations. Arendt can be read as suggesting something similar, albeit in a very different context, in 'Personal responsibility under dictatorship' (2003b: 46–7).

10. An emotion does not have to be shared by all or most members in a group to function as a social cohesive. The evident indignation of some members regarding a shared issue might lead other members to trust them more, even if they themselves do not share the emotion but only the judgement that the issue must be addressed. That said, social cohesion may well be stronger if the emotion is believed to be shared by all members.

11. For a discussion of political activism online from an Arendtian-inspired perspective, see McAfee (2015).

12. For longer discussions on importance of institutions to the Arendtian idea of political action, see Hyvönen (2016); Klein (2014); Waldron (2000).

13. For a discussion of Arendt's views on the potential dangers of political action and her arguably misguided efforts to distinguish these from violence and its effects, see Breen (2012: 144–7).

14. However, contrary to longstanding claims (Kateb 1984; Schaap 2021), I do not think Arendt was an anti-democrat (e.g., Arendt 2018; see also Isaac 2006).

15. Arendt herself occasionally problematised the political use of psychiatric diagnoses, framing the phenomenon as an example of a 'comfortable, speculative or pseudo-scientific refuge from reality' (1972: 130–1; see also 1994: 25–6). Generally, but not unrelatedly, she seemed more concerned with the political implications of psychology (e.g., 1998: 322, 2005b, 1994). For discussions of Arendt's views on psychology and psychiatry, see Norberg (2010); Chakravarti (2014: 96–7).

16. Psychiatric ideas have not gone uncontested. Lawyers have long disputed the authority of psychiatric concepts within the legal arena (Scull 1991: 165, n. 98; Slovenko 2011). Historians, sociologists and social theorists have also been critical of psychiatry. Moreover, as Chapter 6 shows, non-expert citizens have organised politically to contest psychiatric authority as well.

17. As I suggest in the introduction, the authority of psychiatric concepts has itself been constituted through the political actions of psychiatrists and other actors. Relatedly, in a footnote in *The Human Condition*, largely unremarked upon by commentators, Arendt observes the specifically *political* power of scientists: 'An organization, whether of scientists who have abjured politics or of politicians, is always a political institution; where men organize they intend to act and to acquire power. No scientific teamwork is pure science, whether its aim is to act upon society and secure its members a certain position within it or – as was and still is to a large extent the case of organized research in the natural sciences – to act together and in concert in order to conquer nature (1998: 271, n. 26).

18. For a longer account of the political authority of psychiatric diagnosis, see Moncrieff (2010).

19. Arendt is speaking here about psychology, though her words seem to apply equally well, if not better, to psychiatry.

Chapter 3
Disordered Voters: Grieving the Brexit Referendum

In June 2016, the United Kingdom held a referendum on whether to withdraw from the European Union (EU). The protracted Brexit debate that preceded the vote was suffused with negative emotions on both sides, especially anger and fear. Although this may have led some individuals to choose insult over argument, it also generated factors that allowed people to transform their emotions into a public issue, empowering them in ways that many had not experienced before. Among the consequences of this were massive voter turnout, a significant reconfiguration of political allegiances, and one of the biggest upsets in British political history.

The Remain side lost. The morning after the referendum, like many others, I woke up to a result that transformed my understanding of the United Kingdom and my place within it. As an EU citizen resident in the United Kingdom, I had a special stake in the election, and that stake had just been driven into my chest. A new emotion flooded into me, mixing with the fear and anger of the Brexit debate: grief. I had lost. The country had lost. The EU had lost. We had lost. We European denizens of Britain, who had no right to vote in the referendum, were not the only ones experiencing these losses and their attendant emotion. British citizens too expressed an overwhelming sense of grief. Many were grieving more than just a defeat at the polls. They were grieving the impending loss of rights and collectiveness that membership in the EU entailed. They were grieving the loss of a particular understanding of their country and the loss of the identity this understanding had supported (Browning 2018: 341–5). Crucially, though, it was a grief with political potential. Vital questions about Brexit remained unsettled. For a while, it even looked like a second referendum or a legal recourse to prevent Brexit might be possible. The grief could and, to an extent, would be channelled into political action to shape these issues. The medicalisation of negative emotions was an obstacle to these efforts.

In this chapter, I will explore the medicalisation of grief in the context of the Brexit referendum. I will show that the grief of the referendum's losers, who supported remaining in the EU, became subject to medicalising attacks. These attacks created imperatives for people to disconnect themselves from empowering factors, connect to disempowering ones and, ultimately, give up on the idea that their grief and other negative emotions about Brexit were politically relevant, all in order to preserve their health.

Although grief was not the only negative emotion subject to medicalisation in the referendum's aftermath, it deserves special attention for two reasons. First, political theorists have for years been drawing attention to the importance of grief in fuelling the political agency of dissenters (e.g., Butler 2000; Holst-Warhaft 2000). Hence, if medicalisation can and has interfered with grief's capacity to do so, this is of great significance. Secondly, grief seems to be especially vulnerable to medicalisation in political contexts because of its close connection to major depressive disorder. This diagnosis has come under criticism for failing to recognise that, even though severe grief may fulfil the criteria for depression, it is a common and even evolutionarily adaptive response to significant losses. Individuals who have a strong but understandable reaction to the loss of their job, home, marriage or something else they value dearly, therefore, risk being medicalised (Horwitz and Wakefield 2007: 47–51). Changes to the DSM criteria for depression have compounded these concerns. Notably, the so-called 'bereavement exclusion', originally meant to account for the view that severe grief is a non-disordered response to the death of a family member or close friend, has been progressively weakened. That said, anger and fear are closely associated with grief and also played a prominent role in the Brexit referendum. So, while grief will be the main focus in this chapter, anger, fear and, notably, anxiety also come into view. Anxiety, however, figures primarily as a psychiatric concept used to medicalise other emotional reactions to Brexit, rather than as a 'normal' emotion or mood.

I begin by surveying the literature on the politics of grief. Within it, worries about pathologisation are common. But when, why and how framing grief as mental disorder may be politically disempowering to individuals has been under-explored by political theorists working on grief. I address this gap by analysing the medicalisation of negative emotions in the aftermath of the Brexit referendum and its consequences for political agency. The second section sets the scene for this task. It shows how the emotional and meta-emotional rhetoric of the Brexit debate enabled people to transform their emotions into public issues. I then briefly consider the grief that Remainers experienced in response to the referendum loss before showing how mental health experts, journalists, employers and others worked to reframe this grief and other negative emotional reactions as incipient symptoms of mental disorder that required careful management. Strikingly, this management involved emotional citizens and denizens cutting themselves off from empowering factors, like concepts, affiliations and public spaces.

Political and Pathological Grief

Grief can be a powerful political force. It has been a central emotion in the Black Lives Matter movement that emerged in response to the killings of Black people in the United States at the hands of police, catalysing renewed criticism of systemic racism and driving mass activism to address related issues in the United States and across Europe. It was also a central emotion in the 'War on Terror' following the 9/11 attacks, facilitating a realisation of the vulnerability of liberal democratic societies to terrorism and fuelling support for policy efforts to increase resilience. These two examples point to what many political theorists consider grief's main salutary effects, namely, political reflection and solidarity (e.g., Butler 2003; McIvor et al. 2020).

The political theory of grief has understandably focused on examples involving death, like the two just mentioned. Bereavement is probably the most potent source of this emotion and, hence, likely to have the most significant political effect. Yet we grieve matters other than death too. From job losses and divorces in private life to election losses and legislation in public life, these events all seem capable of causing grief, and this grief can have considerable political implications as well.[1] But why should we consider such diverse experiences of loss to involve grief? And what is it about them that makes them capable of fuelling politically potent reflection and solidarity? One answer to the first question could be that all these experiences involve an evaluation that significant loss has occurred. This would help to explain why the emotional responses to both a bereavement and a referendum defeat can be considered grief. Although such an evaluation is plausibly a necessary component of grief, it is not sufficient.[2]

Like Mersault in *The Stranger*, we can *know* that we have experienced a significant loss without *feeling* grief. An individual on the losing side of a referendum, even though they passionately supported their side, might simply feel some disappointment and judge – perhaps for the sake of democracy – that it is time to move on.[3] Or she might feel relief. Or nothing at all. What is absent here is some feeling or set of feelings that constitutes grief as an emotion as opposed to a mere judgement that something important has been lost.[4]

Phenomenological research on grief suggests that there are such feelings or affects and that these can arise in response to a variety of significant losses. Sadness is, unsurprisingly, one of them, but so is unfamiliarity, disruption, uncertainty, confusion, loneliness, meaninglessness, as well as a sensed absence and lack of possibilities (Richardson et al. 2021; Ratcliffe 2016, 2017). Notably, these feelings all seem to involve the kind of unpleasant affect that underpins the motivational, epistemic, communicative and social cohesive features of negative emotions discussed in Chapter 1. Matthew Ratcliffe (2016) gestures at the epistemic value of grief in observing that the sensed absence in grief is often related to searching behaviours. The pain of the absence, we can surmise, drives people to search for whom or what they have lost. These searching behaviours are usually focused on the deceased. But, plausibly, they can, in the presence of politically empowering factors, be directed at a public issue, as when bereaved parents seek meaning in their child's death by identifying and pursuing legal reforms that might address the perceived cause of the death. Along similar lines, grief expressed can communicate the extent to which an individual has been affected by a loss, changing the way others behave towards them (Ratcliffe 2016: 208). This change in interpersonal behaviour usually involves extending empathy and personal support. But, again, in the presence of empowering factors, a person or people's grief can stimulate solidarity among those not touched by grief and mobilise them into action. Unpacking the *feelings* of grief, thus, not only clarifies what it is that experiences as different as losing a loved one and losing a referendum have in common; it also helps us to make sense of the purported political value of grief, particularly its oft-asserted capacity to fuel critical reflection and forge bonds of solidarity.[5]

The feelings of grief help us see why its political value is only potential and that its realisation is far from assured, *contra* Judith Butler's influential assessment of grief in *Precarious Life* (2003: e.g., 22). Consider again the feelings associated with grief. None seem intrinsically empowering politically, though we have seen how they can become empowering under the right circumstances. Some, like loneliness, meaninglessness and a sensed lack of possibilities, seem outright anti-political and politically disempowering. To tap into the political potential of grief, individuals must transform their grief into a public issue, and, to be able to do so, they need access to empowering factors. Other political theorists have also drawn attention to the difficulties of turning grief into political agency and sustaining this transformation. Bonnie Honig (2013) and David McIvor (2016), for example, both elucidate conditions under which grief can be politically empowering, stressing some of the same factors that I have discussed – especially public spaces. Notably, many political theorists also warn of the disempowering effects of the pathologisation of grief and, so, might be said to recognise what I have termed the fragility of political emotions.

In the book's introduction, I mentioned that political theorists regularly raise concerns about the so-called pathologisation of negative emotions. These concerns are widespread among those theorising the politics of grief. Though I have already outlined some reasons why I prefer to speak of medicalisation instead, a closer examination of why political theorists of grief worry about pathologisation will show how my analysis complements and, in some ways, challenges their work.

That pathologisation is a prominent concern in political scholarship on grief is probably due to the foundational position of Sigmund Freud's essay 'Mourning and Melancholia' (1957) within the field. In it, Freud developed a highly influential distinction between the essay's two titular concepts. Mourning, according to Freud, is a normal, healthy reaction to the loss of a loved person or object, involving deeply painful affective and cognitive experiences, but which are focused, manageable and pass in a reasonable amount of time. Melancholia, by contrast, is a *pathological* reaction to loss, in which the painful affective and cognitive experiences become all-consuming, disabling and persistent. Some political commentators have adopted and adapted this distinction for their own purposes (e.g., Butler 1997; Crimp 1989), but few have accepted it uncritically. An oft-cited problem with the distinction is precisely that it threatens to pathologise the sort of intense and persistent negative emotions that may drive political dissent and action (see Eng and Kazanjian 2003b). Hence, regardless of whether Freud is treated as intellectual ally or adversary, his influence has compelled many political theorists of grief to consider the relationship between the political and the pathological, at least in passing.

Although concerns about pathologisation are more prominent within the political literature on grief than on anger and fear, the meaning of that concept is no clearer here than elsewhere. If anything, the widespread use of psychoanalysis in the literature adds to the muddle. For example, David McIvor (2016) raises worries about the pathologisation of grief while diagnosing individual, collective and political pathologies across the canon of political thought and drama. And the authors of an essay aiming to depathologise the Freudian idea of melancholia claim that it is pathologising to label a refugee as an enemy combatant (Eng and Han 2003: 358, 363). In those works and elsewhere, pathologisation and pathology are variously used as medical terms, as theoretical terms of art or simply as hyperbolic metaphors meaning something like 'really bad'. Meanwhile, few theorists appear aware that a version of Freud's distinction between mourning and melancholia has been operant in the DSM and has guided psychiatric research and practice for at least four decades in the form of the bereavement exclusion in MDD – which distinguishes normal grief from disordered grief – much less that this exclusion has been progressively weakened.

Answers to the question of why the pathologisation of grief is politically problematic are not much more enlightening. Political theorists often seem to expect readers to infer the inherent political badness of pathologisation without further details. When they do elaborate on the issue, it is usually only to declare that it is individualising, delegitimising or both. This is problematic. First, uses of the pathology concept within political theory suggest that it is *not* intrinsically disempowering. When McIvor labels certain forms of speech, actions and relationships as pathological, he is pathologising them in a (non-medical) sense. Yet he evidently thinks this serves his goal of delineating conditions and forms of collective mourning that can effectively address social issues. Others who call out political or social pathologies presumably also think that doing so somehow enhances democracy (e.g., Honneth 1996). So, we cannot assume that pathologisation of grief is intrinsically disempowering.

Secondly, while pathologisation sometimes is disempowering, observing that this is because pathologisation individualises or delegitimises can be rather unenlightening. Countless words, actions and processes have these effects. Being called irrational by a political opponent and being diagnosed with depression by a doctor can both be delegitimising for the targeted individual. But not only does the latter, by virtue of its authority, carry far greater (potential) delegitimising force than the former, the diagnosis also imposes or makes more likely a range of other effects. Many are distinctively medical – for example, subjecting people to the authority of doctors and obliging them to undergo certain therapies. Some are individualising – for example, impelling people to identify and treat the cognitive and behavioural causes of their unhealthy feelings. Others are collectivising – for example, obliging others to ensure that the diagnosed person receives appropriate care. All may affect profoundly people's ability to transform their grief into and maintain it as a public issue and, by extension, their political agency. To understand why and how the medicalisation of grief and other negative emotions affects political agency, we must distinguish between at least two types of moves: delegitimising moves unrelated to disease or medicine, such as labelling a refugee as an enemy combatant; and medicalising moves, such as labelling a protester with a mental disorder.

The case of the Brexit referendum will illustrate what can happen to the political potential of grief when it is medicalised in the context of a real-world, democratic contest – as opposed to, say, an ancient play or a psychiatric handbook. Specifically, we shall see how medicalisation can undermine the public shape of people's grief, depriving the emotion of its political valence. I will begin, however, by considering why the Brexit referendum was such a potent catalyst for negative emotions and their political transformation in the first place.

Brexit and the Agents of Emotion

The emancipation of emotions – discussed in Chapter 2 – was in plain view in the lead-up to the referendum. Even before the campaign took off, observers declared that 'deep-rooted emotions and impulses' would rule the debate and determine the outcome (Stephens 2016), warning that it would release passions that had 'been stewing for years' (d'Ancona 2016). The next few months seemingly proved them right. This section explores the meta-emotional rhetoric proliferating in the context of the referendum, suggesting that it reflected and contributed towards factors that invited, or maybe even compelled, people to articulate their own and others' emotions in political terms.

As the volume of the Brexit debate increased in the spring of 2016, each side began denouncing the other for appealing to people's primitive emotions rather than their civilised reason. The Leave side accused the Remain campaign of trying to frighten voters with gloomy forecasts about the consequences of a potential Brexit, a tactic dubbed 'Project Fear' by its opponents (e.g., Delingpole 2016; Slack and Peev 2016). In his opening salvo as a leader of the Leave campaign, Boris Johnson (2016) declared: 'It is now obvious that the Remain campaign is intended to provoke only one emotion in the breast of the British public and that is fear.' He stated that 'intellectually', the reasons to vote leave were clear and urged people to ignore exaggerations peddled by the 'agents of project fear'. The Remain side, of course, argued that their warnings were based on fact or at least the informed assessments of experts. But according to one columnist, 'parading people in authority' was itself a form of 'emotional manipulation' aimed at suppressing the 'rational discussion' that the Leave side wanted (Brolin 2016). Others agreed. The chief executive of the official campaign organisation, Vote Leave, Matthew Elliot (2016), claimed the Remain side was spreading 'scare stories' to avoid 'a rational and reasoned debate on the issues which actually matter'. Remain campaigners reversed the charge; it was the Leave campaign that relied on irrational emotions. One senior Labour MP, Andy Burnham – who later became the first mayor of Greater Manchester – charged Leave campaigners with appealing 'to the baser instincts of the public' (Heffer 2016). Another commentator drew parallels between the Leave campaign and the presidential campaign of Donald Trump, arguing that both whipped up an irrational fear among working-class people worried about holding on to homes and jobs in a globalised world. This commentator warned that a victory of Brexit and Trump was 'a brain-freezing prospect where emotion would eclipse logic' (Smyth 2016). However, the Remain side explicated a point that the Leave rhetoric generally left implicit: those convinced by the arguments for leaving the EU were themselves emotional and irrational. *The Economist* (2016), for example, asserted: 'Those tempted by Brexit are swayed by emotions: fears of foreigners; romantic ideas of sovereignty; Trumpian calls to reverse globalisation.' As far as the Remain campaign was concerned, 'the facts' were indisputably on their side. Reasonable people would thus obviously vote to remain (Mackenzie 2016). Yet as the referendum drew closer, there was a growing recognition that this was insufficient to guarantee victory because, as one commentator put it: 'Brexit is not about facts, it is about feelings and emotions' (Schama 2016; see also Reade 2016).

The commentariat's belief that emotions would determine the outcome of the referendum found plenty of academic support. Simon Jenkins (2016), a prominent columnist, argued in *The Guardian* that 'deep emotions' would determine how people voted, claiming that voters were stumbling helplessly through the haze of facts that had saturated the public discourse: 'Voters are told to think for themselves, and many find this unprecedented and painful.' But their anguish was pointless. It turned out that science had already revealed that reason does not have any role in voters' decision-making. Citing the social psychologist Jonathan Haidt, Jenkins explained that 'hardwired' emotions determine voters' behaviour: 'How they vote depends on how they feel about themselves.' Another commentator invoked Martha Nussbaum's philosophical work on emotions to claim that disgust was the emotion to blame for subverting the role of reason in the referendum debate.[6] Disgust, the commentator maintained, is 'one of the most powerful biological responses we have'. Therefore, voters were defenceless against the 'primitive pull' of political arguments based on disgust (Mahdawi 2016). Even Daniel Kahneman, the behavioural economist and Nobel laureate, entered the debate to warn about the influence of emotions, lending his authority to the Remain side. 'The major impression one gets observing the debate is that the reasons for exit are clearly emotional,' Kahneman said in an interview. 'The arguments look odd: they look short-term and based on irrationality and anger. These seem to be powerful enough that they may lead to Brexit' (Evanspritchard 2016).

Towards the end of the campaign, the predictions that emotions would dominate the debate seemed to have been fulfilled. When one commentator a few days before the referendum observed that the campaign had been 'conducted in a febrile atmosphere of emotion' (*Mail on Sunday* 2016), this was true in two senses. First, rhetoric and people were both emotional. Campaigners had set out to stoke emotions in favour of their respective side, deploying emotional words and images (Hobolt 2016; see also Clarke et al. 2017) – that is, they were using emotional rhetoric. When their side was doing it, campaigners preferred to describe it as appealing to 'the hearts and minds' of the voters or 'making the passionate case' for their side. Meanwhile, they continued to accuse opponents of fuelling primitive passions. Either way, the efforts appear to have been successful. People on both sides developed, or at least expressed, powerful emotions, especially negative ones, about Brexit (Vasilopoulou and Wagner 2020). But the atmosphere was also emotional in a second sense, which this section has focused on: talk *about* emotions – what emotions people have, what emotions do, and what should be done with emotions – that is, meta-emotional rhetoric was pervasive as well.

Meta-emotional rhetoric can be politically problematic. In the context of the Brexit referendum, voters were at times portrayed, at best, as misguided children or, at worst, as emotive animals. While ruling elites have long held views of this kind, citizens thinking of themselves or, as is more likely, others in these terms – that is, as individuals always at the mercy of powerful or even irresistible emotions – has troubling implications. Like our reasoned judgements, our negative emotions sometimes lead us astray and open us up to manipulation. Therefore, we should reflect critically on our emotions and try to resist them if we think they are making us feel, think or act in inappropriate or ineffective ways. But if no one, not even you, believed that you could resist your emotional impulses, then why would you try? The emancipation of emotions, thus, does not necessarily entail empowerment. Once the path for emotions to enter politics openly has been cleared, much depends on how we understand and, especially, how the sciences guide us to understand our emotions. If this understanding leads us to see ourselves as incapable of governing our own emotions, others might do it for us; if it makes us think that some emotions threaten our health, we might ask experts to remove them.

That said, meta-emotional rhetoric also reflects and contributes to empowering factors that permit people to transform their emotions into public issues. It seems to correspond to more permissive attitudes to open emotionality in public life (Moss et al. 2020), at least concerning some issues. Moreover, and perhaps more interestingly, the meta-emotional rhetoric itself contains conceptual resources that can endow emotions with a political valence. That emotions determine political events, that voters are emotional, that their emotions can be influenced, and so on, these ideas drag emotions into the public sphere, encouraging people to understand themselves and their fellow citizens as emotional in politically significant ways. Although this might make political emotions subject to governance in the Foucauldian sense,[7] it also allows individuals to self-consciously reflect on the relationship between their emotions and politics, draw on their emotions for motivation, and communicate the political meaning of their emotions to others.

The empowering concepts of the emotional and meta-emotional rhetoric of the Brexit referendum compounded with the empowering factors that usually come into play or become more prominent during elections referenda, such as official political organisation, forums for public debates, and other resources discussed in Chapter 2. Thus, the referendum and the affiliations, spaces and concepts people found within it enabled many to transform their emotions into public issues, to give their joy or suffering a shared name and explanation – regardless of whether it was immigration or freedom of movement – something which likely helped to fuel one of the largest turnouts in British electoral history. The conjunction of these factors also helps to explain why the public articulations of emotion were so persistent, especially among those who had voted Remain and continued to sustain political bonds, protests, and controversy for the months and years come (see Hobolt et al. 2020). The persistence of these political emotions did not prevent efforts to undermine them, however; in fact, it seems to have promoted them.

Sore Losers

The day after the referendum, on Friday, 24 June 2016, the votes had been counted and a winning side declared; 52 per cent of voters opted for the United Kingdom to leave the EU. London, Scotland and Northern Ireland overwhelmingly voted to remain, whereas much of non-metropolitan England and Wales voted to leave. Prime Minister David Cameron resigned in response to the defeat of the side he had led.

The fear and anger of the campaign soon intermingled with a new emotion among Remain voters, a powerful sense of grief about the loss and its implications, driving a series of massive anti-Brexit protests across the country. This mixture of emotions is palpable in the words of a participant in one such protest: 'I feel personally bereaved by Brexit. I feel like it is a death. I am European, I love Europe, I am part of Europe . . . I feel it is an evil, wicked thing being forced on us' (quoted in Brändle et al. 2018). This protester was one of many acting against what they saw as a threat to the United Kingdom, Europe and the world. To them, the transformation of grief into a public issue was likely seamless, simply an addition to the other intense political emotions they had developed during the campaign, which reinforced and redirected pre-existing motivation, reflection and relationships.

Others' experience of grief seemed less politically valenced, echoing some of the more disempowering feelings of grief that Ratcliffe describes, like loneliness, as well as disruption, unfamiliarity and uncertainty. One British citizen reflecting on the outcome said: 'I feel I no longer have a national identity. It has been robbed from me. I do not recognise my former country which I feel has betrayed me. I am grieving' (quoted in Higgins 2018). Such feelings were, of course, prominent among EU citizens living in the United Kingdom too (Gawlewicz and Sotkasiira 2020; Guma and Jones 2018; Lulle et al. 2019). Some of these people would not find a political response to their grief (Lulle et al. 2018: 7; Vathi and Trandafoiu 2020). But many did (Brändle et al. 2018; Vathi and Trandafoiu 2020), adding their weight to protests, initiatives and organisations that formed to resist Brexit.

These post-referendum political actors were literally *sore* losers, pained by the defeat. Richard Nadeau and his colleagues (2021) have used this term in a technical sense to explore the referendum aftermath. They contrast sore losers, who refused to accept defeat, with 'graceful losers', who readily accepted defeat, idealising the latter as 'politically involved and principled citizens' crucial to 'the stability of democratic regimes' (77). According to Nadeau and his colleagues' research, sore losers were driven by powerful negative emotions and a strong connection to the EU. In contrast, graceful losers were less emotional, ostensibly more informed, and, thus, able to overcome their disappointment over the loss and confer legitimacy to the outcome (90).

Losing well is vital in a liberal democracy. But can graceful losers, who respond to defeat by disengaging from a public issue with profound consequences for the United Kingdom, its citizens and denizens, really be said to lose well? Though the Brexit referendum was over, critical political questions remained. The most general and salient of these was: what did Brexit actually mean? While many sore losers, who refused to let go of their negative emotions, were trying to change the result – through procedural means, it is important to note – they were also trying to shape the UK's post-referendum future. They did so in the face of a government, led by the new prime minister, Theresa May, that seemed intent on challenging the legitimacy of *any* further debate or public involvement on Brexit and denied that there were any further questions to be answered about the issue – notably adopting the bizarre mantra 'Brexit means Brexit'. The intense and political emotions generated in the preceding months potentially imperiled these efforts. However, this problem began to resolve itself as observers started to claim that these emotions were perhaps not political after all, but, rather, incipient symptoms of mental disorder.

The Discovery of Brexit Anxiety

Soon after the referendum, there were reports that the number of people in therapy was surging. Some individuals had apparently been so upset by the result that they required professional mental healthcare. According to a headline in *The Sun*, psychiatrists had seen an 'alarming rise in [the] number of patients seeking help for "Brexit anxiety"' (Lockett 2016). Another tabloid suggested that Brexit anxiety had brought patients queuing for mental healthcare (Prynn 2016). Such assertions were not confined to the tabloids, although their claims were the most hyperbolic. *The Guardian*, *Financial Times* and several other news outlets also suggested that the referendum had caused an increased demand for mental healthcare (e.g., Court 2016; Jacobs 2016; Orbach 2016; Watts 2016). An opinion piece in the *Daily Telegraph* even implied that the increased pressure was pushing psychiatrists to the point of breaking (Fitzpatrick 2016).

What evidence did they have to support these claims? Not much. Among the articles I surveyed, only one cited evidence of an increase in patients; it quoted a staff member at a private mental health institution in London, who claimed that a recent rise in patients was directly attributable to the referendum outcome (Moore-Bridger 2016). Other newspapers relied on blog posts and opinion pieces written by mental health professionals. Among the most notable expert writers on this matter was the renowned feminist author and psychotherapist Susie Orbach (2016). In a piece for *The Guardian*, headlined with her name and the phrase 'in therapy, everyone wants to talk about Brexit', she described the volatile emotions that her clients had expressed about the referendum's outcome, such as anger, despair and – especially – anxiety. Other mental health professionals related similar experiences on blogs and professional websites. But none mentioned anything to support the claim that the number of patients was surging. What some did report was that most *existing* patients wanted to talk about Brexit.

While the queues of psychiatric patients might have been a figment of the journalistic imagination, the idea of 'Brexit anxiety' was not, at least not entirely. The term seems to have first appeared in 2015 when it was used to describe the tendency of investors to withhold or withdraw investments from the United Kingdom due to the economic uncertainties that Brexit meant for businesses and the national economy. In this context, the word 'anxiety' bore little relationship to the emotional experience anxiety – and even less to any mental disorder (cf. Berezin 2009) – but served instead as a shorthand for a particular economic indicator; this continued to be its primary usage in the months after the referendum.[8] That said, the referendum outcome probably did make many people anxious in the emotional sense. Anxiety is, of course, different from grief. Perhaps most obviously, anxiety is future-orientated, involving an evaluation that something bad might happen, while grief is past-orientated, involving an evaluation that something bad has happened. Yet anxiety can bleed into grief, as the grieving person inevitably wonders what their world will look like without the person or thing that has been lost. And grief can bleed into anxiety as well, as the concept of anticipatory grief suggests. Anticipatory grief names the emotion that sometimes occurs when a threatened loss – which may at one point have been the cause of anxiety – becomes understood and felt as unavoidable (see Varga and Gallagher 2020). However, when mental health professionals picked up the concept of Brexit anxiety in the aftermath of the referendum, they did not consider it as a complex and political emotion, potentially imbricated with both perceived threats and losses. Instead, they deployed it with a distinctively medical meaning, capable of encompassing a whole range of negative emotions that people were experiencing in response to Brexit.

Throngs of experts jumped at the chance to offer analyses of and advice on the mental health of the British population in the days after the referendum. Of particular interest were those who had voted to remain and found themselves on the losing side of one of the most emotional and vicious political campaigns in the history of British democracy. Mental health professionals warned about the consequent rise of Brexit anxiety (Burgess 2016; Kurz 2016; Magee 2016; Private Psychiatry 2016; Sieger 2016; The Speakmans 2016). The term's apparent meaning varied somewhat. Some experts seem to have used it to describe the worry that people might have had about the consequences of the referendum (e.g., Burgess 2016). Others employed it more broadly to encompass a range of negative emotions people may have felt in the referendum's aftermath, including grief, fear and anger (e.g., Sanderson 2016). What most had in common was the idea of Brexit anxiety as an incipient form of mental disorder that needed to be managed carefully to avoid serious health consequences. In an article considering the mental health effects of the referendum, one therapy clinic warned that the anxiety and grief people felt in the wake of Brexit were 'symptoms' that should not be ignored:

> They are the biggest causes of mental health problems and one of the main reasons patients come to our practice – they can even cause further problems with physical health if not recognised and treated properly. (Private Psychiatry 2016)

Cautions of this kind were common. On its website, the Mental Health Foundation, one of the oldest mental health charities in the United Kingdom, advised people to manage their negative emotions 'proactively' to avoid mental disorder and 'adjust to whatever the post-Brexit reality brings'. The foundation listed several activities that could aid people in this process, such as exercising, using self-help apps and disconnecting from the news cycle (Rowland 2016; see also LeBon 2016; Sanderson 2016).

The notion that one had to acknowledge one's lack of control in the face of Brexit and instead focus on 'what really matters' – like family and friends, as well as personal and professional success – was a central element in many plans. Among the most colourful examples was a YouTube video in which a therapist showcased his avowed ability to help people to 'get over Brexit' using neuroscience-based hypnotherapy (Cullen 2016a, 2016b). The video shows the client, a middle-aged man, who begins by explaining that he is distraught and angry about the referendum result and how the Brexit debate has divided the country. Halfway through the video, we understand that some kind of treatment has transpired, and the therapist prompts the man to explain how the treatment has helped him. The man responds:

> It's made me realise that I can't do too much about it and it is really what it is. And we need to hope that things can become better. And for me to just accept it and let it go. (Cullen 2016a)

What stands out about this example is not the treatment, which is obviously outlandish. No matter how well-versed in neuroscience, most serious therapists would avoid claims that they could achieve results like this in a single session. What is striking is the patient's response, which is portrayed as the ideal treatment outcome: the patient has realised that he can do nothing about the state of the country; all he can do is accept it and hope it gets better. The cure for his troublesome feelings about the state of politics is, apparently, the insight that he is politically impotent. The fragility of political emotions is on full display here. The man enters the therapist's office full of powerful and explicitly political emotions and seemingly leaves without them.

All Brexit anxiety management plans seemingly aimed for something like this, that is, to reverse the transformation from subjective emotional experience to public issue. They guided people to sever the connection between their emotions and politics, under the premise that failure to do so may lead to serious disease. That recalcitrant political emotions motivate us to think and act politically, to share our views and act with others is part of what makes them so dangerous to our health. They mislead us into believing that we might be able to change the world around us. What we must understand, experts urge us, is that politics is not the cause of our suffering: we are.

However, the Brexit anxiety management plans did not simply entreat the individual to conceptualise his emotions in apolitical, self-directed terms in order to avoid becoming diseased. They also urged him to distance or sever himself from other empowering factors – like agonistic affiliations, ongoing debates and public spaces where shared issues are discussed – and replace them with relationships, spaces and concepts that focus attention on private matters. Without these empowering factors to maintain the public articulation of his emotions, the individual can easily conclude that his emotions were not political after all and that he really is politically powerless – even without the help of neuroscience.

Unhealthy Emotions beyond the Clinic

'But what is the problem?' you might ask. 'Few people read mental health blogs. Those who do read them probably have a history of mental health problems and are especially vulnerable to the emotional fallout of political events.' But we have already seen that newspapers picked up the idea of Brexit anxiety and warnings of other dangerous emotional (over-)reactions to the referendum from these experts, disseminating them far beyond the regular readership of therapy blogs. In some articles, Brexit anxiety even evolved from an incipient if dangerous symptom into a full-blown disorder. For example, at the bottom of *The Sun* report on the 'alarming' spread of Brexit anxiety, an information box titled 'The Official NHS Doctors Guide to Anxiety' provided a list of symptoms and neurological causes of anxiety disorder (Lockett 2016). Thereby, *The Sun* and other publications also propagated the view that people had to manage Brexit-related emotions carefully to avoid mental disorder.

Neither did these ideas merely bounce around in a media echo chamber. Following the referendum, several employers started offering special mental health support for staff who needed help to cope with Brexit. Some universities arranged group counselling sessions for this purpose. For instance, staff at the University of Nottingham who had 'concerns about the potential changes following the Brexit decision and wish[ed] to enhance the ways in which they manage their own well-being' could attend a half-day workshop where they could learn ways 'to navigate the uncertainties of political changes' and 'how to feel more in control when face[d] with uncertainty' (University of Nottingham 2016). In an analogous effort, the University of Leeds published a guide online for dealing with negative emotional reactions to Brexit. The 'tools and strategies' contained in the guide were, not surprisingly, almost identical to those in mental health blogs. They included: appreciating the things one has, limiting exposure to news, avoiding agitating situations, and paying careful attention to the signals and needs of one's body (Staff Counselling and Psychological Support Service 2016). Remarkably similar to the advice of mental health experts discussed in the previous section, these methods too aimed to alienate employees from empowering factors that could enable them to maintain the public shape of their grief and find ways to channel it into action, replacing those factors with disempowering ones that were ostensibly more conducive to good mental health.

Initiatives like these also underline the potential disempowering effects of broader efforts by businesses to manage the mental health of employees in the light of evidence of the economic cost of mental disorder and unhappiness (see Davies 2015: ch. 4). Critics have argued that such efforts – which are backed by the government (Public Health England 2019) and charities (Mental Health Foundation 2020) – mask poor workplace conditions and inadequate labour laws that contribute to suffering, individualising what are best understood as collective problems (e.g., Cabanas and Illouz 2019: 91–2). The medicalisation of grief after the Brexit referendum indicates that employee mental-health management can affect not just people's ability to shape issues related to their workplace, but their political agency concerning other public issues as well. Significantly, besides introducing concepts meant to focus employees' emotions on driving self-change over political change, these efforts reconfigure workplace relationships in potentially disempowering ways. They turn these relationships, which have historically been a crucial source of empowering affiliations, into surveillance networks, which mobilise employees to check whether their colleagues are showing signs of mental disorder and, if so, to report it to the appropriate workplace authority.

The claims and guidance of mental health experts, employers and newspapers may have led people to believe that it was unhealthy to feel too strongly about Brexit, which would have disempowering implications. Not everyone who voted to remain bought into this, of course. As mentioned, after the vote, tens of thousands of people took to the streets to protest the result. Millions signed online petitions for another referendum. These people were probably not thinking about their grief as symptoms of mental disorder. However, even those who did not embrace the idea of medicalised grief and negative emotions were vulnerable to its disempowering effects.

Within the right-wing media, the phenomenon of Brexit anxiety, the provision of therapy for those supposedly suffering from it, and the use of psychiatric concepts to describe distress among Remain voters became a means to delegitimise political opponents. In the days after the referendum, the *Daily Express* and *Breitbart* both emphasised conversations in online forums between young Remain voters. The forum posts showed individuals describing themselves as 'grieving', 'sick' and feeling 'genuinely depressed', leading the *Daily Express* (2016) to assert, without evidence, that thousands of 'whinging students are complaining they're suffering from depression'. Drawing on posts from the same online discussion, *Breitbart* proclaimed that 'students "depressed" and "traumatised" by Brexit say they will fail exams'. The article accused these students of holding 'firmly anti-democratic views' (Deacon 2016). It suggested, in effect, that to experience and express strong emotions about the referendum result was not only irrational but antithetical to democratic value; this suggestion pre-empted Nadeau and colleagues' categorisation of citizens driven by strong emotions to contest the result as politically toxic, sore losers.

Some politicians and pundits pushed similar views. An NHS trust in southeast England was apparently among the first to announce, days after the vote, that it would provide free mental health support for staff emotionally affected by the outcome. Reacting to the announcement, the UKIP MEP Jane Collins called the initiative 'an insult to democracy and an insult to people who expect their NHS to deliver health care for sick people not those having referendum-related tantrums' (Stevens 2016). Whereas mental health bloggers sought to characterise the emotional fallout on Brexit as shared by both sides, Collins had no time for such pretences. In her view, it seems, only a loser would have reason to feel upset. Collins also stated more plainly what *Breitbart* implied: people who respond to Brexit with irrational tantrums undermine British democracy and its core institutions. The previously mentioned initiatives at the universities of Leeds and Nottingham provoked similar reactions when they came to light. 'Democracy has proven too hard to stomach for University of Nottingham academics', a contributor on *The Conservative Woman* blog remarked. 'Sulking snowflakes will enhance their "skills for resilience in response to the Brexit decision" by having half a day off work to sit in a room and moan about the grubby lower classes who upset them in June' (The Conservative Woman 2016; see also Mikelionis 2016).

The harsh rhetoric and *ad hominem* attacks on people who voted remain are not surprising. Left- and right-wing pundits alike have a penchant for attacking opponents' identities and right to a fair hearing rather than their arguments. The more interesting aspect of these attacks from the right is that they show how the medicalisation of grief and other negative emotional responses to Brexit could be utilised as a political weapon, a weapon that struck at the fragility of political emotions. While there were significant differences between the views of the mental health experts and the right-wing commentators on the issue of Brexit anxiety, they functioned similarly. Drawing on psychiatric concepts, they targeted people's doubts about the nature of their own and other people's emotions, claiming that the grief, fear and anger that people experienced in the referendum's wake were irrational feelings resulting from individual flaws rather than legitimate political concerns. Although therapists and right-wing pundits disagreed on the specific methods for how these individuals should overcome their flaws and what they should be called, their message was essentially the same: get over it; move on; normal, healthy citizens do not cause a fuss; they leave politics to the politicians; they keep calm and carry on.

Such medicalising attacks and the idea of citizenship they imply can undermine the political agency of activists regardless of whether they convince the activists themselves. There are two reasons for this. First, by framing political emotions as unhealthy, medicalising attacks increase the apparent cost of political involvement, depriving activists of potential allies for whom these costs are prohibitively high. Secondly, even if activists can maintain the public shape of their grief amongst themselves and, with it, the emotion's motivational, epistemic and social cohesive benefits, the medicalising attacks constrain the political–communicative benefits of grief by turning lamentations over Brexit from a sign of authenticity into a sign of medical disease.

Conclusion

Using the Brexit referendum as a case study, I have in this chapter tried to show how the medicalisation of grief can impact political agency. Like the other negative emotions considered in this book, grief has tremendous political potential. The unpleasant affects involved in grief – like feelings of disruption, uncertainty and absence – can fuel reflection about and action against wrongs in the world; they can ground and strengthen bonds of solidarity between people and help us communicate the depth of our loss and need to others. Yet these feelings and the emotion of which they form part are not intrinsically political. Deep grief often blurs out the rest of the world, drawing our attention and efforts inward. To realise the political potential of grief, we need to transform it into a public shape. This is what many Remainers did with their grief and other negative emotions in the aftermath of the Brexit referendum, tying these experiences to the issue of what the country's future would be and how it would be determined and channelling them into protests, campaigns and new policy organisations. But even in contexts like the referendum in which emotional and meta-emotional rhetoric pervade public discourse and drag emotions into politics, political emotions remain fragile, open to doubts about the 'real' basis of people's emotions. Public responses to the grief of Remainers brought this fragility into sharp relief. Mental health experts, journalists and employers warned that strong emotional reactions to the loss were incipient symptoms of mental disorder and urged individuals to distance themselves from the relationships, spaces and concepts that (mis)led them into believing that their emotions were politically relevant and that they have the power to address the causes of their emotions. Such medicalising attacks were apparently capable of destroying the public shape of individuals' grief. However, the impact of these attacks on the political agency of Remainers was in most instances probably more subtle, working particularly by undermining others' willingness to join them or even hear them out.

Hence, political theorists are right to worry that labelling grief as a disease can undermine political agency, but they are wrong to regard it as just another form of individualisation or delegitimisation. Medicalisation can do more than individualise or delegitimise subjective experiences. It can also alienate people from empowering factors that allowed or could have allowed them to transform those experiences into a public shape, replacing those factors with disempowering ones.

Notes

1. While the political theory of loss has tended to focus on bereavement, theorists have highlighted the political relevance of grief unrelated to bereavement as well. See, for example, contributions in Eng and Kazanjian (2003a) and McIvor et al. (2020).

2. Louise Richardson and colleagues (2021) suggest that loss may not even be a necessary condition for grief. Sometimes, it seems that rather than relating to loss, grief is better understood as relating to 'certain kinds of *change* and *transition*'. One might, of course, argue that change induces grief only if it is so significant as to be experienced as a loss. So, I do not think anything significant about grief as an experience is occluded if we treat loss as a necessary condition for grief.

3. Danielle Allen (2004) and others (e.g., Nadeau et al. 2021) advocate something like this type of reaction to political losses in liberal democracies.

4. The centrality of feeling in grief might seem obvious and many political theorists do recognise it at least in passing. But some influential scholars, like Honig (2013: 89), have dismissed it. As we have seen in previous chapters, political theorists have underestimated the importance the feeling component of other emotions as well.

5. That grief involves so many painful affects might also justify claims that 'the energy of extreme grief may offer a unique opportunity for social mobilization and political action' (Holst-Warhaft 2000: 9). Perhaps the negative affects mobilised in grief can compound in such a way as to engender a such an 'inexhaustible' emotional potential.

6. This commentator might have read Nussbaum's *From Disgust to Humanity* (2010), in which she characterises disgust as an irrational political force. Nussbaum characterises several negative emotions this way, including anger and fear as we shall see in later chapters.

7. Social and feminist theorists have argued for some time that emotions are a central subject and vector of governance under contemporary

capitalism (e.g., Ahmed 2014; Illouz 2007). But the governance of specifically *political* emotions has not been widely recognised.

8. A search in the ProQuest newspaper database for the string <'Brexit anxiety' AND (psychological OR mental OR psychiatric OR therapy)>, indicates that Brexit anxiety was not used to describe mental health before 11 July 2016.

Chapter 4
Mad Protesters: Raging with Occupy

This chapter explores the role of anger and medicalisation in the Occupy movement. Occupy has been among the most widespread protest movements so far in the twenty-first century. It emerged when the Arab Spring was at a high point. In Tunisia and Egypt, people had successfully risen against oppressive and entrenched dictators. Meanwhile, the West was still reeling from the financial crisis of 2007 and 2008. Many were depressed (affectively and economically), worried about the future, and outraged at the extreme inequality that the Great Recession uncovered. Briefly, it seemed as though Occupy could ignite a Western Autumn. That did not happen, of course. Ultimately, as some would have it, 'cooler heads' prevailed and Occupy came to an end. The movement was not a complete failure. For one, it contributed significantly towards the re-politicisation of economic inequality (Bailey 2017: 181), which has been palpable in recent elections both in the United Kingdon and the United States. But in other ways, it did fail. Within six months, the movement's occupations of public spaces across the world had been cleared out, often through court order and the protesters' demands were largely ignored. Many factors might have contributed to these failures. Samuel Burgum (2018), for example, suggests that neoliberal values like individualism were to blame, partly because these values made external publics unreceptive to Occupy's messages, partly because the activists unwittingly reproduced these values in their actions.

In this chapter, I contend that the medicalisation of negative emotions may have been another such factor. More specifically, drawing upon activist accounts, news coverage and court records, I argue that psychiatric concepts functioned as disempowering factors that undermined Occupy protesters' credibility, affiliations and access to public spaces. However, most of the examples in this chapter do not involve the kind of explicit medicalising attacks on negative emotions that we saw in the Brexit case. Instead, they elucidate a more indirect kind of medicalising attack, one that disempowers by emphasising the presence of people with mental disorder within a movement, implying that something must be wrong with the movement if it attracts such people. Such attacks are facilitated by the general medicalisation of negative emotions but do not disempower primarily by medicalising emotions. Nevertheless, these attacks can medicalise emotions just as surely as those that target emotions explicitly.

I begin with a brief discussion of recent philosophical debates on the role of anger in politics. I then highlight the importance of anger in the movement and that Occupy provided people with the resources to transform their anger into public issues. However, I also suggest that opponents exploited the evident emotionality of the protesters to disempower the movement. Subsequent sections examine medicalising attacks on Occupy in the United States and the United Kingdom in turn. In both contexts, observers claimed that a significant contingent of protesters was mentally disordered. I argue that such claims can, on the one hand, disempower people with mental disorder by obscuring their political anger and other reasons they might have for acting politically and casting them as a delegitimising presence in a movement. On the other hand, they can also disempower protesters generally by undermining their credibility *vis-à-vis* external publics, weakening their affiliations to one another, and even justifying their exclusion from public spaces.

Anger, Medicalisation and Politics

That anger can support political agency seems obvious. Philosophers of emotion usually take anger to involve an evaluation that a wrong has been committed. Provided that the anger is warranted, that is, the evaluation that a wrong has been committed is correct, and the reaction is proportionate, it can be productive. Anger focuses our attention on what has gone wrong, drives us to think about why and motivates us to address it. And depending on how we express our anger, it can help other people see that something has gone wrong and perhaps mobilise them to act with us to address it. Under the right circumstances, these features can help effect political change.

Nevertheless, there are sceptics about the positive political potential of anger. Martha Nussbaum (2016) has led the charge against the emotion in recent years. She argues that it is both intrinsically irrational and politically counterproductive. Philosophers of emotion generally agree that an evaluation that a wrong has been committed is a necessary component of anger, but Nussbaum thinks that another necessary component is a desire for the wrongdoer to suffer.[1] Because the wrongdoer's suffering does not restore what the wrongful act damaged, Nussbaum concludes that anger is irrational. Her conceptual analysis of anger is closely linked to her claim that anger politically counterproductive; because anger aims for retribution, it is 'politically futile' (236). She attempts to support this claim empirically through some examples from the history of social movements. Neither Nussbaum's conceptual nor empirical attack on anger is successful. There are good reasons to think that anger can involve a desire for things other than retribution (Brady 2013: 32), such as recognition (Silva 2021; see also Adkins 2020). Furthermore, anger has played a significant and constructive role in numerous social movements, not to mention in the lives of many marginalised individuals who challenged the injustices they faced.[2]

Unsurprisingly, then, Nussbaum's rejection of anger in politics has met with fierce opposition.[3] Indeed, defenders of anger increasingly seem to represent the philosophical and political mainstream. These defenders owe much to feminist and anti-racist scholars and activists who insist on the political value of anger (Goodwin et al. 2001). Notably, they draw attention to the motivational, epistemic, communicative and social cohesive features of negative emotions that I discussed in Chapter 1. As we saw in that chapter, Audre Lorde, for example, emphasised that anger, transformed into an appropriate shape, could motivate action. She also gestures at the emotion's epistemic and communicative features, suggesting that instances of anger can serve as 'spotlights' that confront people with injustice and mobilise them to participate in 'corrective surgery' to address it collectively (Lorde 2007: 124–5; see also Lepoutre 2018). Inspired by Lorde and others, many defenders of anger in politics today focus on its epistemic and communicative features, especially on how social norms and practices that devalue the anger of certain people can curtail these features (e.g., Adkins 2020; Cherry 2018; Srinivasan 2018). Stereotypes about angry Black men and hysterical women, for example, can lead members of these groups to regulate their anger in ways that are harmful to them (see Archer and Mills 2019). One of the ways it may do so is by directing the anger of individuals towards private rather than public life and, hence, leaving injustices unaddressed or even unnoticed (Lepoutre 2018).

Perhaps because there are so many ways in which anger's path into public life may be diverted, analyses exploring how this path is affected by medicalisation specifically are rare.[4] Some commentators even appear to doubt that the sciences of the mind could be used to transform people's anger in psychiatric problems, at least by quali-fied practitioners of those sciences today (e.g., Gallegos 2021: 8).[5] Yet well-known mental disorders do count anger among their symp-toms and have been accused of harmfully medicalising the emotion. For example, '[i]nappropriate, intense anger or difficulty controlling anger' is a symptom of borderline personality disorder (BPD) (663). It is commonly believed that three-quarters of people diagnosed with BPD are women,[6] and many women with the diagnosis have been subject to physical and sexual abuse (Zanarini et al. 1999), leading feminist critics to argue that BPD medicalises these women's justifi-ably angry responses to oppression (Shaw and Proctor 2005; Ussher 2013). Moreover, as Nancy Potter (2009: 38) argues, once someone has been diagnosed with BPD and their disposition to get angry has been labelled as a symptom, any instance of occurrent anger can easily be dismissed as a symptom as well even though it may be warranted. Thereby, a BPD diagnosis can also obscure ongoing mistreatment that non-medicalised anger could have elucidated. Oppositional defiant disorder (ODD) may have similar effects in relation to Black children and adolescents, who are disproportionately diagnosed with the disor-der in the US (Fadus et al. 2020). Anger is a central criterion in ODD, which the DSM describes as involving a 'pattern of angry/irritable mood, argumentative/defiant behavior, or vindictiveness' (APA 2013: 462). Because of racial discrimination and related factors, like poverty, Black children may have more reasons to be angry and externalise their anger, while teachers and healthcare professionals may be more likely to regard these externalisations as symptoms of ODD (Potter 2016: ch. 4). Hence, the diagnosis may obscure the racism and other injus-tices experienced by Black children. I do not mention these diagnoses because political actors are often diagnosed with or accused of having them. Neither BPD nor ODD was, as far as I have found, deployed against activists in the Occupy movement; indeed, despite much talk of mental disorder in the media, specific diagnoses were rarely cited. I mention them because they form part of and point to a wider web of dis/empowering factors that make medicalising attacks on anger and other negative emotions in public life possible and, sometimes, highly effective. It is, as we shall see, a web in which political actors can easily become entangled.

A few political theorists have raised concerns about the political consequences of the medicalisation of anger in instances of transitional justice, but without considering that it may have similar consequences in other contexts. Examining the proceedings of the South African Truth and Reconciliation Commission (TRC), Thomas Brudholm (2008) and Sonali Chakravarti (2014) both identify among TRC officials a tendency to view the anger of witnesses who had suffered the injustices of apartheid as a mental health issue that needed to be overcome for the sake of the witnesses themselves as well as society. This individualised the witnesses' anger, averting full consideration of its systemic causes (Brudholm 2008: 39; Chakravarti 2014: 71–2). Differently put, medicalisation in the TRC undermined the transformation of anger into public issues, directing the emotion's epistemic and communicative features away from public and towards private life. Similar moves were made against the Occupy movement, with hostile commentators deploying psychiatric concepts to discredit protesters' angry actions and reframe their experiences as medical problems.

Occupational Anger

It was on 17 September, a Saturday afternoon in 2011, that the first group of protesters began their occupation of Zuccotti Park, two blocks away from Wall Street. How many gathered in Zuccotti Park that day under the Occupy Wall Street (OWS) banner is unclear, though it was a sizeable number that grew quickly. Soon, hundreds were camped out in the park and tens of thousands joined in associated protest marches. OWS' call to action was not ignored. Within weeks, protesters were occupying public spaces in cities across the United States, the United Kingdom and the world. That negative emotions were a significant driving force within the movement was clear from the start. There was grief over lost jobs, destroyed futures and deprivation; fear for individual and collective futures and about retribution from the authorities for speaking up; and, perhaps most evidently, *anger* – anger at greedy bankers, corrupt politicians, dysfunctional institutions and the injustice of extreme inequality.

The meta-emotional rhetoric that emerged around the movement was ambivalent about protesters' anger. While Occupy's critics and critical sympathisers claimed to understand the anger, they admonished the protesters for the ostensive aimlessness of their emotion (e.g., Kristof 2011a; *Wall Street Journal* 2011). In a typical comment, one US journalist remarked: 'Yes, many people have been hurt by this country's financial system and they are appropriately angry . . . But unless and until this anger is channeled into something that catalyzes a policy debate, it is not particularly newsworthy' (Fiedler 2011). Others similarly called for concrete policy demands, a formal organisational structure, the identification of leaders and official talks with policymakers.

These commentators were not imploring activists to avoid anger. Philosophers have warned that members of marginalised groups are often subject to norms and rhetoric aiming to 'regulate away [their] anger' about injustice (Archer and Mills 2019: 83; see also Srinivasan 2018). One way of doing so is by warning them that their anger is politically counterproductive. However, the Occupy activists were facing calls not to avoid anger but to redirect and reshape it. Indeed, given the apparent emancipation of emotion, we might expect explicit denunciations of emotions in public life for whatever reason to become increasingly rare.

To demand of someone that they redirect and reshape anger can be disempowering too, of course (see Whitney 2018). In the context of OWS, it probably was. After all, commentators were effectively calling for protesters to play by the rules they rejected, to transform their unruly emotions into the rational language and practices of the elite. That was tactically and conceptually problematic for the protesters. The 'rational' language of policy they were being urged to adopt was biased in favour of the institutions and practices they opposed (Wright 2012). It may, therefore, have seemed to the protesters that if they went along with the advice, they would not only disadvantage themselves but legitimise their opponents.[7]

Contrary to the claims of prominent pundits like Nikolas Kristof (2011a, b) though, the protesters were not acting on *raw* emotions. Writings of activists and scholars illustrate that a core function of the Occupy camp in Zuccotti Park was to enable individuals to transform their anger and other negative emotions into politically meaningful thought, speech and action. The title of Michael Taussig's (2013) account of OWS, 'I'm so angry that I made a sign', captured one such transformation. Borrowed from a placard displayed during the protest, that phrase tells us that the sign-maker took something often regarded as private and destructive – anger – and turned it into something public and, arguably, constructive – a protest sign. Thereby, they made more than just a sign; they participated in creating public spaces, affiliations and other empowering factors through which they and others could transform their anger and other negative emotions into public issues and political action. Taussig (2013: 39) recognised the camp's transformative function as well, describing it as a space in which 'the atomized mass of yesterday, without hope . . . crystallized itself through a new language and sense of collective'.

The concepts that were part of this space also facilitated this transformation of negative emotions into public issues and political action. The most important of those concepts was probably the idea of 'the 99%'.[8] During the movement, hundreds of people posted personal stories about everything from healthcare to discrimination to student debt on a blog called 'We are the 99 percent' (Anon. 2013). Many were handwritten, with the authors holding their notes up next to their faces. Each note was signed, 'I am the 99%', affirming the authors' affiliations to one another and the movement. Rather than search for an explanation of their negative emotions in themselves, Occupy permitted these people to find it in the world. As one activist suggested, OWS was simultaneously a 'symbol of distress' and a platform for action (Schmitt and Taylor 2011).

So, participation in Occupy entailed a transformation of anger, but it was not the kind of transformation commentators had in mind. Politicians and business leaders, though doubtlessly emotional, routinely conceal their emotions within a grammar of reasonable interest and economic necessity (see Goodwin et al. 2001; Hirschman 1977). The protesters rejected this 'rationality', appearing unapologetically angry in their calls for equality and justice. The explicit anger of the protesters likely helped to foment and sustain the movement by inviting people to channel the motivational and epistemic force of their emotions into action, by communicating activists' sincere commitment to the movement and by deepening the bonds between them. However, the fragility of emotions meant that it was also a vulnerability that others could use to define and redefine the nature and causes of protesters' experiences and actions.

The Mad Faces of Occupy Wall Street

The following two sections show that psychiatric concepts were deployed against Occupy protesters in disempowering ways. Psychiatric concepts are far from the only resources that can be used to undermine protests. Dissenters in liberal democracies routinely face a range of disempowering factors (Theodossopoulos 2014), which, among other things, challenge the political relevance of their emotions (Gould 2010). But psychiatric concepts are more potent than most other such resources because they imply not just that protesters should be ignored and excluded from public life, but that the concepts, affiliations and spaces that empower protesters should be replaced with diagnoses, doctors and hospitals.

The most obvious way and sometimes the most effective way to disempower a political actor using a psychiatric concept is to deploy it directly against them, labelling them as sick. If the label sticks, it may not only destroy the public shape of their anger but inhibit them from transforming their anger into a public shape in the future, since any future episode of anger can be dismissed as the resurgence of psychiatric symptoms – a problem that women with BPD face, as we have seen. *Fox News*' star host at the time, Bill O'Reilly, launched this type of direct medicalising attack against the Occupy movement on his show when he brought on the psychotherapist Karen Ruskin to comment on the 'psychological make-up' of the protesters. Ruskin claimed that they were mentally unwell and that their actions were further harming their mental health:

> You see, when we feel out of control in our life, that leads us to depression. What they're actually asking for is to be out of control. They're asking for others to take control of their life by giving me – give me, give me, give me – rather than self-empowerment, rather than self-enhancement. That is concerning. And that does lead to mental instability. (O'Reilly 2011)

This example again brings into view the fragility of political emotions. The protesters showed no symptoms of depression. In the video clips that formed part of O'Reilly's segment with the therapist, protesters appeared, if anything, to be angry. Indeed, O'Reilly even formulaically pushed back against Ruskin by suggesting that the protesters felt empowered in action. Ruskin responded that this apparent empowerment simply 'masks' (her word) the true and unhealthy mentalities and processes of the protesters.

The vocabulary and the effort to find the hidden truths of the heart behind the façade of political meaning recalls the unmasking of inauthentic emotions in the French Revolution. It also resonates with one of Arendt's more direct critiques of psychiatry. In the context of the Eichmann trial, Arendt (1994: 26) disparaged 'the comedy of soul experts', that is, psychiatrists, trying and failing to find anything mentally wrong with Eichmann, whom they testified to being a perfectly normal, well-adjusted human being. It was a 'comedy', according to Arendt, because Eichmann's crime could only be understood politically. But psychiatry, which evaluates individuals against and adjusts them to medical norms, was politically blind (Norberg 2010). Perhaps, then, O'Reilly's interview could be considered an example of a *tragedy* of 'soul experts' – a tragedy because it involves mental health experts and others, who are plainly politically cognizant, deploying psychiatric concepts to deprive people's actions of political meaning and return political emotions to the darkness of the heart.

Medicalising attacks are not always as blunt as this and need not be in order to be effective. O'Reilly's light pushback perhaps indicates that he thought even his right-wing viewers needed help swallowing accusations that the emotions and thoughts of Occupy activists were symptoms or precursors of mental disorder. Medicalising attacks also come in subtler forms, which do not look like attacks on political actors and their experiences at all but like observations of fact. The more salient type of medicalising attack on Occupy did not claim that its political actors generally were mentally disordered but that it was, in effect, contaminated by an unusually large number of people who were. Observing the presence of mental disorder within a movement is not necessarily disempowering, of course. For all we know, many of the Occupy protesters did have psychiatric diagnoses. Given the prevalence of mental disorder in general, anywhere between 10 and 20 per cent of the members of any movement might plausibly have been diagnosed with mental disorder. However, as we shall see, news reports hardly provided a neutral account of the prevalence of mental disorder.

With thousands of protesters occupying public spaces around the United states in autumn 2011, people were asking: who were the members of the Occupy movement? What drove them to act? Attempting to answer these questions, *USA Today* proposed that many protesters fell into one of four archetypes: the veteran protester, the student, the poor and the (mentally) troubled (Hampson 2011). As an example of the last archetype, the article cited 29-year-old Nkrumah Tinsley, a protester who had been arrested after an online video surfaced of him threatening to firebomb a New York City department store. Tinsley's parents later claimed that their son suffered from mental health problems, something his erratic behaviour in court apparently confirmed. The *USA Today* article effectively suggested that a significant contingent of the Occupy movement was like Tinsley: mentally disordered and potentially violent.

USA Today was not the only newspaper to paint this picture. New York media reported extensively on Tinsley's arrest and subsequent trial, often reiterating his mental problems and connection to Occupy.[9] The New York *Daily News* followed the case closely. A week after Tinsley had been arrested, the newspaper published an article headlined 'Molotov madman who said on YouTube he would bomb Macy's is out of jail and back at Zuccotti Park' (Grace and Kemp 2011a). It alleged that OWS members had posted his $7,500 bail, implying that they had deliberately put a dangerous madman back on the street. The newspaper repeated this allegation in connection with the arrest of Brandon Watts, a 20-year-old man who was one of the most well-known protesters at Zuccotti Park. Watts had become a poster boy for Occupy after a picture of his face, gruesomely bloodied by a police beating, appeared on the front page of the *Daily News* and in newspapers across the country on 18 November. A week later, the *Daily News* reported that Watts had been arrested for stealing a police officer's hat during a confrontation, resisting arrest and throwing a pen at the police. Once again, OWS posted the bail for one of their own. Watts' own lawyer, Martin Stolar – who represented several other OWS members as well – urged in a statement that his client was not representative of the movement. 'That would brand all of them as people with psychiatric issues – and that is clearly not the case,' Stolar elaborated, even though Watts had no evident mental health issues. His concern proved justified. The *Daily News* subsequently suggested that the protesters' demonstrable willingness to bail out mentally disordered individuals such as Tinsley and Watts was a sign of more widespread psychiatric problems among the movement's members (Grace and Kemp 2011b).

As the protests continued, further reports emerged of quarrelsome protesters being dragged off for psychiatric evaluation.[10] Another seemingly disordered OWS protester, Dylan Spoelstra, made international headlines after mounting a 70-foot sculpture in the park and refusing to come down until his demand for New York Mayor Michael Bloomberg's resignation had been met (*New York Post* 2011; Stevens 2011). After being convinced to dismount the sculpture, Spoelstra was arrested and taken to a hospital for psychiatric evaluation. A police spokesman told the media that Spoelstra was 'emotionally disturbed' and it was uncertain whether he would be prosecuted (Newcomb 2011). Again, some OWS supporters worried that the event would reflect poorly on the movement (Badia and Shapiro 2011). Among some conservatives, it demonstrably did. A conservative journalist remarked that people like Spoelstra 'summed up the lunacy' of OWS, continuing: 'How do you talk rationally with people who spout such idiocy? The answer is, you don't' (Moran 2011).

This reaction typifies the sort of dismissal that theorists of anger and mental disorder alike worry about. The putative mental disorder of some protesters was used to conclude that they, the broader movement and the anger it channelled, should not be heard. This is important because it demonstrates that psychiatric concepts have recently been used to discredit political actors and their anger in the eyes of external publics. It is not an unexpected finding. Many critics of psychiatry have claimed that psychiatric diagnoses are being deployed to this end in contemporary politics, but they often fail to point to examples where it has (e.g., Cohen 2016).

Another, less obvious disempowering dynamic can be discerned in the media coverage of OWS too, namely, that medicalising attacks can contribute to *internal* divisions and thereby undermine protesters' affiliations. As we have seen, participants and allies of Occupy also worried about mental disorder within the movement. They believed that having a large contingent of people with mental disorder within a movement is delegitimising. Worries like these can lead political actors to try to distinguish the healthy and from the sick among them, as though the latter were not authentic actors. Stolar was doing this when stressing that Watts was not representative of the movement. It was also happening on the ground in Zuccotti Park, where it became a source of conflict among the protesters (Bossewitch 2016: ch. 3). In a council to discuss 'protocols' for evicting troublesome people, particularly with certain mental disorders, one protester angrily declared: 'The revolution that I'm interested in participating in is the one that includes everybody and doesn't distinguish between worthy and unworthy protesters' (quoted in Bossewitch 2016: 75). Medicalising attacks can make such distinctions difficult to avoid. If the presence of people with mental disorder within a movement undermines its credibility, differentiating between healthy/authentic actors, on the one hand, and sick/inauthentic ones, on the other, might be a prudential way for protesters to protect their political agency. This tactic has a price, however. It may ultimately weaken the political agency of the movement by alienating actual and potential co-actors with mental disorder. More damningly, it disempowers individuals with mental disorder by effectively practicing the prejudice that they have no place in public life.

Occupy London, a Magnet for Madness

By the end of October 2011, Occupy had spread around the world, including to Britain. Protesters established camps under the Occupy banner in major cities across the United Kingdom, including London, Birmingham and Edinburgh. Of these, Occupy London was the most visible and long-lasting. Participants in these off-shoots were drawing upon the movement's resources to channel into political action the same anger that moved their peers across the Atlantic. At least, that is what Cassie Earl (2018) concluded based on interviews with Occupy London activists. Earl frames the function of the camp in terms strikingly similar to the ones I have used in relation to OWS:

> Occupy opened up the possibilities and Occupiers thought about and confronted ideas that they previously had no space to experiment with. The experience was embodied and performative because of the context and setting, therefore emotionality could hardly have been avoided. Occupy gave its activists an outlet for their anger, whether we concede that it worked or are disappointed by its failure, it attempted to do something positive, whilst avoiding cynicism or unbalanced fury, and it did it with a generous heart. (Earl 2018: 109–10)

Though Occupy London never mobilised as many protesters as OWS, it provoked similar responses from its opponents, including medicalising attacks. Some followed the O'Reilly model of depicting protesters' experiences and actions as disordered (e.g., Gledhill 2011; Williams 2011). The more salient kind of attack, though, was again of the other variety, which highlights and problematises the presence of people with mental disorder within the movement. This section focuses on the use and apparent consequences of the latter. It does so with two aims. The first is to show that the medicalising attacks on Occupy were not a uniquely American phenomenon. The second is to draw out some additional ways in which such attacks can disempower protesters, specifically by mobilising the law against them and creating cumbersome collective responsibilities.

The Occupy London organisers initially called for a march on Paternoster Square outside the London Stock Exchange on 15 October. But after police blocked access to the square, thousands of Occupy protesters instead assembled in front of St Paul's Cathedral, where the demonstration continued into the night. The next day, around 500 protesters gathered and agreed on an 'Initial Statement', consisting of ten points setting out their general position and aims. Among other things, it declared the protesters' intention to develop alternatives to the 'current system', which they perceived as 'undemocratic and unjust' (Occupy London 2011). The number of occupiers quickly declined. By 17 October, two days after the occupation began, only about 150 tents were pitched outside the cathedral. Many of those who remained, however, proved to be tenacious, and their persistence led City officials, apparently with the support of the Church of England (Butt et al. 2011), to pursue eviction proceedings against the camp in court.

Occupy London's ostensive mental health problem started making headlines less than two weeks after the occupation of St Paul's court began. *The Telegraph* reported that organisers in the camp had requested the support of mental health professionals and social workers to help them to cope with an influx of people with mental disorders and addictions. An Occupy spokesperson quoted in the article said that activists planned to set up a 'welfare tent' in the camp to support individuals with such problems (Ward 2011). The article failed to mention that this was praxis within the movement. In Zuccotti Park, OWS activists also established a health tent and other services soon after the occupation began; to the protesters, the provision of such services was integral to the movement's principles (Pickerill and Krinsky 2012: 283). When the plan had been realised, there were reports that it was harming the people it was meant to help. According to *The Times*, the camp had become a 'magnet for homeless people'. Citing charity workers, it described how people were leaving medical and social care behind for the sake of the free food and community spirit of the camp. One source claimed there had also been 'complaints about vulnerable people not taking their meds'. Given these circumstances, the article warned, the conditions of protesters with mental health problems were likely to worsen (Schlesinger 2011). The message was clear. If anyone was to blame for this, it was the protesters. Each day the occupation persisted, more sick people would be drawn to the camp.

The presence of 'vulnerable people' evidently was a problem for some protesters. Five months into the protest, an anonymous protester told a newspaper that the toughest aspect of life in the camp was dealing with inhabitants with mental health, alcohol and drug problems, and claimed that their number was increasing (Holehouse 2012; see also Burgum 2018: 49–53). As far as I have been able to tell, no one tried to estimate the number of people in the camp experiencing mental disorder addiction, or homelessness. For the purposes of this book, though, this number is less interesting than how observers used the idea that the camp was filled with sick people. In January 2012, a court found in favour of the City of London's case to evict the protest – we shall look closer at the court proceedings soon – and, a month later, the protesters lost their appeal. Shortly after the appeal's failure, *The Telegraph* columnist Brendan O'Neill (2012) declared: 'Occupy London is now basically a holding camp for the mentally ill.' He blamed the degeneration of the camp into 'a modern-day Bedlam' on the aimlessness of the early protesters. 'Originally a magnet for leftists bereft of ideas, Occupy London is now a magnet for the mentally unsound,' O'Neill concluded. 'It is no longer a political protest at all, but a health outlet, and as such it should urgently be brought indoors.' In other words, people with mental disorder do not need to be heard politically, they need to be cared for medically, and they cannot have both.

The recurrent descriptions of Occupy London as a magnet are noteworthy. Earlier I discussed how medicalising attacks in the context of OWS may have compelled people within the movement to try to distinguish between healthy/authentic actors and sick/inauthentic ones. As we have seen, this distinction was pursued both externally and internally in the context of Occupy London as well. But the magnet metaphor draws attention to something else that occurred in the latter context: people with mental disorder were reduced to non-agents or objects at the mercy of an irresistible force; their behaviour was *individualised* and the possibility that they may have political reasons for joining the protest ignored. At the same time, *collective* agency and responsibility were attributed to the (healthy) protesters. By creating the camp and attracting individuals with mental disorder, the protesters became responsible for providing care to these individuals and managing the risk their presence posed to the community around them, as well as culpable for any failure to do so. The protesters, possibly to their detriment, effectively accepted this by trying to provide healthcare in the camp. So, even as medicalisation can individualise the problems and emotions of one person, it can collectivise the care for that person. Usually, that collective responsibility falls on doctors and healthcare institutions (Rose 1998), but medicalising attacks can foist it onto political actors ill-equipped to provide it.

Similar ideas found their way into court when the protesters were fighting the City of London to avoid eviction. One newspaper reported that social workers had expressed concern in court 'about the mentally ill, alcoholics and drug addicts who [had] been attracted to the camp' (Kelly 2011). The public court transcript does not mention any such testimonies (*City of London Corp.* v. *Samede* 2012). The transcript includes the testimony of one witness, a charity volunteer, who said he had patrolled the camp at night on several occasions. During these patrols, he said, the camp was generally quiet. What little trouble he saw involved either people 'with mental health issues being noisy or abusive and disruptive' or people with 'alcohol issues being noisy, confrontational and disruptive'. No other witnesses in the trial cited problems with mental disorder in the camp. Considering this, the role that reporters and the judge assigned to mental disorder seems disproportionate. In his judgment, siding with the City of London, Mr Justice Keith Lindblom implied a link between 'anti-social behaviour' – a key theme in the prosecution's case – and mental illness:

> [T]he camp cannot be blamed for the existence in society of problems such as homelessness, mental illness and addiction. But, [as the prosecutor] Mr Forsdick submitted, the occupation of this land by a tented community has stimulated anti-social behaviour and criminal activity. Had the camp not been there, this would not have happened. (*City of London Corp.* v. *Samede* 2012)

This suggests that people with mental disorder were a significant source of anti-social behaviour and crime in the camp and the surrounding area. Although the camp could not 'be blamed for the existence' of mental illness 'in society', according to the judge, the camp, and, by implication, the protesters were collectively culpable for attracting mental illness to the area and the troubles stemming from it. For these reasons among others, Lindblom decided that the protesters should be evicted.

The outcome of the trial highlights several disempowering effects that medicalising attacks can have beyond undermining the credibility of protesters. First, by constructing people with mental disorder as a significant threat to public safety and making other protesters collectively responsible for that threat, medicalising attacks can provide legal justification for depriving a protest of public space. Secondly, medicalising attacks can obscure political meanings. While food and community plausibly motivated some people with mental disorder and other vulnerable individuals to come to the camp, they may simultaneously have joined out of a sense of indignation about inequality and precarity, issues of which they have faced the worst. Even if indignation was not a factor, that vulnerable people willingly abandoned charity-provided food, shelter and medicine to join a makeshift camp is itself an action ripe with potential political meaning.[11] Lindblom, charity workers, journalists and other commentators buried these meanings under psychiatric concepts and other labels for deviance.

Conclusion

The Occupy movement provided empowering factors – including spaces, affiliations and concepts – that allowed people to transform their negative emotions into a public issue, into anger *about* inequality, fuelling political action on a scale not seen for years. In this context, psychiatric concepts came to function as disempowering factors, deployed in medicalising attacks that undermined the public shape of the protesters' anger. However, the main target of these attacks was not the anger of protesters but the empowering factors of the movement. Medicalising attacks on Occupy involved claims that the movement was contaminated by an abnormal number of people with mental disorder, who were too irrational, vulnerable or dangerous to participate in the protests. Attacks like these struck at the credibility and affiliations of the protesters. In the context of Occupy London, they even contributed towards undermining their access to public space and mobilising the law against them. As I have emphasised, the impact of these medicalising attacks was likely particularly severe for individuals with mental disorder, who were frequently framed as non-agents whose proper place is in the medical, not the political, domain. Neither observers nor protesters seemed to consider that such people could be driven by and trying to express the same anger about inequality that animated others in the

Occupy movement. Therefore, when it came to people with mental disorder, their anger did not even have to be named to be deprived of its fragile public shape because it was quietly crushed beneath the weight of their putative diagnoses.

Notes

1. Nussbaum is not alone in claiming that anger necessarily involves a desire for the wrongdoer to suffer. Pettigrove (2012), Callard (2020) and Ben-Ze'ev (2000), for example, all agree with her. However, Ben-Ze'ev has recently argued, in response to Nussbaum, that the 'normative value [of anger] is not determined by the presence of a wish, such as revenge, but rather by the implementation of this wish'. So, even a desire for the wrongdoer to suffer would be a necessary component of anger, it would not justify Nussbaum's moral and political condemnation of anger.
2. For work showing the importance of anger in social movements and revolutions against oppressive governments, see, for instance, Eklundh (2019); Gould (2001); Saxonberg (2013). In Chapter 1, I provide several examples of the role of anger in the lives of civil rights leaders and activists (see also Degerman 2018). Lepoutre (2018) provides other noteworthy illustrations of this.
3. See, for example, Srinivasan (2018) and the growing literature building on her idea of affective injustice, as well as the contributions in Cherry and Flanagan (2018).
4. In her now canonical essay 'A Note on Anger', Frye (1983) highlights that calling women crazy has been one of the ways in which their anger has been deprived of uptake. However, what she seems to be concerned with is a metaphorical usage of the term crazy, whereby the implied meaning is that the object is unreasonable rather than ill (see also Whitney 2018). Although this usage can obviously be disempowering too, it is different from the worry that anger might be understood as a literal symptom of mental disorder.
5. Protevi (2018) notes in passing that what he calls berserker rage could be understood as a symptom of intermittent explosive disorder (see APA 2013: 466), but he does not consider what the medicalisation of such rage might mean.
6. Many critics cite the *DSM-IV-TR* section on BPD as a source for the claim that 75 per cent of people diagnosed with the disorder are women (APA 2000: 708). But recent studies suggest that there is no gender disparity in the prevalence of BPD (Sansone and Sansone 2011).
7. For an influential discussion of this kind of dynamic, see Young (2001).
8. Fenton (2015) describes the idea of 'the 99%' as an articulation of 'anti-corporate anger'.

9. See, for example, Conley (2011); Kemp et al. (2011); *The New York Times* (2011).
10. For additional examples, see Fasick (2011); Harrington and Dreier (2011); McNerthney (2011).
11. For a discussion of the practical challenges and political opportunities in the relationship between Occupy and homeless people, see Schein (2012).

Chapter 5
Primitive Populists: The Fear of UKIP

This chapter examines another political organisation whose members' experiences, opinions and actions appear to have been vulnerable to medicalisation: the UK Independence Party (UKIP). UKIP differs significantly from the other groups explored in this book, that is, the Occupy movement, Remainers and the user/survivor movement. Unlike those, UKIP is a political party, and, in the period from 2005 to the Brexit referendum in 2016 that I focus on in this chapter, it was a notable one. Despite its belligerent rhetoric and controversial aims, it participates in the traditional fray of politics – formal political systems of local, national and international government. As such, UKIP relies on a stricter and more centralised organisational structure than, for example, Occupy. The party can also lay claim to the kind of concrete achievements that eluded Occupy. In the 2014 European Parliamentary elections, UKIP won the most seats of any UK party. And, its raison d'être, a British exit from the EU has come to pass, arguably, in no small part because of UKIP's efforts.

What makes the rise of UKIP a relevant case to study in the present context, notwithstanding these differences, is that the party and its supporters seem likely targets of medicalising attacks. The animating emotion of the party's rhetoric, policies and supporters was arguably fear. Fear is not just one of the most vilified emotions in contemporary political theory (Degerman et al. 2020; Enroth 2017). It has also undergone considerable medicalisation in recent decades (Horwitz and Wakefield 2012), with the prevalence of fear-related mental disorders more than doubling since 1985 (Bandelow and Michaelis 2015). Furthermore, UKIP's opponents have long claimed that its policies are xenophobic and regressive, views which have been targets of medicalising attacks in the past. Notably, Theodor Adorno and his co-authors asserted in *The Authoritarian Personality* that xenophobia and 'resistance to [progressive] social change' were pathological

(Adorno et al. 1950: 157), and despite criticism of its medicalising project (Lasch 1991: 453), the book's thesis continues to be influential (e.g., Altemeyer 1988; Jost et al. 2003).[1] Perhaps relatedly, sociologists have claimed that we are seeing an ongoing medicalisation of racism (Gilman and Thomas 2016). Given this, UKIP, its supporters and their fear were seemingly ripe for medicalisation.

In this chapter, analysing news coverage of UKIP, I show that the party's opponents sought to delegitimise the fear that ostensibly animated its supporters through what I call hyper-emotionalising attacks rather than medicalising ones. I begin by considering how fear can support political agency. I then proceed to argue that because political theorists have been preoccupied with denouncing fear in politics, they have failed to recognise the empowering potential of fear as well as the disempowering potential of its medicalisation. The remainder of the chapter focuses on UKIP. After considering the role of fear in the rise of UKIP, I show that medicalising attacks against the party and its supporters appear to have been rare. Instead, hostile commentators accused them of being possessed by primitive fear and other negative emotions that had usurped their reason, claims that found backing in neuroscience and political theory. In conclusion, I summarise the chapter and suggest that, even if we think that fear is politically dangerous, efforts to exclude it from public life through hyper-emotionalisation or medicalisation are misguided.

The Politics of Fear

Fear can be a symptom of numerous different mental disorders, with anxiety disorders being the most obvious. In *DSM-5*, anxiety disorders are defined by fear that is excessive or disproportionate to the actual danger (APA 2013: 189). Several specific diagnoses are distinguished by what they take as the object of fear. For example, social anxiety disorder involves fear of social situations (202); specific phobias involve fear of a 'specific object or situation' (197); and generalized anxiety disorder, which does not actually involve objectless fear but 'excessive anxiety . . . about a number of events or activities'. These disorders have come to pervade society. In 1985, the estimated lifetime prevalence of anxiety disorders was 14.6 per cent. Two decades later, an authoritative epidemiological study put it at 33.7 per cent (Bandelow and Michaelis 2015). That the explosive surge in anxiety disorders is due to a sudden increase in, say, brain dysfunctions seems unlikely. More plausibly, what has changed is our understanding of and approach to dealing with certain fears, as Allan Horwitz and Jerome Wakefield (2012) have argued. That is, fear has become increasingly medicalised.

But what is fear, and why should its medicalisation concern us politically? Philosophers of emotion generally agree that it encompasses several components, including a threat evaluation, unpleasant feelings, physiological reactions and behaviours. However, they disagree on which components are essential to fear (Scarantino and De Sousa 2018). Many political and social theorists of fear focus on the evaluative component of fear and on behaviours they construe as threat responses (e.g., Furedi 2018; Robin 2004; Wodak 2015).[2] But, although the evaluative component seems essential to fear, a threat evaluation and avoidant behaviour alone do not entail fear. While I look both ways before I cross the street because I know that cars are a threat, I am not afraid whenever I am about to step onto the road. Missing here is some unpleasant feeling or feelings of fear signifying that the threat is particularly salient to me. Accounting for these feelings is not just conceptually important. As discussed in Chapter 1, these feelings also help to explain fear's capacity to focus our thoughts on a particular threat, motivate us to act to remove it, communicate effectively and efficiently to others the presence of a severe threat, and mobilise others to help us.

That fear, at least in our personal lives, can have these epistemic, motivational, communicative and social cohesive functions seems uncontroversial. Psychological research even suggests that these are biologically evolved functions of fear (Mobbs et al. 2015), and it is easy to see how they can help ensure survival. Given the poor political reputation of fear, however, claiming that these features can translate into public life is controversial, as we shall see. Yet empirical studies of fear in politics show that they indeed can, given the right resources. The political psychologist George Marcus (2002: 116) draws on voter polling data in the United States to argue that, given the right conditions, fear enables the mind 'to dream, to create, to speculate, introspect, deliberate, calculate, theorize' about political matters.[3] Marcus' work, thus, emphasises particularly the epistemic features of the emotion in public life. Sociologists, meanwhile, have provided evidence of fear's motivational, social cohesive and communicative features in social movements. Jack Gladstone and Charles Tilly (2001) observe that fear has been a mobilising force among marginalised people from the French Revolution to apartheid South Africa (see also Barbalet 2004: 160–1). Extending their analysis, Ron Aminzade and Doug McAdam (2001) show that fear can also help to generate and sustain solidarity within movements, while fearful reactions can communicate the potential costs of inaction to others subject to the same threat.

As with grief and anger, these features of fear are not guaranteed a political valence. Many factors can (re)direct fear towards changing ourselves rather than the world around us. The anxiety diagnoses mentioned above are examples of such factors. Labelling fear as an anxiety disorder can focus the emotion's epistemic and motivational features on self-change through medical means, while turning its communicative features into signs of disease and mobilise others to encourage medical treatment. And, of course, treating fear medically may eliminate the emotion and its potential political benefits altogether. The sheer pervasiveness of anxiety disorders today seems to put political actors' fear at risk of medicalising attacks. Recent changes to the diagnostic criteria for these disorders may have increased this risk further. *DSM-5* removed a long-standing criterion in social anxiety disorder and specific phobias requiring people above the age of eighteen to recognise that their fear is unreasonable in order to be diagnosed (APA 2013: 811). The implication of this change was effectively that the individual's own thoughts about the causes of their fear are medically irrelevant. Despite this, the pathologisation of fear has been exempt from the kind of concerns that we have seen political theorists raise about the pathologisation of anger and grief. That is probably because fear itself is widely regarded as a social or political pathology that has infected the polity and requires (political) treatment.

Fear has had its defenders within the canon of political theory, as Robin (2004) shows. But, notwithstanding important exceptions like Judith Shklar (1989) and Rebecca Kingston (2011), contemporary thinkers defending the role of fear in politics seem a rare breed.[4] Critiques of fear, by contrast, abound. They generally follow one of three models. The first argues that fear is inherently harmful to democracy, the second that fear is an oppressive political technique, and the third that fear is a sign of social or political decay.[5] A closer look at these helps to explain why the medicalisation/pathologisation of fear has not been a concern within political theory, but also why responses to UKIP supporters' putative fear took the shape they did.

Representing the first type of analysis, Martha Nussbaum has delivered what is perhaps the most profound recent indictment of fear in her recent book *The Monarchy of Fear* (2018). According to her, the problem with fear extends beyond its potential for political exploitation into its core. Fear, she says, is a primitive, intrinsically narcissistic emotion, antithetical to democratic citizenship and institutions. It lies in the nature of fear to distort our reasoning, open us up to manipulation and fuel intolerance (Nussbaum 2018: 44–60). Moreover, fear is not simply one bad emotion among others; it is the master villain. Other emotions that ostensibly threaten democracy, especially anger, envy and disgust, all derive from fear, according to Nussbaum (9). Therefore, we are better off avoiding it whenever we can, or, when we cannot, divesting ourselves of it as soon as possible.

An exemplar of the second type of critique can be found in the work of Corey Robin (2004). Pointing to examples ranging from the war on terror to the relationship between employees and bosses in white-collar workplaces, Robin argues that fear is a device that elites construct, maintain and use to control non-elites. Notably, he claims that elites deploy fear to obscure political issues, such as the West's responsibility for the grievances that motivated the 9/11 attacks (159). Robin recognises that elites also experience fear; indeed, this is often what drives them to use fear as a means of control (e.g., 183–4; cf. Barbalet 2004: 164–8). The origins of elite fear, however, are different from normal fear. On Robin's account, elites own their fear insofar as it derives from their autonomous assessment of the world, a feat of which others are apparently incapable.

The third type of analysis, in which fear is a sign of social or political pathology, is perhaps the most variable of the three since much hinges on what the analyst takes the pathology to be. Still, analyses of this kind apparently have in common the claim that fearful people – especially on the right – are generally ignorant of the true causes of their fear. We find good examples of this in a recent essay by Brigitte Bargetz (2021). Highlighting the putative role of fear in right-wing populism, Bargetz argues that this fear is actually a consequence of the simultaneous decay of the sovereignty of nation-states and citizens' continued longing for sovereignty. But fearful people (on the right) are not simply mistaken about the true causes of their fear. Bargetz contends that the decay of sovereignty, which is the true cause of fear, is itself tied to an illusory conception of sovereignty and its benefits. So the mistake of fearful political actors goes all the way down, so to speak, from the conscious to the unconscious. Later on, we shall see that this resonates with claims that UKIP supporters' fear is a figment of underdeveloped brains.

These accounts are not mutually exclusive. Some version of the idea that fear is intrinsically bad in public life figures both in analyses that take fear as a tool of oppression and those that take it as a symptom of political pathology. Robin (2004), for example, assumes that there is something about fear that makes it an effective means of elite control and ensures it never fuels dissent. And while fear is primarily a symptom of a deeper pathology in Bargetz' analysis, she also suggests that fear unavoidably fuels destructive, right-wing politics. Indeed, for this reason, Bargetz rejects the notion that fear can sustain reflection and constructive political action (Bargetz 2021: 22). Along similar lines, Robin's worry that fear creates opportunities for authoritarian manipulation figure in both Nussbaum and Bargetz' assessments. We shall see that versions of these analyses, often intermingled with each other, appeared in public responses to the rise of UKIP.

Fear, UKIP and Right-wing Politics

UKIP was founded in the early 1990s. Securing the UK's withdrawal from the EU was a central aim from the party's founding, though, as few people cared about the EU then, the party widened its policy aims over the years. Among other things, this included taking a hardline stance to curb immigration. More than a decade would pass before UKIP came to mainstream political notice. But a strong performance in the 2004 EU parliament election was followed by a failure to secure any seats in the 2005 general election. As the dust of disappointment began to settle, a new leader emerged: Nigel Farage. He would take the party into a new era that saw the party win the 2014 EU elections, become the third-most-popular party in Britain, and the UK vote to withdraw from the EU. Even though UKIP never held more than two seats in Parliament and had, as of 2022, been reduced to a marginal force once again, this record amounts to a success unmatched by a new political party in Britain, at least since the Social Democratic Party in the 1980s.

There is widespread agreement among political scholars that fear was a key factor in driving support for UKIP and its politics. However, research showing that UKIP supporters actually experience fear is in short supply. Few studies of the party have explicitly asked supporters if they feel afraid or anxious about immigration or pointed to supporters explicitly acknowledging having these emotions. Instead, like many political theorists of fear, students of UKIP often assume that the party's supporters must have been fearful because its policies and rhetoric deal with issues characterised as threats, like immigration and EU regulation (e.g., Kinvall 2018; Skey 2014; Wodak 2015). Survey-based studies have asked UKIP supporters if they perceive, for example, Muslims or globalisation as threats, and affirmative answers have been interpreted as proof of fear (e.g., Ashcroft 2012; Carter 2018; de Vries and Hoffman 2016). Yet, as I observed earlier, a threat evaluation does not necessarily entail fear. UKIP supporters who say immigration is a threat may feel no particular emotion about it at all, or they might feel something other than fear, like anger (see Marcus 2021). Indeed, judging from the party's social media activity at the peak of its popularity in 2014 and 2015, officials wanted to associate anger with its policies and supporters, while fear was an emotion they sought to project onto their opponents rather than admit to themselves.[6] Therefore, a greater measure of epistemic humility about what was happening in the hearts of UKIP supporters would be appropriate.[7]

Nevertheless, many UKIP supporters were plausibly afraid. Matthew Goodwin and colleagues conclude that fear was a crucial driver of UKIP support; they do so based on a wealth of interviews with party officials and supporters as well as first-hand observations from party events (Ford and Goodwin 2014a; Goodwin and Milazzo 2015). Their evidence may well include people explicitly expressing fear of immigration. But, more importantly, Goodwin and colleagues show that many people who supported UKIP seemingly had good reasons to be afraid. The party's base consisted primarily of 'older, working-class, white voters who lack educational qualifications and skills needed to adapt and thrive amid a modern post-industrial economy' (Ford and Goodwin 2014b: 278; see also Ford and Goodwin 2014a: ch. 5). Many of these voters are cognizant of their poor prospects and live in areas of England that have been declining since the 1970s. They are also considerably more likely than other groups to feel they have no say in government, to be distrustful of politicians, and to have been politically disengaged for many years (Ford and Goodwin 2014b; see also Jennings et al. 2014). As Ford and Goodwin argue, these people had been 'left behind' in more ways than one. Add to this the perception that certain dangers, like immigration, threaten to strike at these very vulnerabilities, and fear certainly seems a probable response.

Whatever UKIP might have done to manipulate this fear through focusing it on particular threats and ways to avert them, we should acknowledge that the party also gave these marginalised people a political voice, empowering them to participate and shape public life in ways that many of them may never have experienced before. Putting it in terms of my Arendtian framework, UKIP provided many people with the resources – including concepts, spaces and, of course, affiliations – to transform their fear and other negative emotions into public issues and action.

A Party of 'Loonies and Closet Racists'

How did UKIP's opponents react to its growing political fortunes? Did they draw on the wealth of applicable psychiatric concepts to medicalise the fear that arguably fuelled support for the party? A search through newspaper reports on UKIP suggests that medicalising attacks were uncommon. But, as we shall see, some critics did deploy metaphors of madness.

Despite its uneven performances up until the 2005 election, UKIP's successes had unsettled politicians and observers in the media. In April 2006, David Cameron, a few months after assuming leadership of the Conservative Party, denounced UKIP in a radio interview, saying that the party consisted mainly of 'fruitcakes, loonies and closet racists'. The remarks outraged supporters of the party. Nigel Farage, then UKIP's leader in the European Parliament but not yet of the party, demanded an apology for the accusation of racism. The other words, he claimed to take as a badge of honour: 'I don't mind him calling us loonies – I don't mind him calling us fruitcakes. We are big enough and ugly enough and we have a sense of humour.' To Farage, these epithets were evidence that his self-described party of outsiders were becoming a real threat to the establishment parties (Assinder 2006). Indeed, while Cameron probably intended to ridicule his opponents and, thereby, delegitimise them, it is doubtful that he was suggesting that UKIP supporters required therapy. Whatever clinical connotations fruitcake and loony may once have had to laypeople, these words today denote eccentricity and even misunderstood ingenuity rather than mental disorder. And the latter two were attributes that Farage and his supporters happily accepted (Cohen 2015).

When UKIP supporters were called 'insane', it was usually in a hyperbolic and metaphorical sense rather than clinical one. This still caused some problems for UKIP. Though commentators noted that 'fruitcakes and loonies' exist within all parties (Hope 2012; Thomas 2014), there was a sense that they were over-represented within UKIP (Bell 2013; Boffey 2013; see also Franklin 2014; Segalov 2015). Some members of the party shared this view. In 2014, one senior party official told a newspaper: 'half my time is spent weeding out the lunatics', partly by administering 'psychological tests' on prospective MPs and MEPs to ensure that they were 'vaguely sane' (Shipman 2014). Magazine features and television documentaries also propagated the idea that UKIP supporters, while not clinically unwell, were not quite normal. The most notable example of this is the BBC documentary *Meet the Ukippers* (2015), which aired a few months before the 2015 UK general election. The documentary's portraits of colourful UKIP members included a clown-collecting press officer and a forthrightly racist council member. That said, while the documentary invited ridicule and outrage in the media (e.g., Hyland 2015; Singh 2015), no one – as far as I have been able to find – suggested publicly that these people were mentally ill.

Some intellectuals writing in newspapers came closer to medicalising UKIP, with at least one doing so outright. Like others, they were asking themselves: how had a populist, anti-immigrant and, arguably, xenophobic party been able to amass so much support? A few proposed that the rise of UKIP was the manifestation or a symptom of a kind of societal mental disorder. In an early newspaper commentary on the party's rise, Paul Gilroy (2005a), a prominent cultural theorist, sketched out a psychoanalytically-inspired explanation that related the increasing popularity of UKIP to a collective neurosis rooted in the loss of the British Empire. In this analysis, the rise of UKIP was a culmination of a disease, and while all Britons were carriers, only UKIP supporters had fallen ill. It is basically a medicalised version of the 'fear is a symptom of social or political pathology' analysis discussed earlier.[8] Other commentaries also fell within this type of analysis but with a still stronger medical dimension. For example, an opinion piece in *The Guardian* began as follows:

> UKIP cleans up in a nationwide poll; Britain tops 1.4m zero-hours contracts; anti-depressant prescriptions soar. It might seem fanciful to wrap these three recent headlines in a single syndrome. But an age of anxiety is making itself felt in disparate ways. (Clark 2014)

On the one hand, analyses such as these may help to politicise the spread of anti-depressants and zero-hours contracts, issues which might otherwise have been matters of medical and economic expertise, respectively. On the other, the inclusion of UKIP among the symptoms seems to have the opposite effect. It suggests that the political views of UKIP supporters are not meaningful as such – that is, as legitimate contributions to the political debate worthy of direct responses – but only as symptoms of a deeper social or political pathology that wiser people should seek to cure or quarantine.

Overall, however, medicalising attacks on UKIP and its supporters were uncommon, even including the looser metaphorical form.[9] That is surprising given the apparent medicalisation of fear and xenophobia and the ready availability of psychiatric diagnoses – including anxiety disorders, but also other diagnoses like paranoid personality disorder and anti-social personality disorder (ASPD) – which seem to fit the emotions and actions of UKIP supporters.

The scarcity of medicalising attacks on UKIP is one reason to be suspicious of analyses that try to extrapolate the political impact of medicalisation from diagnostic criteria, as many critics of medicalisation have done. Recall, for example, that Cohen (2016) contends that ASPD medicalises dissent. Among the symptoms of ASPD are 'impulsivity or failure to plan ahead', 'irritability and aggressiveness', 'reckless disregard for safety of self or others' and 'lack of remorse, as indicated by being indifferent to or rationalizing having hurt, mistreated, or stolen from another'. Even a disinterested observer could attribute these symptoms to UKIP supporters. Controlled by fear and anger, UKIP supporters were arguably acting impulsively and against their long-term interests by pursuing the UK's withdrawal from the EU. They refused to heed warnings of how this would harm others and themselves – notably, opponents of Brexit described it as an act of 'self-harm' (e.g., *Financial Times* 2016; cf. Davies 2020: 44). Moreover, once they had achieved their goal, they were remorseless about having plunged the nation into deep uncertainty; in fact, they celebrated it. But while 'Ukippers' were called many things, mentally ill was generally not one of them.

Fearful Brains

Attempts to delegitimise and disempower UKIP instead followed a more traditional model, with a cutting-edge scientific twist. Instead of levelling accusations of insanity, critics claimed that the emotions fuelling UKIP were too irrational, primitive and dangerous for public life, effectively recycling the dichotomy between politically salutary reason and destructive emotions that political scholars and commentators have used in some form since Plato to exclude certain people – including working-class men, women and Black people – from public life. While critics of UKIP, unsurprisingly, did not place themselves within this long political tradition, the resonances are obvious.[10] Crucially, however, they framed the dichotomy using a new resource: the brain sciences.

Numerous recent books have sought to explain political differences in psychological and neuroscientific terms, with many suggesting directly or indirectly that people on either end of the left–right political spectrum are mentally deficient. These books often boast expert authors and have become bestsellers on both sides of the Atlantic. One influential example is *The Political Brain* (2008) by Drew Westen, an American professor of psychology and psychiatry and avowed supporter of the US Democratic Party (Bacon 2010).[11] *The Political Brain* became popular with Democrats, receiving the endorsement of former President Bill Clinton among others. In the United Kingdom, it was read and cited by politicians and commentators on the left and the right (e.g., Harris 2014; Henderson 2008; Huhne 2014; Rowson 2014; Sylvester 2007). Westen's core argument is that the reason the Democrats have so often faced defeat by the Republicans is that the former rely on reason whereas the latter rely on emotion in their political messaging and rhetoric; and 'when reason and emotion collide, emotion invariably wins' (2008: 35). According to Westen, evolution has granted the emotional part of the brain dominance over the rational part. However, it seems evolution has not made all brains equally subject to the despotism of emotion. Many Americans vote for the Democrats despite their 'irrational commitment to rationality' and the supposed lack of emotional rhetoric and imagery in their communications (15). Hence, one could conclude that (the brains of) Democrats are more rational and advanced, whereas (the brains of) Republicans are more emotional and primitive. That was at any rate how *The Guardian* columnist Chris Huhne (2014) interpreted the book. Drawing on Westen's claims, Huhne sought to explain why the Liberal Democrats – whom Huhne formerly represented in Parliament – were losing ground to UKIP. Whereas Liberal Democrats are reasonable, well-educated people, Huhne said, 'Ukip's supporters are old, fearful and anxious.' It was thus no wonder that Farage's emotive rhetoric was so seductive to these poor people. Paraphrasing his source, Huhne observed that in 'evolutionary psychology, fear . . . trumps reason'. Westen himself did not openly assert that something was wrong with or unreasonable about right-wing voters. The conclusion that UKIP supporters are irrational was Huhne's own. Nevertheless, Westen's ideas have potentially worrying implications for political agency and liberal democratic citizenship. For instance, based on his own brain-imaging research, he concluded that many brains – as many as 60 per cent – are neurologically locked into their political views. In this research, Westen also found that 'the partisan brain' not only eschewed information that conflicted with its extant political opinions but actively sought information that confirmed them. Apparently, this mirrored the processes found in the brains of drug addicts, leading Western to remark that this gave 'new meaning to the term political junkie' (xiv).

For observers like Huhne, Westen's book validated the belief that UKIP's base consisted of 'loonies and closet racists', people who had given in to emotion and abandoned reason. This idea extended beyond *The Guardian*'s readership. Since it appeared that UKIP was stealing votes from the Conservatives and Labour, commentators on the right also had an interest in pushing the stereotype of the emotional/irrational UKIP supporter. In an opinion piece for *The Times*, Rachel Sylvester (2013) compared UKIP supporters to cavemen. She asserted that the real driver of UKIP's burgeoning popularity was 'fear of change': what UKIP offered voters was the false promise of stopping progress and turning back time; seduced by this 'fantasy', UKIP supporters become unable to distinguish between 'myth and reality' – a claim that prefigures Bargetz' analysis of fear. All political parties may have supporters who fear change, but no party had more than UKIP, according to Sylvester. In the face of change, these people gave in to fear, and, hence, failed to see the benefits of progress. Thus, in some ways, they were even more primitive than cavemen, or so Sylvester appeared to suggest: 'The cavemen were terrified when they first played with fire – but then they learnt to harness its power.' Though Sylvester forwent the concepts of neuroscience and psychiatry for more colourful metaphors, her claims resemble those of Huhne and Westen. UKIP voters did not think; they felt. Like wild animals and prehistoric humans, they were slaves to their instincts. At least Sylvester did not seem to think that they were a lost cause. If the cavemen learned to see the benefits of fire, then UKIP supporters could perhaps eventually learn – or be taught by their betters – to understand the benefits of immigration, free markets, and progress.

To many commentators, science proved that UKIP supporters were not like other voters. A passage from an opinion piece in *The Observer* well-summarised what many seemingly perceived as the main differ-ence: 'Most people's voting intentions are a product of a mix of the rational and emotional sides of the brain. A Ukip vote, more than any other, is a visceral response' (Rawnsley 2014; see also Parris 2014). In other words, among UKIP supporters, emotion had ostensibly defeated reason.

Though disempowering, these various but overlapping represen-tations of UKIP are not medicalising. After all, they do not invoke the concepts of psychiatric or medical disease. What they amount to instead are 'hyper-emotionalising' attacks. They *deform* political emo-tions into apolitical ones by treating people's views and actions as mere epiphenomena that are far less important than the emotional processes that give rise to them. The emotions emerging from this deformation can then be reassigned political meaning, a meaning that may be unre-lated to the people's original views and actions. For instance, UKIP supporters' stated complaints about immigration become reduced to neurologically primitive fear, which then becomes a symptom of the flaws of capitalism. The neuro-rhetoric we have seen above attempts to ground such claims in science by implying that certain political views are neurologically advanced while others – for example, the views of UKIP supporters – are neurologically primitive. If neuroscientific research has shown that something in the brains of people on the right renders them unsusceptible to scientific evidence, it is easy to conclude that something is also wrong or undesirable with those brains as well as the citizens who host them. Certain views of the world then effec-tively become evidence of neurological underdevelopment.

Political theory is complicit in the production of this meta-emo-tional rhetoric of fear in politics. Amalgams of the three types of political analyses of fear can be detected in many news commentar-ies on UKIP's rise. Nussbaum's understanding of fear as inherently harmful to democratic politics is most prominent, though Bargetz' understanding of fear as a symptom of deeper political issues and Robin's understanding of fear as a means of elite manipulation fea-ture as well. In all these analyses, individuals driven by fear are non-agents, mere leaves tossed around in a fearful storm whipped up by forces they fail to see. From this, the conclusion that these people need to be politically managed but not heard is a small step away.

This points towards the darker side of the emancipation of emo-tion.[12] While the proliferation of meta-emotional rhetoric in politics has likely made it easier for people to channel their emotions into political action, it has also created new ways to use the fragility of political emotions against their subjects. By drawing on sources like neuroscience, commentators can unmask people's political emotions, revealing them as a mere façade – not unlike the French revolutionaries did, according to Arendt (see Chapter 1). Behind this façade, we find the real reasons or, rather, real emotions that cause people to act politically, emotions that we should care more about than what these people say. Such unmasking through hyper-emotionalisation can disempower people as surely as medicalisation. Neuroscience, psychology and political theory have produced disempowering concepts that can lead people to understand fear – their own or other people's – as brain processes devoid of political meaning or as phenomena that are politically meaningful only insofar as their appearance in public life signifies deception or a social issue that those who are fearful fail to see. These constrain people's access to other empowering factors. Particularly notable is how it can affect affiliations, not just by alienating potential allies but also by subjecting political actors to the authority of experts claiming to understand what the meaning of actors' emotions and actions mean better than they do themselves.

However, that emotionalisation may also be disempowering does not mean that we should treat it as equivalent to medicalisation, reducing both to some broader process or strategy like pathologisation or neoliberalisation. Although labelling someone as irrationally emotional can be disempowering, it does not entail judgements about health or disease. It does not imply that they need medical care. It does not raise questions about the need to force medication. And it is highly doubtful that a court would consider it an acceptable reason for evicting a protest. Psychiatric concepts, as we have seen, can do all these things. Because they are enmeshed in a complex and sticky web that includes, but is not limited to, psychiatric and medical institutions, mental health professionals and therapeutic technologies, the purpose of which is to discover, diagnose and treat individuals who experience mental disorder. When we label someone as mentally disordered, we are not simply saying that they are a bit odd or an inconvenient, but permissible, deviation from a norm; we are saying that they are sick and need medical treatment to get better.

Conclusion

UKIP provided some individuals who had long felt politically powerless – especially white, working-class ones – with empowering factors that enabled them to transform their fear and other negative emotions into public issues, that is, for example, into fear of immigration, job insecurity, globalisation and changing social norms. This likely helped to turn UKIP into the considerable political force that it once was. Yet it also exposed the party and its supporters to attacks seeking to deform the public shape of their fear. These attacks were not primarily of a medicalising kind, however. Instead, hostile commentators hyper-emotionalised the party's supporters, claiming that science showed that Ukippers were governed by primitive emotions rather than reason. Showcasing the darker side of the emancipation of emotion – discussed in Chapter 2 – hyper-emotionalising attacks can, like medicalising ones, be profoundly disempowering, striking both at the fragile public shape actors have given their emotions and the empowering factors they draw on.

The case of UKIP raises an important question: If fear is politically dangerous, why should we care if it is hyper-emotionalised, medicalised or delegitimised in some other way? Limiting the political agency of people who are mistaken about the causes of their fear and, by extension, the agency of political leaders who stoke and manipulate that fear for odious ends is arguably desirable. If so, the fragility of political emotions is an opportunity, and political theorists are justified in contributing to the hyper-emotionalisation of fear and ignoring its medicalisation. (Similar points could be made about grief and anger as well, though left-leaning readers might be less likely to consider them in relation to Remainers, Occupy and other instances of emotional political action whose causes they agree with.)

However, the problem with trying to exclude fear (and other negative emotions) from politics is that such efforts risk disempowering other political actors as well, actors whose fears and aims are warranted. *Pace* Bargetz (2021), fear does not *only* fuel destructive political thinking and action. *Pace* Robin (2004), fear does not *only* serve political elites, distract people from the 'real' political issues or preserve structural injustices. In case the historical examples mentioned earlier in this chapter should strike some readers as outdated, contemporary examples of fear's capacity to fuel political agency in the service of more recent, laudable causes are available. During the COVID-19 pandemic, for example, fear fuelled not just a radical change in ingrained habits and rejection of neoliberal public policies, but also collective action in support of vulnerable people and strained institutions (Degerman et al. 2020). If that example is unsatisfying because it involves submission to authority and action that preserves rather than changes the status quo, consider the environmental movement instead. Interview-based studies have shown that activists are avowedly fearful and experience their fear as an emotion that sustains their participation in the movement. Furthermore, they self-consciously use fear, believing that it can drive people to reflect on the dangers of climate change, change their behaviours and join the movement (Kleres and Wettergren 2016). Research on the efficacy of the environmental movement's fear appeals indicates that activists are correct (Meijnders et al., 2006).

Perhaps it can be shown that fear on balance drives more 'harmful' than 'beneficial' political action. On a charitable reading, this is what political critics of fear have concluded (though it seems that many have simply overlooked instances in which fear is politically beneficial). But even if we were confident efforts to exclude fear from public life primarily prevent 'harmful' actions, it is unclear this is the right course given the potential costs. We could, after all, simply criticise what people on the right say and do rather than what they feel.

Notes

1. In another possible legacy of *The Authoritarian Personality*, a government-led survey in Scotland recently investigated whether negative attitudes to immigration were correlated to mental health problems (Reid et al. 2014: 43).
2. Others have criticised scholars of fear in politics for inferring that the presence threat and avoidant behaviours means that people are afraid. Brubaker and Laitin (1998: 442–3) rightly observe that 'analyzing rhetorical processes, symbolic resources, and representational forms' of which threats are constructed – a task which preoccupies most aforementioned scholars – though cannot tell us 'whether, when, where, to what extent, and in what manner the posited beliefs and fears were actually held' (see also Best 2020).
3. Marcus technically speaks of anxiety in the quoted passage, but he puts little stock in the distinction between anxiety and fear (Marcus et al. 2019: fn. 11), and has treated the two terms as interchangeable across his work (see Marcus 2002; Marcus and Mackuen 1993; Marcus et al. 2019). I think he is wrong to dismiss the distinction. But since Marcus understands fear/anxiety as involving, among other things, a specific threat evaluation and a negative affect, his work actually seems focused what I and most philosophers of emotion would call fear anyway.
4. Barbalet (2004) has made a similar observation.
5. The second and third types of fear analyses are inspired by Enroth's (2017) typology of political fear narratives. Though Enroth bases

this typology on a comprehensive and careful review of recent literature on the politics of fear, he overlooks Nussbaum's type of critique.

6. This is at least what the following data seems to suggest: between 2014
    and the general election in 2015, UKIP's official Facebook page pub-
    lished twenty-seven posts using the words 'fear', 'frightened', 'afraid' or
    'scared'. Of these, nineteen described UKIP's opponents as feeling fear.
    This includes statements like 'Labour are now running scared of UKIP',
    one of the most shared posts during the period. None described UKIP
    officials or supporters as afraid, though some used the phrase 'I'm afraid'
    or 'I fear' idiomatically – for example, 'I fear that you may have been
    reading too much into a statistical sample'. Meanwhile, sixteen posts
    published in the same period used the words 'anger', 'angered', 'angry',
    'outrage', 'outraged', 'fury' or 'furious'. Of these, ten described the anger
    of UKIP officials – such as 'UKIP's Health spokesman, Louise Bours is
    "utterly outraged"' – or anger about institutions, policies or statements
    that UKIP opposes – such as 'Outrage as thousands of migrants living
    abroad are still claiming sick pay' (CrowdTangle Team 2021).

7. I elaborate on this issue in political research on emotions in Degerman
    (2020a).

8. Notably, Bargetz (2021: 30) aligns her analysis with Gilroy's *Post-
    colonial Melancholia* (2005b), which is, effectively, a book-length
    version of the argument Gilroy makes in the newspaper commentary.

9. To illustrate: a Nexis newspaper database search in *The Guardian* for
    the string [((UKIP) AND (insane OR "mentally ill" OR "mental ill-
    ness" OR "mental disorder" OR "mentally disordered" OR crazy OR
    lunatic OR madness))] between 2006 and 2016, which yielded 296
    results; a search for the string [((UKIP) AND (emotion OR emotional
    OR anger OR fear))] in the same period turned up 2,645 articles. A
    sampling of these results indicated that often neither set of terms was
    used to describe UKIP or its supporters. Nevertheless, the quantita-
    tive disparity suggests that emotions were more closely associated with
    UKIP than mental disorder

10. UKIP's critics are, of course, not the only ones who have used the
    reason–emotion dichotomy to try to discredit their opponents. As we
    saw in Chapters 3 and 4, this practice remains rife across political
    fault lines in the United States and the United Kingdom.

11. Another noteworthy example is Haidt's best-selling book *The Righ-
    teous Mind* (2012), which, like *The Political Brain*, claims that there
    is neuroscientific evidence for the idea that people on the right are
    inherently more emotional – specifically, more fearful – than people
    on the left (278–9). As it turns out, this evidence is in fact very weak
    (LaFollette and Woodruff 2015).

12. Leys (2017: ch. 7) and Zerilli (2015) discuss related and other risks of
    the affective turn.

Chapter 6
Maladjusted Patients: The Agency of the User/Survivor Movement

The chapters so far have focused on cases in which people's mental and emotional fitness for public life has been disputed. In the Brexit referendum and the Occupy movement, we saw psychiatric concepts being deployed in medicalising attacks against political actors. Although some observers claimed that Occupy disproportionately attracted individuals with mental disorders, there was no *prima facie* reason to think that either Occupy or Remainers were defined by mental disorder. Certainly, neither took this to be one of their collective characteristics. A central concern about the medicalisation of negative emotions is that the words and deeds of 'normal' political dissenters might be dismissed on medical grounds. But there is another important type of case to consider. Some political actors acknowledge that they have been diagnosed with a mental disorder, and are, hence, already acting or trying to act politically under the stigma of mental disorder. Where better to look than at these very actors if we want to understand how the medicalisation of negative emotions affects political agency?

Many people diagnosed with mental disorder have rejected the current state of mental healthcare. Some are acting with others to challenge the authority of psychiatry and the public perception of mental disorder. These individuals and the groups they have formed are sometimes collectively referred to as the psychiatric service user/survivor movement, indicating that it consists of mental health service users and self-described survivors of psychiatric services and social exclusion. This movement's members face empowering and disempowering factors that can inform our understanding of the political impact of the medicalisation of negative emotions. Not only have many been formally medicalised through a diagnosis, they also self-consciously struggle to politicise

experiences and issues that sit within the supposedly apolitical relationships and spaces of psychiatry and medicine (see Lewis 2006).[1]
As I suggested in Chapter 2, medicalisation constitutes a strong
background condition of political action for users/survivors. While
most have not been deprived of legal rights, we shall see that users/
survivors face other forms of marginalisation, which are maintained and exacerbated by various aspects of public and psychiatric
discourse.[2] The case of the user/survivor movement is of broader
importance for two reasons. First, it elucidates the obstacles to
political action facing the growing number of people whose negative emotions and other forms of suffering have been medicalised.
Secondly, it suggests what a future in which politics is increasingly
fought out in medical terms portends for the political agency of
citizens in general.

Drawing on the writings of user/survivor activists and organisations, newspaper articles and psychiatric professional publications, this chapter examines the factors that shape the political
agency of users/survivors. Unlike the subjects of the other case
studies, this is an ongoing and fast-changing movement. The historical timeframe and source selection of this book mean that
some more recent activities and certain dis/empowering factors do
not come into view in this examination. Social media, for example, plays an important and often empowering role in the lives
of users/survivors. However, by focusing on other sources, such
as on what traditional print media say or do not say about the
user/survivor movement, this chapter elucidates factors that shape
the political agency of users/survivors *vis-à-vis* other but no less
important publics, such as medical professionals, policymakers
and other groups of citizens who may determine the success of the
movement's causes.

After introducing some major user/survivor groups and organisations, along with notable activities and achievements, I examine
how British news media have represented user/survivor groups,
highlighting parallels to how US psychiatrists have responded
to their critics. I then consider how the appropriation of user/
survivor concepts in mainstream policy and mental health affects
the political agency of activists and others diagnosed with mental
disorder. With some qualifications, I argue that this appropriation
can empower these activists by enabling them to make collective
and more effective demands on private corporations and public
institutions.

Welcome to the Movement

There is a diverse range of groups in the United Kingdom and other parts of the world that contest various aspects of psychiatry.[3] Some – such as the Canada-based Coalition Against Psychiatric Assault (2019) and its internationally-prominent intellectual leader Bonnie Burstow (2015) – advocate for abolishing psychiatry. Others – such as the Hearing Voices Network (2019) – challenge the standard uses of psychiatric diagnoses and treatments. Still others – such as the National Survivor User Network (2019) – focus on advocating for increased service-user involvement in psychiatry and mental health policy, meaning that they want those with first-hand experiences of mental distress to shape its concepts and practices. This simplified outline overlooks many views represented within the movement, but it gives us a sense of the lay of the land. The term 'user/survivor movement' might itself be slightly misleading since some groups that fall within its scope may have few values or goals in common. However, they share political ambitions to reshape relationships, spaces, laws and concepts that many outside the movement perceive as apolitical and scientific. Activists within the movement (e.g., Gorman et al. 2013; MindFreedom International 2011: 20; see also Coleman 2008) have often invoked Martin Luther King's praise of maladjustment in the face of injustice:

> Psychologists have a word which is probably used more frequently than any other word in modern psychology. It is the word 'maladjusted' . . . Well, there are some things in our social system to which I am proud to be maladjusted and to which I suggest that we ought to be maladjusted. I never intend to adjust myself to the viciousness of lynch-mobs . . . the evils of segregation and discrimination [or] the tragic inequalities of an economic system which takes necessities from the masses to give luxuries to the classes . . . History still has a choice place for those who have the moral courage to be maladjusted. (King 1997)

In the spirit of these words, user/survivor activists have rejected the idea that the causes of their suffering reside solely within their bodies and can be dealt with through medical means alone; they have determined that the causes of their suffering are at least partly political and must be dealt with as such, in effect, regarding themselves as maladjusted to injustice.

User/survivor groups constitute empowering factors in their own right, by providing medicalised and suffering individuals with affiliations, that is, others with whom to explore and act on shared issues. They also give individuals access to other empowering factors linking the individual into a 'web of relationships' that, potentially, reaches far beyond any given gathering and amplifies the effects of their actions. We can discern these factors and the political agency they can give rise to in the relatively short-lived but prominent British user/survivor group Mad Pride. Started in the United Kingdom in 1999, its founders saw the struggle of users/survivors as a continuation of the civil rights struggles of the twentieth century (Abraham 2016). The ethos of Mad Pride was summed up by one of its co-founders Simon Barnett (2008) as follows: 'If you've got a problem with mad people it's your problem.' Much like the Black and Gay Pride movements, Mad Pride activists see the re-appropriation of words used to shame and discriminate as central to their movement both as a means and an end. Activists have pursued this through a variety of provocative names, slogans and practices. For example, between 2006 and 2008, they held an annual arts and mental health festival in London named 'Bonkersfest'. It is also common for activists in anglophone countries to refer to themselves and their peers as 'mad', 'bonkers' or 'nutter'. As we shall see, some commentators have pushed back against this tactic in particular. Mad Pride activists are aware of this: 'Many people will find our casual use of words like "mad" and "nutter" strange,' an anonymous activist wrote in a local UK newspaper in 2010. 'However, we feel that reclaiming the language of madness is empowering. It is hard for someone to belittle you as "mental" when you are already saying, "Yeah, I'm mad. Officially"' (*Bath Chronicle* 2010). Notwithstanding, or perhaps because of, their controversiality, such repossessed terms formed a central part of the empowering factors of Mad Pride and remain crucial to the user/survivor movement. They are concepts that activists can use to relate their negative emotions to established issues and elucidate shared experiences of discrimination and injustice. These concepts also constitute and reconstitute affiliations between individuals and organisations like Mad Pride and scholarly networks like Mad Studies.

After several well-publicised events and protests in the first decade of the twenty-first century, Mad Pride fizzled in the United Kingdom. By 2012, it was largely inactive. One reason for this was apparently the founders' inability to maintain the organisation over the longer term (Abraham 2016). Another likely reason is that the push to include users/survivors in the research and development of psychiatric practice – advocated by Mad Pride, among others – has been quite successful in the United Kingdom (cf. McDaid 2010). Users/ survivors are increasingly being involved in the research and the clinical aspects of mental healthcare in the United Kingdom. The Department of Health (1999) has long emphasised the need to enhance user involvement, and, in recent years, even adopted a variation on one of the user/survivor movement's core tenets: 'no decision about me without me' (2012) – although the individualising shift from the activist slogan 'nothing about us without us' is notable. Another arguable success is the popularisation of what is called 'recovery' or 'the recovery model'. Often contrasted against the medical model of diagnosis and treatment – which critics say myopically focuses on symptoms and biological functioning – the recovery model favours a holistic approach, de-emphasising the use of medications, aiming to help suffering individuals to (re)gain a 'personal process, way of life or attitude, involving the growth of new meaning and purpose beyond the effects of mental illness' (Deegan 2003). The recovery model has been widely endorsed by mental health charities (Mountain and Shah 2008), NHS Trusts (Boardman et al. 2010), as well as the government (Department of Health 2011). This 'mainstreaming of recovery' (Rose 2014) is not unproblematic, however. Later in the chapter, I shall consider further how the uptake of the recovery model and user involvement in healthcare affects the political agency of user/survivor activists.

No matter the reason, the timing of Mad Pride's flagging in the United Kingdom is notable, given the debates raging at the time over the forthcoming *DSM-5*. In the United States, the DSM revision process had become a catalyst for protest, involving several user/survivor groups (Bossewitch 2016). Nevertheless, the actions of Mad Pride continue to shape the world, as illustrated, for example, by activists from Germany to India raising the Mad Pride banner. So, beyond whatever concrete influence it may have had on policy, Mad Pride contributed towards establishing and developing empowering concepts that frame the negative emotions of people with mental disorders as political rather than helping them and others to undermine the 'illusion' that their emotions are purely a medical concern.

Users/Survivors in the Media

We shall now examine what we can learn about these dis/empowering factors from news coverage of the user/survivor movement. News media have been central sources in each of the preceding chapters, and they will here as well. But, in the present case, this focus requires some further justification. Mad studies scholars have specifically highlighted the importance of social media, podcasts and other alternative media for the user/survivor movement. For example, Angela Woods and colleagues (2019) stress the role of such spaces in 'illuminating aspects of experiences that are painful and difficult to articulate'. Since many of these spaces are deliberately hidden and exclusionary, they do not seem to conform to Arendt's (1998: 51) own idea of public space as a place admitting all citizens and subjecting everything within it to 'the implacable, bright light' of collective scrutiny. As I observed in Chapter 2, the dimmer, shared spaces of social media or a basement meeting room can also be empowering. However, Arendt's warning about the disempowering potential of such intimate and homogeneous spaces seems particularly apt in relation to the user/ survivor movement. Much like Jews did in Europe before the Second World War, according to Arendt (1995: 12–14), user/survivors may understandably treat participation in online spaces as an end rather than as a means to launch into the mainstream because of stigma about both what they are and what they believe.

With these considerations in mind, much can be gained from focusing on traditional news media, which conform more closely to Arendt's idea of public space as an arena of intense visibility. While news media are, of course, exclusionary as well – though in ways that are quite different from those of, for example, closed Facebook groups – their representations of the user/survivor movement and associated ideas both shape and are shaped by the attitudes of larger and more privileged publics than those found on user/survivor social media. Therefore, it is notable that user/survivor groups have received scarce attention in British newspapers over the past decade.

In what little in-depth coverage the movement attracted in British media, judgements were mixed. References to the Hearing Voices Network (HVN) were generally positive. HVN is a support and advocacy group for people 'who hear voices, see visions or have other unusual experiences'; it challenges the idea that those experiences are necessarily symptoms of mental disorder that require cure or treatment. Articles mentioning the organisation often represented it as an central resource for individuals who experience voice-hearing. Advice columns in *The Sun* and *The Guardian* even recommended HVN to letter-writers who worried about friends or partners who hear voices (Blair 2006; Sanders 2016). Some uncritically relayed one of the organisation's most controversial principles, namely, that voice-hearing need not be a symptom of mental disorder – a claim which has enraged some US psychiatrists. The newspapers usually portrayed HVN as a support group without mentioning its political advocacy for reforming mental healthcare. This partly explains why HVN has largely avoided the criticism that groups like Mad Pride faced in certain quarters of the British media. However, the conspicuous absence of political context in these articles also shows how news media, as public spaces, can disempower activists within HVN and the user/survivor movement generally. There are deep tensions between HVN's approach to mental disorder and mainstream psychiatric practice (Pilgrim 2005: 19). The failure to mention these tensions and the political contestation surrounding them gives the impression that HVN is simply a complementary component of the wider British mental healthcare system.

Some commentators have been explicitly critical of user/survivor groups. Among these is *The Guardian* columnist Clare Allan (2006, 2007), who has written regularly about mental health issues for over a decade and discussed Mad Pride at times, from the perspective of someone who has herself struggled with mental disorder. Since Allan and Mad Pride activists appear to share views on multiple issues, Allan's repeated use of her national platform to criticise Mad Pride is surprising. Her criticism of the group appears to stem primarily from its claim that what psychiatrists call mental disorder can be a central aspect of people's identities. In one column, Allan argued that these efforts romanticise mental disorder. '[M]ental illness is not an identity,' she declared. 'Mental illness is an illness, just as cancer is an illness; and people die from both' (Allan 2006; see also Rashed 2019: 28–9). Invoking a common metaphor between mental disorder and cancer – long promulgated by the pharmaceutical industry and condemned by user/survivor activists and critics of psychiatry – Allan implies that Mad Pride activists fail to understand the true nature of suffering that they and others with mental disorder experience.

Criticism of this kind – which suggests that user/survivor activists and other critics of psychiatry misguidedly and dangerously romanticise, trivialise and stigmatise mental disorder because of a failure to understand what mental disorder *really* is – seems to be rare in Britain. Allan's criticism does resonate, however, with views expressed in US news media (e.g., Friedman 2012; Glaser 2008; Simon 2008; *Wall Street Journal* 2014; see also Coleman 2008), as well as by some leading US psychiatrists (e.g., Krystal 2012; Lieberman 2013;

Pies 2015). By contrast, British psychiatrists do not generally appear to engage in these kinds of attack on critics of psychiatry, user/survivor activists included. The relative absence of open hostility is probably related to – though not wholly explained by – user involvement in mental healthcare and research in the NHS, which has been institutionalised over more than two decades (see Rose 2015). Consequently, British psychiatrists are probably more likely than their US counterparts to encounter and have to consider user/survivors' criticism of their profession and its methods. The institutionalisation of user involvement, recovery and other concepts that have emerged from the user/survivor movement seemingly pose different threats to the political agency of activists with mental disorders, however, which we shall look at next.

Depoliticising Recovery

User/survivor activists may not suffer overt attacks from British psychiatrists, but they do face subtler disempowering factors. I suggested earlier that re-appropriated concepts such as 'mad' and 'bonkers' serve as empowering factors for user/survivor activists, helping them to articulate their negative emotions as public issues. Other more complex terms have served the same role. I have already mentioned two important examples: user involvement and recovery. The user activist and scholar Premila Trivedi (2010) has observed that these are concepts 'born out of service user/survivors['] experiences, anger, hope, creativity and wisdom', and intended to revolutionise the mental health care system. User/survivor activists and critical scholars warn that, over the past few years, these terms have been co-opted by mental health professionals and policymakers.

Take recovery, for example. The idea of recovery in mental healthcare and policy seems to have originated in the user/survivor movement (Rose 2014). Within the movement, the term was used partly to frame structural problems facing people with diagnosed mental disorders or in severe emotional distress and to highlight that recovery lay in addressing these problems rather than in – or at least in combination with – changing the sufferers. This entailed enhancing the individual's say in treatment, exploring non-medical conceptions of and approaches to mental suffering, strengthening community membership and reducing stigma, as well as improving and safeguarding political rights (Pilgrim 2008; McWade 2016). The concept of recovery challenged conventional understandings and treatments of the suffering associated with mental disorder, which focused on individual problems and symptoms and how these could be ameliorated by intervening on the person. It was a way for individuals to link their suffering to the public issues pursued by the user/survivor movement, enabling them, in effect, to 'cut loose' from the medical frame and access the empowering factors of the movement.

However, critics have charged that as the idea of recovery has been taken up as a concept in mainstream mental healthcare and policy, it has been emptied of its critical, demedicalising and politicising meanings (e.g., Morrow 2013; Pilgrim 2008). Recovery has been a buzzword in the mental health policy reforms of British governments since the 1990s, signifying an ongoing transition to a more personalised approach to care that places an increased emphasis on patients' voices (McWade 2016). As mentioned, charities and NHS trusts alike have supported or adopted the idea of recovery. But rather than recognising the tensions between recovery and psychiatric approaches, these institutions have tended to represent them as unproblematically complementary, such that recovery might simply be appended to the existing mental healthcare system (Harper and Speed 2012). Indeed, the fact that two British psychiatrists, Deborah Mountain and Premal Shah (2008), were able to conclude that there are no incompatibilities between recovery and the medical model – without mentioning the relationship between recovery and social or political context – is an indication of how far the meaning of recovery has drifted from its activist origins and instantiation. Mountain and Shah suggest that the principles of recovery are integral to the medical model that psychiatrists already employ, and they primarily highlight points where existing practices could be strengthened. Mountain and Shah's characterisation of empowerment, which they identify as a core component of recovery, is also noteworthy. They state that empowerment is about: 'Promoting self-control, self-management and personal responsibility and supporting patients to believe that they can shape their future' (243). Strictly speaking, this conception of empowerment may not be incompatible with the collective power and political change sought by activists, but it emphasises the individual and personal change in a way that seems likely to steer users away from political action than towards it.

The individualisation of recovery has been noticed and criticised by activists and critical scholars (e.g., Harper and Speed 2012; Howell and Voronka 2012). The implementation of recovery in parts of the

NHS has entailed more practical interventions and aims than may have been common previously, such as helping people with mental disorders develop skills for and secure work and independent living. But the focus has remained mainly on the individual, her defects and how medical experts can make her better (Rose 2014). Meanwhile, what David Pilgrim (2008) refers to as the 'forces of social exclusion', that is, the 'prejudice, stigma, and institutional discrimination against those with mental health problems' – which the activist instantiation of recovery brought into view – have remained peripheral in mental healthcare and debates about mental disorder. This seemingly has negative implications for the political agency of user/survivor activists and others diagnosed with mental disorders. Using terms that recall my characterisation of disempowering concepts, David Harper and Ewen Speed (2012: 10) argue that recovery now 'obscure[s] the social and political links between distress and structural injustice'. That is, what used to be an empowering concept has arguably become a disempowering one.

For reasons I shall discuss shortly, it is not entirely accurate to call recovery a disempowering concept, but its depoliticised instantiation does have disempowering effects. Trivedi's statement illustrates that the activist instantiation of recovery could function as an empowering concept for users/survivors. It facilitated connections to other empowering factors; perhaps most significantly, it helped to establish and maintain affiliations between a diverse range of individuals and groups (see also Woods et al. 2019: 10–11). The depoliticisation of recovery in policy and healthcare means that it no longer – at least not without clarification – reliably enables users/survivors to illuminate, for example, shared experiences of social exclusion and the importance of addressing this problem either amongst themselves or to outsiders. Internally, some activists – notably, the Recovery in the Bin collective (2019) – have distanced themselves from the term, which they perceive as corrupted; others insist that it is useful despite its misappropriation (Morrow and Weisser 2012); and, presumably, still others are satisfied with its mainstream uptake. Hence, affiliations between them may begin to fray. It is in relation to external publics that the effects are likely to be most significant, however. The depoliticised mainstream meaning of recovery deprives user/survivor activists of an empowering factor that they had developed to express coherently and constructively the political dimensions of their suffering to doctors, politicians and other stakeholders. There is some room for disagreement within the frame of this mainstream meaning, such that recovery can mean somewhat different things to different people (Woods et al. 2019). It may, for example, be tolerable for individuals to differ on whether recovery requires medication or behavioural change. These disagreements maintain that mental disorder and recovery are what Mills (1959: 8–9) called 'personal troubles' pertaining to 'the character of the individual' and 'his immediate relations with others'. Meanwhile, many, though not all, meanings that would make or tie recovery to a public issue – such as substantively reforming psychiatry or addressing inequality – which demands political action and structural change may seem intolerable. For activists to insist on politicised meanings of recovery in the face of the expert-endorsed mainstream meaning is hard work and threatens to weaken their extant affiliations or prevent them from forming new ones, but abandoning the concept means giving up a hard-won empowering concept.

Users/survivors are not alone in facing this kind of problem. The appropriation of the user/survivor movement's concepts to name arguably shallow reforms may be just one instance of the capacity of social and political systems to assimilate and neutralise radical critique (Boltanski and Chiapello 2005: 27; cited in McNay 2014). But we should bear in mind that unlike the subjects of other case studies in this book, user/survivor activists are acting from a position and drawing upon experiences that have already been medicalised. Not only does this mean they face the problem of trying to politicise the ostensibly apolitical. As a result of their diagnosis and symptoms, they also face negative stereotypes that are likely to undermine their political agency. For example, a comprehensive 2014-survey in England found that 39 per cent of respondents associated mental disorder with a tendency for violence (TNS BRMB 2015: 24). Such perceptions are clearly not conducive to political affiliations. Other prejudices suggest that people with mental disorder do not even have the basic capacities necessary for political action. Almost half the survey respondents said that an individual with mental disorder usually cannot 'be held responsible for his or her own actions'. A further 40 per cent associated mental disorder with the inability to 'make simple decisions' about one's own actions (TNS BRMB 2015: 24).

So far, we have seen several ways in which the political agency of user/survivor activists and individuals with mental disorders, along with the empowering factors available to them, are undermined, for example, by psychiatric diagnoses and the mainstream appropriation of user/survivor concepts. However, what critics of psychiatry often fail to recognise is that the political agency of diagnosed individuals can be enhanced by psychiatric concepts and associated affiliations and institutions in certain contexts.

The Promises and Pitfalls of 'Psycho Politics'

The uptake of user/survivor concepts in the healthcare system – which in a sense medicalises them – does not uniformly or necessarily disempower users/survivors. With respect to recovery, for instance, one could argue that its appropriation by the government and in the NHS has created new opportunities and resources for shaping mental healthcare and the rights of people who experience severe emotional distress or other symptoms of mental disorder. Its uptake gives activists a conceptual foothold in these institutions and healthcare debates. Some commentators even appear to see it as an opportunity for 're-inventing' recovery, replacing its mainstream meaning with its original, politically radical and demedicalising meanings (Morrow and Weisser 2012). A more modest hope would be that by continuing to contest the concept, activists may be able to complement the mainstream instantiation of recovery with concerns about political context. This is why I suggested earlier that it may not be accurate to call recovery a disempowering concept.

A better, though still controversial, example of how the appropriation of a user/survivor concept in policy and healthcare can generate or strengthen political agency is user involvement. As mentioned, user involvement is another central tenet of the movement that has been implemented in mental healthcare policy, research and practice. It is meant to give an institutional voice to individuals who have lived experiences of being on the receiving end of psychiatry, recognising the role that these 'experts-by-experience' should have in providing and shaping mental healthcare. Since the 1990s, a series of policies established and extended formal requirements for user involvement across the NHS. Users/survivors were called to serve as members on hospital boards, as support workers and consultants, research advisers and researchers. User involvement has received its share of criticism over the years. Doctors and users/survivors alike have complained that many user roles that have emerged over the years are simply figurehead positions (e.g., Trivedi 2010). Members and allies of the latter group have also charged that user involvement has marginalised the more radical voices of survivors in favour of the more reformist voices of users and has yielded little in terms of actual political power (McDaid 2010). Yet some critics seem to underestimate the empowering potential of the spaces that user involvement has pried open, especially given that other spaces that may once have served as sites for establishing affiliations, sharing experiences and formulating public issues – such as inpatient facilities – have been disappearing. Even if hospital boardrooms do not provide opportunities to contest broader issues within mental healthcare effectively, they allow users/survivors to express critical opinions on issues to potentially receptive and influential professionals. Furthermore, as Tehseen Noorani (2013) observes, 'rights-demanding activism [is] often conducted through service user involvement spaces' (see also Newbigging and Ridley 2018: 41–2). Users/survivors in peer-support roles, for example, can and do sometimes facilitate the kind of connections just mentioned. And partly by drawing on concepts such as recovery (Woods et al. 2019: 15), they can do so as experts-by-experience, whose authority has, to an extent, been formally recognised by the very institutions they contest.[4] I do not mean to dismiss the criticism of user involvement, which highlights how institutional compromises may hinder activism. I only want to underline that it is empowering with regard to certain matters.

But this is a crucial point, which relates to a key claim made in Chapter 2: receiving a diagnosis of mental disorder does not always diminish an individual's political agency. Although the medicalisation of his suffering might constrain his ability to contest the authority of psychiatry or to raise political claims that might be perceived as doing so, his diagnosis may also empower him to act more effectively with respect to other issues, such as matters relating to healthcare. Recall that Peter Sedgwick (1982) argued that the anti-psychiatry thinkers of the 1960s and 1970s who sought to deconstruct and challenge the idea of mental illness failed to see and indeed obscured the potential for psychiatric concepts to work as focal points for a new kind of political contest – a contest that Sedgwick dubbed 'psycho politics'. He indicated that the concept of illness could empower individuals collectively to '*make demands* upon the health service facilities of the society in which we live' (1982: 40). Differently put, it can enable the politicisation of mental suffering.

A psychiatric diagnosis transforms subjective suffering into a certain kind of public shape. It is not a public issue, to be sure. But it provides people with shared terms that allow them to discuss their experiences, and it can connect people to empowering factors that do allow them to articulate their suffering as a public issue. Indeed, even if one rejects the way a diagnosis defines an experience, as user/survivor activists often do, psychiatric concepts can enable individuals to engage with others and articulate their suffering as a collective maladjustment to the injustices of the societies in which they live. This is a point that is obscured even in some of the more nuanced contemporary criticism of psychiatry. For example, in a recent paper, Svend Brinkmann (2014) proposes a distinction between different languages of suffering, including diagnostic language and political language. Diagnostic language, for Brinkmann, apparently encompasses the diagnostic categories of the DSM, as well as psychiatric aetiologies and treatments. Unlike some critics, he acknowledges that diagnoses may lead to 'externalisations' of an individual's problems. These can, in turn, empower the individual to act politically through patient groups, for example. Yet he insists that externalising resources 'come from outside the diagnostic language itself', for instance, from political language – whose character remains vague in Brinkmann's scheme. Although the distinction between diagnostic and political language partly resonates with some of the earlier reflections of this paper, it is overdrawn. Psychiatric concepts *can* be externalising and, hence, straddle Brinkmann's categories, because psychiatric concepts are enmeshed in a network of affiliations, spaces, laws, institutions and other concepts. These and other connections give psychiatric concepts their authority; they are why psychiatric concepts have such a powerful impact on us.

For individuals who become the targets of diagnoses, these connections are in some cases empowering and in others disempowering. In the United Kingdom and elsewhere, a diagnosis of mental disorder entitles the individual to services from institutions, which are subject to ongoing political debate and visible political governance. When these institutions fail the individual, she may find the resources for understanding and acting upon this failure as a public issue through the connections in which her diagnosis has entangled her. This includes user/survivor groups, of course, but also factors that are part of the medical system, such as regulations stipulating care standards, treatment records and medical staff. By gathering with others in a space where they will be heard and seen and can state that they have a diagnosed disorder for which they have been denied proper treatment, medicalised individuals are raising an issue of shared concern through institutional channels and collective action – that is, they are exercising political agency.

Brinkmann (2014: 642–3) might object that what I have described here entails political language in addition to diagnostic language; he would be right. My point is that some apparently political concepts – like the *right* to healthcare – and other potentially empowering factors are partly constituted by psychiatric concepts and authority. That means that the same factors that make the act of diagnosis so powerful can make the actions of the diagnosed powerful as well.

Notwithstanding the potentially empowering effects of psychiatric concepts and, by extension, medicalisation, Sedgwick's 'psycho politics' has its pitfalls. Sedgwick urged the politicisation of 'medical goals', albeit in what he hoped would be an increasingly socialised healthcare system. But the range of experiences and issues that one can credibly raise within the context of the medical system or frame as medical goals seems relatively narrow. Doing so might empower activists to shape the healthcare system to an extent. However, it may also put an upper bound on their political agency, by constraining the range of empowering factors available to them. We have seen, for example, that while there are narrower and 'dimmer' spaces – ranging from social media groups to hospital board rooms – within which users/survivors can explore and act on experiences and issues, wider and 'brighter' spaces like the news media have had little room for them. Similarly, the psychiatric concepts and affiliations that users/survivors draw on may be empowering when they raise certain issues. Yet these factors also make users/survivors and their political actions particularly vulnerable to medical expertise. We have seen examples of the kinds of powerful resistance from psychiatrists and pundits as well as governments and healthcare systems that can be engendered by users/survivors' attempts to politicise mental disorder.

Beyond this, there is, of course, also the concern at the heart of much contemporary criticism of psychiatry, and King's earlier words about maladjustment to injustice, namely, that most people who have been diagnosed with a mental disorder will simply adjust themselves, with the help of therapy and medication, to the injustices that may have caused their medical suffering in the first place, never considering the possibility of political action. Sedgwick dismissed this concern: 'It is as though people believe there is only a finite pool of grievances for radicals to work with.' This is absurd, he suggested, 'for no matter how many maladjustments may become adjusted through expert techniques, the workings of capitalism will ever create newer and larger discontents, infinitely more dangerous to the system than any number of individual neuroses or manias'. Such an appeal to what Arendt (1961: 61) might call the 'iron law' of ideology – which in Sedgwick's case was Marxism – is suspect in itself. But even if we could take it for granted that capitalism will continue to produce new and non-medicalised forms of suffering and other experiences that can fuel political action, Sedgwick's argument has a troubling implication. It suggests that we do not have to worry about the disempowering effects of medicalisation because people will eventually find the resources for political action. Yet the price for this faith in a future political salvation is paid by individuals whose suffering is being medicalised now, whose complaints about discrimination and marginalisation are met with diagnoses and medications – individuals who could have added their power to the user/survivor movement, or indeed some other political action, and perhaps changed the world for the better today.

Conclusion

In this chapter, I have examined the movement of psychiatric service users/survivors contesting the authority of psychiatry. This move- ment consists of numerous groups that both constitute and provide empowering factors for individuals who reject psychiatric under- standings of their mental suffering. These groups offer access to political affiliations, spaces and concepts, empowering factors that can help people to transform negative emotions into public issues and action. Yet we have also seen that both before and after joining any group, individuals diagnosed with mental disorder face disem- powering factors as well. These people are vulnerable to prejudices about mental disorder, which, for example, impeach their capacity for reason and responsible action before and during political action. Relatedly, users/survivors may struggle to find concepts and other empowering factors that permit them to understand and act on their suffering politically. Concepts that frame their concerns as public issues and make demands on governments and healthcare systems have in notable instances been appropriated and depoliticised by these institutions. One example of this is recovery, which in its main- stream instantiation has largely been purged of the demedicalising and political meanings it has (or once had) for activists. This under- mines the conceptual resources available to individuals who experi- ence mental and emotional distress – rendering it more difficult for them to understand their problems as political in the first place – as well as the political agency of users/survivors who are currently trying to reshape psychiatry and mental healthcare. However, I have also argued that neither the appropriation of user/survivor ideas nor psychiatric diagnosis necessarily diminishes political agency. It can also be empowering. A diagnosis – and psychiatric concepts more generally – can enable individuals to make more effective and collective demands on healthcare services and the people responsible for them, as well as businesses, schools, governments and other institutions that are responsible for the health of some communities.

Even this benefit must be qualified because not everyone can or wants to frame their concerns in medical terms and evidence. Those who do not may be more vulnerable to the kind of medicalising attacks we saw in previous chapters. Considering that in the twenty-first century psycho politics has to an extent become just ordinary politics, this is cause for concern. In Britain, it seems that not a day passes without mental health being used to justify, explain or criticise a political event or policy in the news. This is unlikely to change. Recent trends indicate that psychiatric and especially neuro-psychiatric concepts may become even more pervasive in public discourse (Konnoth 2020; Rose and Abi-Rached 2013). Some users/survivors will find this politically empowering, but many will not. Looking beyond these groups and their concerns, and towards the people and issues explored in the previous chapters, we also need to keep another question in mind, given that certain public issues probably cannot be adequately expressed in psychiatric or medical terms at all. In a society where political matters increasingly have to be framed in medical terms or another expert language to be heard, how will suffering and disadvantaged people be able to participate effectively in politics? We might have seen one possible answer to this question already in recent elections and referenda, as politicians ostensibly speaking for the working class have declared that people have 'had enough of experts', a reaction that is hardly without its own dangers.

Notes

1. An important recent work on the user/survivor movement is Mohammed Rashed's *Madness and the Demand for Recognition* (2019). Our respective investigations have different but complementary foci. Whereas the concept of political agency guides my analysis, Rashed's guiding notion is recognition. His objective is to justify philosophically that mental disorder can be a basis for identity and that user/survivor activists' demand

for recognition on this basis has legitimate normative force. For the sake of contrast, my own concern in this chapter could be reframed as how and why user/survivor activists' demands with respect to recognition or other issues obtain or fail to obtain significant uptake and support their political agency.

2. In the United Kingdom, some people have been and continue to be deprived of their formal political rights through what is known as 'sectioning'. Opposition to sectioning and 'drugging' – that is, forced medication – have long been among the key issues of the user/survivor movement (Pilgrim 2005). The laws governing these practices in England and Wales were reformed with the introduction of the Mental Health Act 2007. However, the reform has been controversial among some users/survivors and commentators, who argue that it may render people more vulnesrable to compulsory detention and treatment (Shah 2009; see also Mackay 2011); in fact, between 2005/6 and 2015/16 detentions rose by 40 per cent (CQC 2018). In another notable legislative act, Parliament in 2012 also repealed a component of mental health law that stripped MPs of their seats if they were sectioned for more than six months.

3. For a comprehensive historical survey of the user/survivor movement in Britain, see Crossley (2006).

4. My reflections on the empowering effects of user involvement draw on Noorani's (2013) empirical research and analysis.

Conclusion:
Political Agency after COVID-19

Philosophers, historians and sociologists have long warned of the adverse political effects of medicalisation. Some political theorists have raised similar concerns. Yet their criticism has often been sweeping and seldom attended to political agency, much less to political agency and emotion together. In studies that do consider the impact of medicalisation on political agency, we find little, if any, evidence that psychiatric concepts have actually been deployed against political actors. I have sought to provide a better understanding of how the medicalisation of negative emotions impacts political agency. Drawing upon an Arendtian framework for understanding the relationship, I have analysed four instances of political action in which people's emotional and mental fitness for public life has been called into question.

These cases have shown how political actors can draw upon empowering factors to transform their emotional experiences into public issues and take concerted action, but also how their political opponents can disempower them by undermining the fragile public shape of their emotions through medicalising attacks and other means. Four features of negative emotions make them vital to political agency. They can motivate us to reflect on the causes of our experiences, drive us to address them, communicate our authentic concern with a particular issue, and help constitute and sustain social cohesion between us and other people. To this, the Arendtian perspective developed here contributed a central insight: emotions are not inherently political. Recalling Arendt's (1998: 50) own words, before emotions have been 'transformed, deprivatized and deindividualized' they 'lead an uncertain shadowy kind of existence'. To fuel political agency, negative emotions must be transformed into something political, that is, articulated as public issues. In some of the cases, the process of transforming emotions into public issues was implicit. But actors in all cases clearly struggled in different ways with the problem of maintaining the public shape of their emotions. A related Arendtian insight, which I developed with the help of feminist theorists like Sue Campbell, is that the public shape of emotions is fragile. Even after an individual has articulated her negative emotion as a public issue, she and others may easily begin to doubt the connection between the two. Throughout the book, I have tried to show how empowering factors can facilitate and maintain such articulations, whereas disempowering factors prevent and undermine them. When psychiatric concepts are deployed in public discourse, they tend to function as the latter, but do not always.

The cases I have explored, thus, confirm some worries that critics of psychiatry have raised about the dangers of medicalisation. But they have also given us some reasons to be hopeful. The case studies support the Arendtian thesis that political action can emerge in the most unfriendly and unlikely of places. To many readers, the most unexpected instance of political action is probably the user/survivor movement and its struggle with psychiatry. Since mental disorder is widely regarded as 'a disease like any other' (TNS BRMB 2015: 4), it is reasonable for people to think that psychiatry is like any other area of medicine. They might well agree with the indignant observation of a former president of the American Psychiatric Association that 'being "against" psychiatry' is no different and no less absurd 'than being "against" cardiology or orthopedics or gynecology' (Lieberman 2013). In Chapter 2, I observed with Arendt that, in order to act politically, individuals must renounce 'the comfortable protection of nature' (Arendt 2007: 284), which leads them to believe that particular problems are beyond the political grasp of ordinary people. We usually think of medical issues as such problems, that is, matters that must be left to certified experts and kept out of the hands of ordinary people. This idea is as old as the Western political tradition itself, with Plato famously using the physician's authority over medical issues as a template for stateman's authority over matters of government (e.g., 2004: 389b–c; see also Stalley 1980). Arendt is, therefore, on the right track when she states that scientists 'move in a world where speech has lost its power' (1998: 4; see also Dallmayr 2009: 88–9), though I would modify her statement as follows: doctors, including psychiatrists, are used to moving in a world where the speech of ordinary people has little power. We have seen that in practice, some of this power has been recovered as user involvement and expertise-by-experience. However, most people probably regard psychiatry as a domain that should be free from the influence of non-scientists. The user/survivor movement, for example, may therefore not only *appear* unexpected to ordinary people, but, in a more substantive sense, *is* unexpected, considering the disempowering factors – most saliently in the form of medical concepts, relationships and spaces – that user/survivors face.

Crucially, the user/survivor case showed that psychiatric concepts and the medicalisation of negative emotions can be empowering and disempowering, affirming Sedgwick's claim that psychiatric diagnoses can form the basis for political action. Others have made stronger claims along the same lines. Nikolas Rose (2006: 132) has argued that we have entered an era of 'biological citizenship', referring to forms of citizenship based on biological knowledge about ourselves. Medicalisation is not a term that Rose (2007) favours due to its arguably negative connotations. However, medicalisation – again, understood as the 'process by which medical definitions and practices are applied to behaviors, psychological phenomena, and somatic experiences not previously within the conceptual or therapeutic scope of medicine' (Davis 2010) – clearly plays a vital role in the production of this knowledge. Although Rose (2006) states that biological citizenship has existed in some form for centuries, linked to biologically informed notions of the individual, family, gender, race and species, among others, he also observes that recent medical and technological developments have produced knowledge and technologies that have vastly expanded the possibilities for thinking about and acting on ourselves and others biologically (140–1). While some of these shifts are individualising, Rose emphasises that they are often collectivising as well. They enable people to relate to one another and make shared claims using the burgeoning resource of biological concepts (134–5). He rightly observes that people suffering from various diseases and health problems have been able, for example, to fight stigma, claim rights and support others affected by disease (144).

Yet I think Rose is too blithe about the adverse political effects of these developments. Despite recognising that the expanding realms of biological citizenship can be individualising, he appears unconcerned about the threat this may pose to political agency – a term he does not use. On the contrary, Rose concludes that '[b]iological citizenship requires those with investments in their biology to *become* political', that is, to engage in various kinds of political action

(2006: 149; original emphasis). He is undoubtedly mistaken. Rose observes that the political actions entailed by his conception of biological citizenship 'often involve quite specialized scientific and medical knowledge of one's condition' (134–5). This, as I have sought to underscore, is something that many people lack in a politically, or even a personally, empowering form. Although nearly everyone might be able to access the internet and, thus, medical information, it does not mean that they are able to use it for any other purpose than to obtain a doctor's appointment – and perhaps not even that.

Non-medical concepts that enable individuals to perceive and describe negative emotions as public issues are by no means easy for everyone to access or use either. As Arendt (1961) highlights, concepts that we traditionally think of as political – for example, freedom as the right to non-interference – can also be disempowering if they prevent individuals from perceiving the need and opportunities for concerted action. But for all their flaws and ambiguities, concepts that are widely recognised as political, like freedom, equality, justice, democracy, citizenship and many others, maintain deep, diverse and direct connections to a range of empowering factors by virtue of their traditional role in political thought and practice (but cf. Brown 2015: 208). While diagnoses are also tied to some empowering factors, these are comparatively obscure and difficult to find and use.

To clarify: I recognise, with Rose, that medicalisation and psychiatric concepts are not intrinsically disempowering. A diagnosis of mental disorder can, through its connections to affiliations, spaces, laws, etc., provide access to empowering factors that enable individuals to transform negative emotions into public issues and political action that are taken seriously by others. However, critiques of medicalisation and psychiatric diagnoses such as Brinkmann's (2015) indicate that some connections are more easily and often taken up than others, and those closest at hand may be the most disempowering. For instance, the link between the concept of depression and neurochemical aetiology seems to be stronger than the connection between depression and structural explanations. Consequently, an individual diagnosed with depression is more likely to think of and act on her negative emotions as a personal trouble rather than a public issue. And because of the connections between psychiatric concepts and psychiatrists, hospitals, medications and so on, this individual is also more likely to think and act as though her suffering can be addressed only by psychiatrists working in a hospital and using medication. This enables the individual to make personal claims on the healthcare system, and – if this system fails her and others – possibly empowers her to make political demands for improvement. Yet, in other circumstances, these connections are likely to be disempowering. We have, for example, seen that people with mental disorder who act politically against psychiatric interpretations of their negative emotions face disempowering factors that inhibit their ability to articulate their negative emotions as public issues and their credibility *vis-à-vis* external publics. Similarly, we have seen that in some instances, psychiatric concepts have been deployed in public discourse to destroy the fragile public shape that passionate political actors have given their emotions by suggesting that what these actors need is not political change but mental healthcare.

Hopefully, this book will encourage political theorists to re-engage with medicalisation and the relationship between the medical and the political more broadly. As we have seen, the medicalisation of negative emotions has received much less scrutiny than the flourishing interest in the political role of negative emotions calls for. However, others could benefit from attending more to the medical too, including scholars exploring the decay of liberal democracy. At least since the Great Recession, theories of democratic decay have focused on how the extension of economic rationality, or neoliberalisation, undermines the conditions for substantive, participatory democracy. Consider, for example, Wendy Brown's highly influential narrative of democratic decay in *Undoing the Demos* (2015). In this book, she defines neoliberalism as an 'order of normative reason' within which all aspects of human life are understood as economic markets and humans themselves are conceived as entrepreneurs who seek to maximise their own value in these markets (30). This produces a subject that 'approaches everything as a market and knows only market conduct', who 'cannot think public purposes or common problems' (39). Following Foucault, Brown calls this subject *homo oeconomicus*. She warns that, as neoliberal reason spreads and becomes ascendant, the *homo oeconomicus* replaces the 'already anemic' *homo politicus* (35), which rules with others through deliberation, collaboration and contest (79, 221–2).[1] In spite or maybe because of the influence of Foucault, medicalisation or medical power does not figure in Brown's analysis. While Foucault is one of the foremost theorists of the medical, he also appears to have regarded medicine as a mere handmaiden of neoliberalism. So perhaps Brown assumes that medicalisation is simply a more specific form of neoliberalisation, but one that ultimately follows the same economic rationality and produces the same disempowering effects. However, as I have argued throughout this book, we should avoid reducing medicalisation to other disempowering processes, whether that be hyper-emotionalisation, some vague notion of pathologisation or, as in Brown's case, neoliberalisation, because it obscures the particular causes, pathways and effects of medicalisation.

Our political experiences during the COVID-19 pandemic have provided further reasons to avoid such oversimplifying reductions. In the crisis, the political power of medicine was not only in full view, but medical rationality was sometimes opposed to neoliberal economic rationality. This was most dramatically exemplified in the public confrontations between then-President Donald Trump and Dr Anthony Fauci, the Director of the National Institute of Allergy and Infectious Diseases, a key figure on the US government's coronavirus task force. In these confrontations, Trump was largely the champion of the economic and Fauci the champion of the medical. One of the reasons for this collision of rationalities is quite apparent: the end of maintaining health is not always compatible with the end of building wealth. Another is that their authority stems from different webs of empowering factors. Whereas medical authority is bound up in, for example, hospitals, medical research, medications, doctor–patient relationships and, crucially, health; economic authority is bound up in, for example, financial data, money, shareholders and employees and, crucially, wealth.

Given the difference between economic and medical authority, those who like Brown work in a Foucauldian tradition might want to consider alongside *homo politicus* and *homo economicus* a third subject archetype: *homo medicus*. As my late introduction of this concept suggests, it is not one that I favour. Nevertheless, it helpfully illustrates how an analysis of medicalisation can complicate and perhaps complement stories of democratic decay. While *homo medicus* is ordinarily taken to refer to the doctor – this is how Foucault (2006b: 358, 504) himself used it – it has more recently been used to name a subject driven by the imperative of health and that, hence, approaches everything in terms of maximising health and minimising risks to it (Peretti-Watel and Moatti 2009). In a way, the pandemic turned us all into *homo medicus*, actively evaluating the people and things around us in medical terms and asking questions, such as: are the people in front of me at the supermarket contagious? Will my children become sick if I send them to school? Should I wear a mask?

Unlike Brown's *homo economicus*, however, *homo medicus* is clearly capable of 'thinking public purposes', as the example of the 750,000 British citizens and denizens rallying around the National Health Service in the crisis highlights. Although, as I noted in Chapter 2, this is not an instance of the revolutionary kind of political action that radical democrats idealise, the actors involved are thinking a public purpose, even if this purpose is in a sense also medical. While this level of mobilisation around the NHS was unprecedented, we saw in Chapter 6 that users/survivors have long found issues and spaces within the NHS to organise around collectively. Nevertheless, *homo medicus* raises democratic concerns too. Because of its overriding commitment to maintaining health, *homo medicus* may place too much trust in medical experts, especially in their capacity to develop and execute solutions to public issues. In this regard, this subject might find some common ground with *homo economicus*. For though *homo medicus* may at times need to defend politically the resources that enable health, it seems to desire freedom from politics. We saw this in the stream of polemical editorials accusing political leaders of not listening to the experts or of not giving them sufficient power, as though simply allowing medicine or science to rule would cure our ills – something which was a common refrain in some quarters before the crisis as well. The frequency and ferocity of such calls are surprising given that the coronavirus crisis showed that speaking of 'medicine' or 'science' as monoliths capable of providing specific solutions to any problem imaginable is a fantasy, and that, just as in softer fields, reasonable disagreements are both possible and common, particularly when it comes to policy. Hence, exploring the relationship between the medical and the political can inform more nuanced stories of democratic decay and, critically, help us better understand the factors undermining democracy and how we can counteract them.

The fallout of the pandemic will shape our politics for many years to come. Saliently, we will have to reckon with new wellsprings of negative emotions, especially fear, grief and anger. These are emotions that have emerged in response to the effects of and government management of the pandemic as well as the pre-existing, systemic injustices brought into view by the crisis. Contests over the political relevance of these emotions are ongoing, and we must pay careful attention to whose emotions are shaped by whom and how. The influence of governments and corporations is one concern. Their push for a 'new' normal seems to involve bracketing collectivism as an artefact of the crisis while reaffirming pre-crisis individualism, which may crush many fragile and nascently political emotions. But we must be attentive to how medicalisation is shaping these emotions too. This is perhaps more urgent than ever, given the expansion of the political power of medicine during the pandemic and the explicit efforts of the leading medical professionals to consolidate and increase this power (e.g., Davies 2020). Mental health experts and charities claimed from the start that the negative emotions that arose during the pandemic were precursors to serious mental health problems, portending a pandemic of mental disorders on the heels of the COVID-19 crisis. Medicalising these emotions will doubtlessly help many people get the care they need and engage others in political action to ensure the availability of care. Yet it may also mean that many people will never find the resources to transform their emotions into public issues and that the injustices that may have caused these emotions continue to fester.

Note

1. In her most recent book, *The Ruins of Neoliberalism* (2019), Brown extends her analysis beyond *homo oeconomicus* and the rationality it embodies, but she does not abandon it (see 182, 143–60). Strikingly, Brown still has nothing to say about medical power, even though the politics of pregnancy is one of her central cases.

Bibliography

Abraham, A., 2016. 'Remembering Mad Pride', *Vice*, 18 November, available at: https://www.vice.com/en_uk/article/mad-pride-remembering-the-uks-mental-health-pride-movement, last accessed 16 April 2018.

Adams, W. L., 2015. 'The Enemy Within', *The Independent*, 26 January, p. 31.

Adkins, K., 2020. 'We Will March Side by Side and Demand a Bigger Table': Anger as Dignity Claim', *Global Discourse* 10(2/3), pp. 191–210.

Adorno, T. W., Frenkel-Brunswik, E., Levinson, D. J. and Sanford, N., 1950. *The Authoritarian Personality*. New York: Harper & Row.

Ahmed, S., 2010. *The Promise of Happiness*. Durham, NC: Duke University Press.

Ahmed, S., 2014. *The Cultural Politics of Emotion*, 2nd edn. Edinburgh: Edinburgh University Press.

Ahuja, A., 2006. 'Listen to Your Inner Voices', *The Times*, 19 September, p. 2.

Akrich, M., 2010. 'From Communities of Practice to Epistemic Communities: Health Mobilizations on the Internet', *Sociological Research Online*, 15(2).

Allan, C., 2006. 'Misplaced Pride', *The Guardian*, 27 September, p. 1.

Allan, C., 2007. 'Loose-talking Psychophobes Show Nothing but Contempt', *The Guardian*, 5 December, p. 6.

Allen, A., 1999. *The Power of Feminist Theory*. Boulder, CO: Westview.

Allen, A., 2002. 'Power, Subjectivity, and Agency: Between Arendt and Foucault', *International Journal of Philosophical Studies* 10(2), 131–49.

Allen, D., 2004. *Talking to Strangers*. Chicago: University of Chicago Press.

Alleyne, R., Hall, J. and Burton, L., 2011. 'St Paul's Cathedral Announces Closure due to "Occupy" Protesters', *Daily Telegraph*, 4 November, available at: http://www.telegraph.co.uk/news/religion/8841430/St-Pauls-Cathedral-announces-closure-due-to-Occupy-protesters.html, last accessed 7 January 2017.

Altemeyer, B., 1988. *Enemies of Freedom*. London: Josey-Bass.

American Psychiatric Association [APA], 1980. *Diagnostic and Statistical Manual of Mental Disorders (DSM-III)*, 3rd edn. Washington, DC: American Psychiatric Association.

American Psychiatric Association [APA], 1994. *Diagnostic and Statistical Manual of Mental Disorders (DSM-IV)*, 4th edn. Washington, DC: American Psychiatric Association.

American Psychiatric Association [APA], 2000. *Diagnostic and Statistical Manual of Mental Disorders (DSM-IV-TR)*, 4th edn, text revision. Washington, DC: American Psychiatric Association.

American Psychiatric Association [APA], 2013. *Diagnostic and Statistical Manual of Mental Disorders (DSM-5)*, 5th edn. Washington, DC: American Psychiatric Association.

Aminzade, R. and McAdam, D., 2001. 'Emotions and Contentious Politics', in R. R. Aminzade, J. A. Goldstone, D. McAdam, E. J. Perry, W. H. Sewell, S. Tarrow and C. Tilley (eds), *Silence and Voice in the Study of Contentious Politics*. Cambridge: Cambridge University Press, pp. 14–50.

Anon., 2013. *We Are the 99 percent*, available at: http://wearethe99percent. tumblr.com, last accessed 12 April 2017.

Archer, A. and Miller, G., 2019. 'Anger, Affective Injustice, and Emotion Regulation', *Philosophical Topics* 47(2), pp. 75–94.

Arendt, H., 1958a. 'Totalitarian Imperialism: Reflections on the Hungarian Revolution', *Journal of Politics* 20(1), pp. 5–43.

Arendt, H., 1958b. *The Origins of Totalitarianism*, 2nd edn New York: Meridian Books.

Arendt, H., 1961. *Between Past and Future*. New York: Viking Press.

Arendt, H., 1972. *Crises of the Republic*. New York: Harcourt Brace Jovanovich.

Arendt, H., 1977. 'Public Rights and Private Interests', in M. Mooney and F. Stuber (eds), *Small Comforts for Hard Times: Humanists on Public Policy*. New York: Columbia University Press, pp. 103–8.

Arendt, H., 1978. *The Life of the Mind*, vol. I. New York: Harcourt Brace Jovanovich.

Arendt, H., 1982. *Lectures on Kant's Political Philosophy*. Chicago: University of Chicago Press.

Arendt, H., [1964] 1994. *Eichmann in Jerusalem: A Report on the Banality of Evil*. New York: Penguin.

Arendt, H., [1968] 1995. *Men in Dark Times*. New York: Harcourt, Brace & World.

Arendt, H., [1929] 1996. *Love and Saint Augustine*. Chicago: University of Chicago Press.

Arendt, H., [1957] 1997. *Rahel Varnhagen: The Life of a Jewess*, trans. R. Winston and C. Winston. Baltimore, MD: Johns Hopkins University Press.

Arendt, H., [1958] 1998. *The Human Condition*. Chicago: University of Chicago Press.

Arendt, H., [1959] 2003a. 'Reflections on Little Rock', in J. Kohn (ed.), *Responsibility and Judgement*. New York: Schocken.

Arendt, H., [1964] 2003b. 'Personal Responsibility under Dictatorship', in J. Kohn (ed.), *Responsibility and Judgement*. New York: Schocken.

Arendt, H., [1956–9] 2005a. 'Introduction into Politics', in J. Kohn (ed.), *The Promise of Politics*. New York: Schocken, pp. 93–200.

Arendt, H., [1955] 2005b. 'Epilogue', in J. Kohn (ed.), *The Promise of Politics*. New York: Schocken, pp. 201–4.

Arendt, H., [1964] 2005c. 'What Remains? Language Remains', in J. Kohn (ed.), *Essays in Understanding: 1930–1954: Formation, Exile, Totalitarianism*. New York: Schocken, pp. 1–23.

Arendt, H., [1954] 2005d. 'On the Nature of Totalitarianism', in J. Kohn (ed.), *Essays in Understanding: 1930–1954: Formation, Exile, Totalitarianism*. New York: Schocken, pp. 328–60.

Arendt, H., [1963] 2006. *On Revolution*. New York: Penguin.

Arendt, H., [1944] 2007. 'The Jew as Pariah: A Hidden Tradition', in J. Kohn and R. H. Feldman (eds), *The Jewish Writings*. New York: Schocken, pp. 275–97.

Arendt, H., [1963] 2018. 'Nation-state and Democracy', in J. Kohn (ed.), *Thinking Without a Banister: Essays in Understanding 1953–1975*. New York: Schocken.

Aristotle, 2004. *Nicomachean Ethics*, trans. R. Crisp. Cambridge: Cambridge University Press.

Armstrong, D., 1983. *Political Anatomy of the Body*. Cambridge: Cambridge University Press.

Ashcroft, Lord, 2012. *'They're Thinking What We're Thinking'*. London: Lord Ashcroft.

Assinder, N., 2006. 'UKIP and Cameron's War of Words', *BBC News*, 4 April, available at: http://news.bbc.co.uk/1/hi/uk_politics/4875502.stm, last accessed 30 January 2017.

Atkins, A., 2021. 'On Grief's Sweet Sorrow', *European Journal of Philosophy*, forthcoming, available at: https://www.academia.edu/45184109/On_Griefs_Sweet_Sorrow.

Averill, J. R., 1982. *Anger and Aggression: An Essay on Emotion*. New York: Springer.

Badia, E. and Schapiro, R., 2011. 'A Day in the (weired) [sic] Life at Zuccotti Park', *Daily News*, 23 October, p. 8.

Bacon, P., 2010. 'Language Lessons for Democrats, from the Political Brain of Drew Westen', *Washington Post*, 18 May, available at: http://www.washingtonpost.com/wp-dyn/content/article/2010/05/17/AR2010051703823.html, last accessed 24 April 2018.

Bailey, D. J., 2017. *Protest Movements and Parties of the left*. London: Rowman & Littlefield.

Baker, B., 2006. 'Response Laughter Can Help Make Sense of Mental Health', *The Guardian*, 4 October, p. 31.

Bandelow, B. and Michaelis, S., 2015. 'Epidemiology of Anxiety Disorders in the 21st Century', *Dialogues in Clinical Neuroscience* 17(3), pp. 327–35.

Barbalet, J. M., 2004. *Emotion, Social Theory, and Social Structure.* Cambridge: Cambridge University Press.

Bargetz, B., 2021. 'Haunting Sovereignty and the Neurotic Subject: Contemporary Constellations of Fear, Anxiety and Uncertainty', *Citizenship Studies* 25(1), pp. 20–35.

Barnett, S., 2008. 'Bonkersfest', *New Statesman,* 8 July, available at: http://www.newstatesman.com/health/2008/07/became-bonkersfest-mental, last accessed 10 May 2017.

Bath Chronicle, The, 2010. 'Mad Hatters Group Feel Reclaiming Language of Madness "Empowering"', *The Chronicle,* 14 October 2010, p. 36.

Baugh, B., 1989. 'Heidegger on *Befindlichkeit*', *Journal of the British Society for Phenomenology* 20(2), pp. 124–35.

BBC News, 2014. 'I Respect Nigel Farage, says George Osborne', *BBC News,* 24 May, available at: http://www.bbc.co.uk/news/uk-politics-27554556, last accessed 27 September 2018.

Bedford, C., 2011. 'Batman Takes on His Darkest Villain Yet: Occupy Protesters', *Daily Caller,* 20 December, available at: http://dailycaller.com/2011/12/20/batman-takes-on-his-darkest-villain-yet-occupy-protesters-video, last accessed 12 January 2017.

Bell, I., 2013. 'Ukip's Emergence from the Fringe is no Laughing Matter', *The Herald,* 1 May, p. 13.

Benhabib, S., 2003. *The Reluctant Modernism of Hannah Arendt,* rev. edn. Oxford: Rowman & Littlefield.

Ben-Ze'ev, A. 2000. *The Subtlety of Emotions.* Cambridge, MA: MIT Press.

Ben-Ze'ev, A., 2020. 'Anger and its Interaction with Love and Hate: The Constructive Role of Balanced Anger in Our Society', Mosse Lecture, Humboldt University, delivered 19 November 2020, available at: https://www.youtube.com/watch?v=hlElaprpPj8.

Beresford, P., 2011. 'The "Hidden" Have Found Their Protesting Voice', *The Guardian,* 5 January, p. 4.

Beresford, P., 2015. 'Distress and Disability: Not You, Not Me, But Us?' in H. Spandler and J. Anderson (eds), *Madness, Distress and the Politics of Sisablement.* Bristol: Policy Press, pp. 245–59.

Berezin, M., 2009. 'Exploring Emotions and the Economy: New Contributions from Sociological Theory', *Theory & Society* 38(4), pp. 335–46.

Berlant, L., 2005. 'Unfeeling Kerry', *Theory & Event* 8(2), available at: https://muse.jhu.edu/article/187843, last accessed 14 January 2018.

Biden, J., 2020. 'Transcript of Joe Biden's video message for George Floyd's funeral in Houston, Texas', *Medium*, 10 June, available at: https://medium.com/@JoeBiden/transcript-of-vice-president-joe-bidens-video-message-for-george-floyd-s-funeral-in-houston-texas-c427064ad51.

Blackie, J. S., 1867. *On Democracy*, 5th edn. Edinburgh: Edmonston & Douglas.

Blair, L., 2006. 'My Friend Hears Voices', *The Guardian*, 3 August, p. 28.

Blencowe, C., 2010. 'Foucault's and Arendt's "Insider View" of Biopolitics: a Critique of Agamben', *History of the Human Sciences* 23(5), pp. 113–30.

Bloch, S., 1989. 'Soviet Psychiatry and Snezhnevskyism', in van Voren, R. (ed.), *Soviet Psychiatric Abuse in the Gorbachev Era*. Amsterdam: IAPUP, pp. 55–61.

Boardman, J., Craig, T., Goddard, C., Henderson, C., McCarthy, J., McInerny, T., Cohen, A., Potter, M., Rinaldi, M. and Whicher, E., 2010. *Recovery Is For All*. London: South London and Maudsley NHS Foundation Trust and South West London and St George's Mental Health NHS Trust.

Board of Trustees, 2016. *APA financial statement, disclosure of affiliations and conflict of interest policy*. Washington, DC: American Psychiatric Association.

Boffey, D., 2013. 'The Party that Came in from the Fringe: Why Ukip scares Tories', *The Observer*, 25 April, p. 8.

Bohman, J., 1997. 'The Moral Costs of Political Pluralism: The Dilemmas of Difference and Equality in Arendt's "Reflections on Little Rock"', in L. May and J. Kohn (eds), *Hannah Arendt: Twenty Years Later*. London: MIT Press, pp. 53–80.

Boltanski, L. and Chiapello, E., 2005. *The New Spirit of Capitalism*. London: Verso.

Bonnie, R. J., 2002. 'Political Abuse of Psychiatry in the Soviet Union and in China: Complexities and Controversies', *Journal of the American Academy of Psychiatry and the Law* 30, pp. 136–44.

Bossewitch, J., 2016. 'Dangerous Gifts: Towards a New Wave of Mad Resistance', PhD thesis, Columbia University, New York.

Boyle, M., 2011. 'Making the World Go Away, and How Psychology and Psychiatry Benefit', in M. Rapley, J. Moncrieff and J. Dillon (eds.), *De-medicalizing Misery*. London: Palgrave, pp. 27–43.

Best, J., 2020. 'Review – Frank Furedi, How Fear Works: Culture of Fear in the Twenty-first Century', *International Sociology*, available at: https://doi.org/10.1177%2F0268580920906750.

Bradshaw, L., 2008. 'Emotions, Reasons, and Judgments', in L. Ferry and R. Kingston (eds), *Bringing the Passions Back In*. Vancouver: UBC Press, pp. 172–88.

Brand, J., 2007. 'Glad to be "Mad"'? *The Guardian*, 8 May, p. 14.

Brady, M. S., 2013. *Emotional Insight*. Oxford: Oxford University Press.

Brady, M. S., 2018. *Suffering and Virtue*. Oxford: Oxford University Press.

Brady, M. S., 2019. *Emotion*. London: Routledge.

Brändle, V., Galpin, C. and Trenz, H-J., 2018. 'Marching for Europe? Enacting European Citizenship as Justice during Brexit', *Citizenship Studies* 22(8), 810–28.

Breen, K., 2012. *Under Weber's Shadow*. London: Routledge.

Breen, K., 2019. 'Arendt, Republicanism, and Political Freedom', in K. Hiruta (ed.), *Arendt on Freedom, Liberation, and Revolution*. Cham: Palgrave Macmillan, pp. 47–78.

Brinkmann, S., 2014. 'Languages of Suffering', *Theory & Psychology* 24(5), pp. 630–48.

Brockes, E., 2013. 'Book of the Week', *The Guardian*, 9 February, p. 6.

Brolin, M., 2016. 'When Europhiles Start Parading their "Experts" You Know They've Lost the Argument', *Daily Telegraph*, 28 March, available at: https://www.telegraph.co.uk/news/2016/03/28/when-europhiles-start-parading-their-experts-you-know-theyve-los, last accessed 7 April 2017.

Brown, W., 2015. *Undoing the Demos*. New York: Zone Books.

Brown, W., 2019. *The Ruins of Neoliberalism*. New York: Columbia University Press.

Browne, H., 2011. 'The Best New Year Resolution is to Ignore Politicians', *Sunday Times*, 2 January, p. 11.

Browning, C. S., 2018. 'Brexit, Existential Anxiety and Ontological (In)Security', *European Security* 27(3), pp. 336–55.

Brubaker, R. and Laitin, D. D., 1998. 'Ethnic and Nationalist Violence', *Annual Review of Sociology* 24(1), pp. 423–52.

Brudholm, T., 2008. *Resentment's Virtue*. Philadelphia, PA: Temple University Press.

Burgess, M., 2016. 'Brexit Anxiety' *Hypnotherapy Directory*, 25 June, available at: http://www.hypnotherapy-directory.org.uk/hypnotherapist-articles/brexit-anxiety, last accessed 9 December 2016.

Burgum, S., 2018. *Occupying London*. London: Routledge.

Burke, H., 2016. 'Post-Brexit Shame: What Therapy Clients are Feeling. *Welldoing*', 1 July, available at: https://welldoing.org/article/post-brexit-shame-what-therapist-clients-are-feeling, last accessed 9 December 2016.

Burling, S., 2012. 'Former Patients Protest Psychiatrist Convention', *The Philadelphia Inquirer*, 6 May, available at: https://www.philly.com/philly/health/20120506_Former_patients_protest_psychiatrist_convention.html, last accessed 7 June 2017.

Burstow, B. 2015. *Psychiatry and the Business of Madness*. New York: Palgrave.

Busfield, J., 2011. *Mental Illness*. Cambridge: Polity.

Busfield, J., 2017. 'The Concept of Medicalisation Reassessed', *Sociology of Health & Illness* 44(4), pp. 603–16.

Butler, J., 1997. *The Psychic Life of Power*. Stanford, CA: Stanford University Press.

Butler, J., 2000. *Antigone's Claim*. New York: Columba University Press.

Butler, J., 2003. *Precarious Life*. London: Verso.

Butler, J., 2015. *Notes Toward a Theory of Performative Theory of Assembly*. London: Harvard University Press.

Butt, R., Malik, S. and Davies, L., 2011. 'St Paul's Cathedral Canon Resigns', *The Guardian*, 27 October, available at: https://www.theguardian.com/uk/2011/oct/27/st-pauls-cathedral-canon-resigns, last accessed 7 January 2017.

Cabanas, E. and Illouz, E., 2019. *Manufacturing Happy Citizens*. Cambridge: Polity.

Calhoun, C., 1997. 'Plurality, Promises, and Public Spaces', in C. Calhoun and J. McGowan (eds), *Hannah Arendt and the Meaning of Politics*. Minneapolis, MN: University of Minnesota Press, pp. 232–62.

Callard, A., 2020. 'On Anger', in A. Callard (ed.), *On Anger*. Cambridge, MA: Boston Review, pp. 9–30.

Cannon, W., 1927. *Bodily Changes Pain, Hunger, Fear and Rage*. New York: Appleton.

Campbell, S., 1994. 'Being Dismissed: The Politics of Emotional Expression', *Hypatia* 9(3), pp. 46–65.

Care Quality Commission [CQC], 2018. *Mental Health Act: The Rise in the Use of the MHA to Detain People in England*. London: CQC.

Carel, H. and Kidd, I. J., 2014. 'Epistemic Injustice in Healthcare: A Philosophical Analysis', *Medical Health Care and Philosophy* 17(4), pp. 529–40.

Carter, R., 2018. *Fear, Hope and Loss*. London: Hope not Hate Charitable Trust.

Catherwood, C., 2014. 'Racism, Austerity and the Political Response', *The Guardian*, 3 June, p. 33.

Chakravarti, S., 2014. *Sing the Rage*. Chicago: University of Chicago Press

Charland, L. C., 2013. 'Why Psychiatry Should Fear Medicalization', in K. W. M. Fulford, M Davies, R. G. T. Gipps, J. Z. Graham, G. Stanghellini and T. Thornton (eds), *The Oxford Handbook of Philosophy and Psychiatry*. Oxford: Oxford University Press, pp. 159–75.

Cherry, M., 2018. 'The Errors and Limitations of Our "Anger-evaluating" Ways', in M. Cherry and O. Flanagan (eds), 2018. *Moral Psychology of Anger*. New York: Rowman & Littlefield, pp.49–65.

Cherry, M. and Flanagan, O. (eds), 2018. *Moral Psychology of Anger*. New York: Rowman & Littlefield.

City of London Corp. v. *Samede* [2012] EWHC 34 (QB).

Clark, L. A., Cuthbert, B., Lewis-Fernández, R., Narrow, W. E. and Reed, G. M., 2017. 'Three Approaches to Understanding and Classifying Mental Disorder: ICD-11, DSM-5, and the National Institute of Mental

Health's Research Domain Criteria (RDoC)', *Psychological Science in the Public Interest* 18(2), pp. 72–145.

Clark, N., 2018. 'REMAINIACS: Middle-class Remoaners "so upset by Brexit they've developed a psychological disorder", Top Doctors Warn', *The Sun*, 20 August, available at: https://www.thesun.co.uk/news/7055100/middle-class-remoaners-so-upset-by-brexit-theyve-developed-a-psychological-disorder-top-doctors-warn, last accessed 10 October 2018.

Clark, T., 2014. 'Age of Anxiety May be Here to Stay', *The Guardian*, 17 June, p. 7.

Clarke, A. E., Shim, J. K., Mamo, L., Fosket, J. R. and Fishman, J. R., 2003. 'Biomedicalization: Technoscientific Transformations of Health, Illness, and US Biomedicine', *American Sociological Review* 68(2), pp. 161–94.

Clarke, H. D., Goodwin, M. and Whiteley, P., 2017. *Brexit: Why Britain Voted to Leave the European Union*. Cambridge: Cambridge University Press.

Clifford Simplican, S., 2015. *The Capacity Contract*. Minneapolis, MN: University of Minnesota Press.

Coalition Against Psychiatric Assault, 2019. 'Attrition Model', *Coalition Again Psychiatric Assault*, available at: https://coalitionagainstpsychiatricassault.wordpress. com/antipsychiatry/attrition-model, last accessed 24 November 2019.

Cohen, B. M. Z., 2016. *Psychiatric Hegemony*. London: Routledge.

Cohen, N., 2015. 'The Purple Revolution: The Year that Changed Everything Review', *The Observer*, 29 March, available at: https://www.theguardian.com/politics/2015/mar/29/purple-revolution-nigel-farage-self-pity-nick-cohen, last accessed 23 April 2018.

Coleman, E. G., 2008. 'The Politics of Rationality: Psychiatric Survivors' Challenge to Psychiatry', in B. da Costa and K. Philip (eds), *TacticalBbiopolitics Art, Activism, and Technoscience*. London: MIT Press, pp. 341–64.

Conley, K., 2011. 'OWS Protester Busted for Allegedly Threatening to Hurl Molotov Cocktails at Macy's', *New York Post*, 17 November, available at: http://nypost.com/2011/11/17/ows-protester-busted-for-allegedly-threatening-to-hurl-molotov-cocktails-at-macys, last accessed 10 January 2017.

Conrad, P., 1992. 'Medicalization and Social Sontrol', *Annual Review of Sociology* 18, pp. 209–32.

Conrad, P., 2007. *The Medicalization of Society*. Baltimore, MD: Johns Hopkins University Press.

Conrad, P., Bandini, J. and Vasquez, A., 2016. 'Illness and the Internet: From Private to Public Experience', *Health* 20(1), pp. 22–32.

Conservative Woman, The, 2016. 'Lefty lunacy: Precious Dons get Brexit Counselling', *The Conservative Woman*, 5 December, available at:

http://www.conservativewoman.co.uk/lefty-lunacy-precious-dons-get-brexit-counselling, last accessed 14 April 2017.

Cooper, D., 1980. *The Language of Madness*. Harmondsworth: Penguin.

Cooper, K., 2015. 'The Psychology of Voting: An Emotional Matter?. *BBC News*, 6 May, available at: http://www.bbc.co.uk/news/election-2015-32537661, last accessed 7 February 2017.

Court, E., 2016. 'The Real Brexit Winners? British Therapists', *MarketWatch*, available at: http://www.marketwatch.com/story/the-real-brexit-winners-british-therapists-2016-07-06/print, last accessed 8 December 2016.

Crace, M., 2017. *I, Maybot*. London: Guardian Faber.

Cresswell, M. and Spandler, H., 2016. 'Solidarities and Tensions in Mental Health Politics: Mad Studies and Psychopolitics', *Critical and Radical Social Work* 4(3), 357–73.

Crichton, P., Carel, H., and Kidd, I. J., 2016. 'Epistemic Injustice in Psychiatry', *BJPsych Bulletin* 41(2), pp. 1–6.

Crimp, D., 1989. 'Mourning and Militancy', *October* 51, pp. 3–18.

Crossley, N., 2006. *Contesting Psychiatry*. New York: Routledge.

CrowdTangle Team, 2020. *CrowdTangle*. Facebook, Menlo Park, California: 1580078, 1580093.

Cullen, M., 2016a. 'Coping with Brexit', *YouTube.com*, 5 July, available at: https://www.youtube.com/watch?v=gXvUBu4UUKI, last accessed 12 December 2016.

Cullen, M., 2016b. 'How it Works', *Unchain Your Mind*, available at: http://unchainyourmind.co.uk/how-it-works, last accessed 12 December 2016.

Cvetkovich, A., 2012. *Depression: A Public Feeling*. London: Duke University Press.

Dahl, R., 1957. 'The Concept of Power', *Behavioral Science* 2(3), pp. 201–15.

Daily Express, 2016. 'Poor Lambs! After Trigger Warnings and Safe Spaces Students Now Depressed over Brexit', *Daily Express*, 29 June, available at: https://www.express.co.uk/news/uk/684590/Brexit-student-depression-young-people-protest-Remain-free-movement-immigration-Twitter, last accessed 7 December 2016.

Daily Mail, 2013. '26 Cases of Attempted Suicide Here Every Day', *Daily Mail*, 6 September, p. 17.

Dallmayr, F., 2011. *The Promise of Democracy*. New York: State University of New York Press.

Daly, G., 2013. 'Savouring the Secret Ingredient', *Sunday Times*, 14 July, p. 6.

d'Ancona, M., 2016. 'Even if Cameron Seals the Deal, Tories Will be Divided over Europe', *London Evening Standard*, 17 February, p. 14.

Davies, C., 2011. 'Occupy London Protest Continues into Second Day, *The Guardian*, 16 October, available at: https://www.theguardian.

com/uk/2011/oct/16/occupy-london-protest-second-day, last accessed 7 December 2016.

Davies, J., 2012. 'Label Jars, Not People', *New Scientist*, 16 May, available at: https://www.newscientist.com/article/mg21428653.700-label-jars-not-people-lobbying-against-the-shrinks, last accessed 26 September 2018.

Davies, W., 2015. *The Happiness Industry*. London: Verso.

Davies, W., 2020. *Nervous states*. London: Vintage.

Davis, J. E., 2010. 'Medicalization, Social Control, and the Relief of Suffering', in W. C. Cockerham (ed.), *The Wew Blackwell Companion to Medical Sociology*. Oxford: Wiley-Blackwell, pp. 211–41.

Deacon, L., 2016. 'Students "Depressed" and "Traumatised" by Brexit Say They Will Fail Exams', *Breitbart*, 1 July, available at: http://www.breitbart.com/london/2016/07/01/students-depressed-traumatised-brexit-say-will-fail-exams, last accessed 9 December 2016.

Dean, J., 2014. 'Tales of the Apolitical', *Political Studies* 62(2), pp. 452–67.

Deegan, G., 2003. 'Discovering Recovery', *Psychiatric Rehabilitation Journal* 26(4), pp. 368–76.

Degerman, D., 2018. 'Anger and Forgiveness: Resentment, Generosity, and Justice', *Contemporary Political Theory* 17(1) (suppl.), pp. 9–12.

Degerman, D., 2019a. 'Within the Heart's Darkness: The Role of Emotions in Arendt's Political Thought', *European Journal of Political Theory* 18(2), pp. 153–73.

Degerman, D., 2019b. 'Brexit Anxiety: A Case Study in the Medicalization of Dissent', *Critical Review of Social and Political Philosophy* 22(7), pp. 823–40.

Degerman, D., 2020a. 'Introduction: Negative Emotions in Dark Times', *Global Discourse* 10(2/3), pp. 163–8.

Degerman, D., 2020b. 'The Political is Medical Now: Covid-19, Medicalization, and Political Theory', *Theory & Event* 2 (4) (suppl.), S61–S75.

Degerman, D., 2020c. 'Maladjusted to Injustice? Political Agency, Medicalization, and the User/Survivor Movement', *Citizenship Studies* 24(8), pp. 1010–29.

Degerman, D., Flinders, M. and Johnson, M. J., 2020. 'In Defence of Fear: COVID-19, Crises, and Democracy', *Critical Review of Social and Political Philosophy*, available at: https://doi.org/10.1080/13698230.2020.1834744.

Delingpole, J., 2016. 'Why do the Vicious Remain Campaigners Value Emotion Over Reason? *The Spectator*, 21 May, available at: https://www.spectator.co.uk/2016/05/why-are-remain-campaigners-so-vicious-and-rude, last accessed 13 April 2017.

Demertzis, N. (ed.), 2013. *Emotions in Politics*. New York: Palgrave.

Department for Business, Energy and Strategy, 2017. *Trade Union Membership 2016*. London: Department for Business, Energy and Strategy.

Department of Health, 1999. *National Service Framework for Mental Health*. London: HMSO.

Department of Health, 2011. *No Health Without Mental Health*. London: HMSO.

Department of Health, 2012. *Liberating the NHS: No Decision About Me, Without Me*. London: HMSO.

De Vos, J., 2013. *Psychologization and the Subject of Late Modernity*. Basingstoke: Palgrave Macmillan.

De Vos, J., 2016. *The Metamorphoses of the Brain*. Basingstoke: Palgrave Macmillan.

Dixon, T., 2015. *Weeping Britannia*. Oxford: Oxford University Press.

Dolan, F. M., 2005. 'The Paradoxical Liberty of Bio-power: Hannah Arendt and Michel Foucault on Modern Politics', *Philosophy & Social Criticism* 31(3), pp. 369–80.

Duffy, F., 2013. 'I Hear Voices in My Head', *Daily Express*, 31 December, available at: https://www.express.co.uk/life-style/health/451252/I-hear-voices-in-my-head-How-a-mental-health-nurse-helps-others-live-with-the-condition, last accessed 8 June 2017.

Döring, S. A., 2010. 'Why be Emotional?' in P. Goldie (ed.), *The Oxford Handbook of Philosophy of Emotion*. Oxford: Oxford University Press, pp. 283–302.

Driver, S., Hensby, A. and Sibthorpe, J., 2012. 'The Shock of the New? Democratic Narratives and Political Agency', *Policy Studies* 33(2), 159–72.

Economist, The, 2016. 'Schumpeter: Their Eyes on Albion', *The Economist*, 11 June, available at: http://www.economist.com/news/business/21700382-most-european-bosses-are-twitchy-about-brexit-few-spy-opportunity-their-eyes-albion, last accessed 13 April 2017.

Earl, C., 2018. *Spaces of Political Pedagogy*. London: Routledge.

Earp, B., Sandberg, A. and Savulescu, J. 2015. 'The Medicalization of Love', *Cambridge Quarterly of Healthcare Ethics* 24(3), pp. 323–36.

Ehrenreich, B., 2009. *Smile or Die: How Positive Thinking Fooled America and the World*. London: Granta.

Eklundh, E., 2019. *Emotions, Protest, Democracy*. Abingdon: Routledge.

Ekman, P., 1999. 'Basic Emotions', in T. Dalgleish and M. Power, *Handbook of Cognition and Emotion*. London: John Wiley, pp. 45–60.

Elliott, M., 2016. 'Why Britain Will Choose the Safer Option and Vote Leave', *Open Democracy*, 8 March, available at: https://www.opendemocracy.net/brexitdivisions/matthew-elliott/why-britain-will-choose-safer-option-and-vote-leave, last accessed 13 April 2017.

Elpidorou, A. and Freeman, L., 2015. 'Affectivity in Heidegger I: Moods and Emotions', *Being and Time. Philosophy Compass* 10, pp. 661–71.

Eng, D. L. and Han, S., 2003. 'A Dialogue on Racial Melancholia', in D. L. Eng and D. Kazanjian (eds), *Loss: The Politics of Mourning*. London: University of California Press, pp. 343–71.

Eng, D. L. and Kazanjian, D. (eds), 2003a. *Loss: The Politics of Mourning*. London: University of California Press.

Eng, D. L. and Kazanjian, D., 2003b. 'Introduction: Mourning Remains, in D. L. Eng and D. Kazanjian (eds), *Loss: The Politics of Mourning*. London: University of California Press, pp. 1–28.

Enroth, H., 2017. 'Fear as a Political Factor', *International Political Sociology* 11(1), pp. 55–72.

Evanspritchard, A., 2016. 'Irritation and Anger May Lead to Hasty Choice', *Daily Telegraph*, 6 June, p. 1.

Fadus, M. C., Ginsburg, K. R., Sobowale, K., Halliday-Boykinds, C. A., Bryant, B. E., Gray, K. M. and Squeglia, L. M., 2020. 'Unconscious Bias and the Diagnosis of Disruptive Behavior Disorders and ADHD in African American and Hispanic Youth', *Academic Psychiatry* 44, pp. 95–102.

Fasick, K., 2011. 'Deranged Homeless Man goes on Violent Rampage in Zuccotti Park', *New York Post*, 4 November, available at: http://nypost.com/2011/11/04/deranged-homeless-man-goes-on-violent-rampage-in-zuccotti-park, last accessed 5 January 2017.

Feldman, R. H., 2007. 'Introduction', in J. Kohn and R. H, Feldman (eds), *The Jewish Writings*. New York: Schocken.

Feldman Barret, L., 2017. *How Emotions are Made*. New York: Houghton Mifflin Harcourt.

Fenton, J. K., 2015. '"Anyone Can be Angry, That's Easy": A Normative Account of Anti-corporate Anger', *Business & Professional Ethics Journal* 34(3), pp. 329–51.

Ferry, L. and Kingston, R. (eds), 2008. *Bringing the Passions Back In: The Emotions in Political Philosophy*. Vancouver: UBC Press.

Fiedler, T., 2011. 'Occupy Wall Street: How Should it be Covered Now? *The New York Times*, 4 November, available at: https://publiceditor.blogs.nytimes.com/2011/11/04/occupy-wall-street-how-should-it-be-covered-now, last accessed 12 April 2017.

Financial Times, 2016. 'Britain Should Vote to Stay in the EU', *Financial Times*, 15 June, available at: https://www.ft.com/content/3748166e-3151-11e6-ad39-3fee5ffe5b5b.

Finlay W. M. L., 2010. 'Pathologizing Dissent: Identity Politics, Zionism and the "Self-Hating" Jew', *British Journal of Social Psychology* 44(2), pp. 201–22.

Fisher, M., 2009. *Capitalist Realism*. Winchester: Zero Books.

Fisher, P., 2002. *The Vehement Passions*. Princeton, NJ: Princeton University Press.

Fitzpatrick, M., 2016. 'Why You Can Make Your GP Feel Dizzy', *Daily Telegraph*, 27 July, p. 18.

Ford, R. and M. Goodwin, 2014a. *Revolt on the Right: Explaining the Support for the Radical Right in Britain*. London: Routledge.

Ford, R. and Goodwin, M., 2014b. 'Understanding UKIP: Identity, Social Change and the Left Behind', *Political Quarterly* 85(3), pp. 277–84.

Jennings, W., Stoker, G., Clarke, N. and Moss, J., 2014. 'Political Disaffection is Rising, and Driving UKIP Support', *YouGov*, 29 October, available at: https://yougov.co.uk/topics/politics/articles-reports/2014/10/29/political-disaffection-not-new-it-rising-and-drivi.

Foster, E. A., Kerr, P. and Byrne, C., 2014. 'Rolling Back to Roll Forward: Depoliticisation and the Extension of Government', *Policy & Politics* 42(2), pp. 225–41.

Foucault, M., 1977. *Discipline and Punish*, trans. A. Sheridan. New York: Vintage.

Foucault, M., [1976] 1980. 'Two Lectures', in C. Gordon (ed.), *Power/Knowledge: Selected Interviews and Other Writings 1972–1977*, trans. C. Gordon. New York: Pantheon.

Foucault, M., [1965] 1988. *Madness and Civilization*. New York: Vintage.

Foucault, M., 1991. 'Governmentality', in G. Burchell, C. Gordon and P. Miller (eds), *The Foucault Effect: Studies in Governmentality*. Chicago: University of Chicago Press, pp. 87–104.

Foucault, M., [1976] 2000. 'Truth and Power', in J. D. Faubion (ed.), *Power: Essential Works of Foucault 1954–1984*, vol. 3, trans. C. Lazzeri. London: Penguin.

Foucault, M., [1973] 2003a. *The Birth of the Clinic*, trans. A. Sheridan. London: Routledge.

Foucault, M., 2003b. *'Society Must be Defended': Lectures at the Collège de France 1975–1976*, ed. M. Bertani and A. Fontana, trans. D. Macey. New York: Picador.

Foucault, M., [1961] 2006a. *History of Madness*, trans. J. Murphy and J. Khalfa. London: Routledge.

Foucault, M., 2006b. *Psychiatric Power: Lectures at the Collège de France, 1973–1974*, trans. G. Burchell. New York: Palgrave Macmillan.

Franklin, P., 2014. 'UKIP Derangement Disorder: Time for a Second Opinion', *Conservative Home*, 5 May, available at: https://www.conservativehome.com/the-deep-end/2014/05/ukip-derangement-disorder-time-for-a-second-opinion.html, last accessed 7 February 2017.

Fraser, N., 1981. 'Foucault on Modern Power: Empirical Insights and Normative Confusions', *PRAXIS International* (3), pp. 272–87.

Fraser, N., 1990. 'Rethinking the Public Sphere: A Contribution to the Critique of Actually Existing Democracy', *Social Text* 25/26, pp. 560–80.

Freeman, J., 1973. 'The Origins of the Women's Liberation Movement', *American Journal of Sociology* 78(4), 792–811.

Fricker, M., 2007. *Epistemic Injustice*. Oxford: Oxford University Press.

Friedman, M., 2012. 'Creativity and Madness: Are They Inherently Linked?' *Huffpost*, 5 April, available at: https://huffpost.com/us/entry/1463887, last accessed 20 April 2018.

Friel, J., 2011. 'John McCarthy was Told He had Motor Neurone Disease Just after Doctors Removed a Cancer', *Daily Mail,* 17 September, p. 22.

Freud, S., [1917] 1957. 'Mourning and Melancholia', in *The Complete Psychological Works of Sigmund Freud*, vol. XIV, ed. and trans. J, Strachey. London: Hogarth, pp. 243–58.

Frye, M., 1983. *The Politics of Reality*. Freedom: Crossing Press.

Furedi, F., 2018. *How Fear Works*. London: Bloomsbury.

Gallegos, F., 2021. 'Affective Injustice and Fundamental Affective Goods', *Journal of Social Philosophy*, available at: https://doi.org/10.1111/josp.12428.

Gandhi, M., [1920] 1999. 'Speech on Non-co-operation Resolution, Calcutta Congress', in *The Collected Works of Mahatma Gandhi*, vol. 21. New Delhi: Publications Division Government of India, available at: http://gandhiashramsevagram.org/Gandhi-literature/mahatma-gandhi-collected-works-volume-21.pdf, last accessed 20 August 2018.

Gartner, J. and Buser, S., 2018. *Rocket Man: Nuclear Madness and the Mind of Donald Trump*. Ashville, NC: Chiron.

Gawlewicz, A. and Sotkasiira, T., 2020. 'Revisiting Geographies of Temporalities: The Significance of Time in Migrant Responses to Brexit', *Population, Space, and Place*, 26 (1), e2275.

Gilman, S. L. and Thomas, J. M., 2016. *Are Racists Crazy?* New York: New York University Press

Gilroy, P., 2005a. 'Why Harry's Disoriented about Empire', *The Guardian*, 18 January, p. 20.

Gilroy, P., 2005b. *Postcolonial Melancholia*. New York: Columbia University Press.

Ginsborg, P. and Labate, S., 2019. *Passion and Politics*. Cambridge: Polity.

Gladstone J. A. and Tilly, C., 2001. 'Threat (and Opportunity): Popular Action and State Response in the Dynamics of Contentious Action', in R. R. Aminzade, J. A. Goldstone, D. McAdam, E. J. Perry, W. H. Sewell, S. Tarrow and C. Tilley (eds), *Silence and Voice in the Study of Contentious Politics*. Cambridge: Cambridge University Press, pp. 179–94.

Glaser, G., 2008. '"Mad Pride" Fights a Stigma', *The New York Times*, 11 May, p. ST1.

Gledhill, R., 2011. '"Jesus Might Not be on the Protesters' Side," Archbishop Suggests', *The Times*, 6 December, p. 14.

Goodwin, J., Jasper, J. M. and Poletta, F., 2001. 'Introduction: Why Emotions Matter', in J. Goodwin, J. M. Jasper and F. Poletta (eds), *Passionate Politics*. Chicago: University of Chicago Press, pp. 1–25.

Goodwin, M. and Milazzo, C., 2015. *UKIP: Inside the Campaign to Redraw the Map of British Politics*. Oxford: Oxford University Press.

Gorman, R., Saini, A., Tam, L., Udegbe, O. and Usar., O., 2013. 'Mad People of Colour: A Manifesto', *Asylum* 20(4), 27.

Gould, D., 2001. 'Rock the Boat, Don't Rock the Boat, Baby: Ambivalence and the Emergence of Militant AIDS Activism', in J. Goodwin, J. M. Jasper and F. Poletta (eds), *Passionate Politics*. Chicago: University of Chicago Press, pp. 135–57.

Gould, D., 2010. 'On Affect and Protest', in J. Staiger, A. Cvetkovich and A. Reynolds (eds), *Political Emotions*. London: Routledge, pp. 18–34.

Gould, D., 2012. 'Political Despair', in S. Thompson and P. Hoggett (eds), *Politics and the Emotions*. London: Bloomsbury, pp. 95–112.

Grace, M. and Kemp, J., 2011a. 'Molotov Madman is Out He Vowed to Burn Store but is Free & in Zuccotti', *Daily News*, 23 November, p. 6.

Grace, M. and Kemp, J., 2011b. 'OWS Bails Out One of their Own Charged with Swiping Cop Hat, Sprung by Pals', *Daily News*, 24 November, p. 14.

Greif, M., 2011. 'Drumming in Circles', in A. Taylor et al. (eds), *Occupy! Scenes from Occupied America*. London: Verso, pp. 55–62.

Grossman-Kahn, R., 2021. 'Beyond the Rubble of Lake Street: Minds in Crisis in a City in Crisis', *New England Journal of Medicine* 384, pp. 1286–7.

Guma, T. and Jones, R. D., 2018. '"Where are We Going to Go Now?" European Union Migrants' Experiences of Hostility, Anxiety, and (non-) Belonging during Brexit', *Population, Space, and Place* 25(1), e2198.

Hacking, I., 1986. 'Making Up People', in T. Heller, M. Sosna and D. Wellbery (eds), *Reconstructing Individualism*. Stanford, CA: Stanford University Press, pp. 222–36.

Haidt, J., 2012. *The Righteous Mind*. London: Penguin.

Hall, C., 2005. *The Trouble with Passion*. New York: Routledge.

Hampson, R., 2011. '"Occupiers" Not Cut from the Same Cloth', *USA Today*, 28 November, available at: http://usatoday30.usatoday.com/news/nation/story/2011-11-27/occupy-wall-street-protesters-defy-simple-description/51429518/1, last accessed 10 January 2017.

Han, B-C., 2017. *Psychopolitics*. London: Verso.

Hannan, D., 2011. '"March for the Alternative"? WHAT Alternative?' *Daily Telegraph*, 26 March, available at: https://bucf.wordpress.com/2011/03/26/a-word-from-mr-hannan, last accessed 12 January 2017.

Harcourt, B. E. 2013a. 'Political Disobedience', in *Occupy: Three Inquiries in Disobedience*. Chicago: University of Chicago Press, pp. 45–92.

Harcourt, B. E. 2013b. 'Introduction', in *Occupy: Three Inquiries in Disobedience*. Chicago: University of Chicago Press, pp. vii–xv.

Harper, D. and Speed, E., 2012. 'Uncovering Recovery: The Resistible Rise of Recovery and Resilience', *Studies in Social Justice* 6(1), pp. 9–25.

Harrington, T. and Dreier, H., 2011. 'Occupy Oakland Protesters to Join Occupy Cal Action Tuesday', *Oakland Tribune*, 14 November, available at: http://search.proquest.com/docview/903801689?accountid=11979, last accessed 10 January 2017.

Harris, J., 2012. 'Occupy London: What Went Wrong?' *The Guardian*, 13 February, available at: https://www.theguardian.com/commentisfree/2012/feb/13/occupy-london-what-went-wrong, last accessed 7 December 2016.

Harris, J., 2014. 'Forget about the Money'. *The Guardian*, 11 January, p. 30.

Havis, D. and Mosko, M., 2019. 'Managing Individuals and Populations through Psychiatric Classification', in Ş. Tekin and R. Bluhm (eds.). *The

Bloomsbury Companion to Philosophy of Psychiatry. London: Bloomsbury, pp. 391–412.

Hearing Voices Network, 2019. 'Our Values', Hearing Voices Network, available at: http://www.hearing-voices.org/about-us/hvn-values, last accessed 24 November 2019.

Heffer, G., 2016. 'Now Even Top Labour MP Andy Burnham Admits: I'm Betting on Brexit', *Daily Express*, 14 March.

Heins, V., 2007. 'Reasons of the Heart: Weber and Arendt on Emotion in Politics', *European Legacy* 12, pp. 715–28.

Henderson, M., 2008. 'Trust Me, I'm Sincere', *The Times*, 5 November, p. 28.

Higgins, K. W., 2018. 'National Belonging post-Referendum: Britons Living in other EU Member States Respond to "Brexit"', *Area* 51(2), pp. 277–84.

Hilpern, K., 2007. 'How I Tamed the Voices in My Head', *The Independent*, 6 March, p. 8.

Hirschman, A. O., 1977. *The Passions and the Interests*. Princeton, NJ: Princeton University Press.

Hobolt, S. B., 2016. 'The Brexit Vote: A Divided Nation, A Divided Continent', *Journal of European Social Policy* 23(9), pp. 1259–77.

Hobolt, S. B., Leeper, T. J. and Tilley, J., 2020. 'Divided by the Vote: Affective Polarization in the Wake of the Brexit Referendum', *British Journal of Political Science*, available at: https://doi.org/10.1017/S0007123420000125.

Holehouse, M., 2012. '"Exhausted" St Paul's Protesters Plead for Back-up', *Daily Telegraph*, 13 February, p. 13.

Holmes, M., 2004. 'Feeling beyond Rules: Politicizing the Sociology of Emotion and Anger in Feminist Politics', *European Journal of Social Theory* 7(2), pp. 209–27.

Holmes, M., 2012. 'Building on a Firm Foundation of Tolerance and Love? Emotional Reflexivity in Feminist Political Processes', in S. Thompson and P. Hoggett (eds), *Politics and the Emotions*. London: Bloomsbury, pp. 115–38.

Holst-Warhaft, G., 2000. *The Cue for Passion*. Cambridge, MA: Harvard University Press.

Honig, B., 1995. 'Towards an Agonistic Feminism: Hannah Arendt and the Politics of Identity', in B. Honig (ed.), *Feminist Interpretations of Hannah Arendt*. University Park, PA: Penn State University Press, pp. 135–66.

Honig, B., 2013. *Antigone, Interrupted*. Cambridge: Cambridge University Press.

Honig, B., 2017. *Public Things*. New York: Fordham University Press.

Honohan, I., 2002. *Civic Republicanism*. London: Routledge.

Honneth, A., 1996. 'Pathologies of the Social: The Past and Present of Social Philosophy', trans. J. Swindal in D. Rasmussen (ed.), *The Handbook of Critical Theory*. Oxford: Blackwell, pp. 369–98.

Hope, C., 2012. 'Some Tories are "Loonies, Fruitcakes and Closet Racists", says Michael Fabricant MP', *Daily Telegraph*, 26 November, available at: http://www.telegraph.co.uk/news/politics/conservative/9703847/Some-Tories-are-loonies-fruitcakes-and-closet-racists-says-Michael-Fabricant-MP.html, last accessed 30 January 2017.

Horwitz, A. V., 2015. 'How Did Everyone Get Diagnosed with Major Depressive Disorder?' *Perspectives in Biology and Medicine* 58(1), pp. 105–19.

Horwitz, A. V. and Wakefield, J. C., 2007. *The Loss of Sadness*. Oxford: Oxford University Press.

Horwitz, A. V. and Wakefield, J. C., 2012. *All We Have to Fear*. New York: Oxford University Press.

Howell, A. and Voronka, J., 2012. 'Introduction: The Politics of Resilience and Recovery in Mental Health Care', *Studies in Social Justice* 6(1), pp. 1–7.

Hughes, K., 2016. 'Psychology', *Mail on Sunday*, 1 May, p. 38.

Huhne, C., 2014. 'A Vision of a Better Yesterday won't give Farage the Future', *The Guardian*, 31 March, p. 28.

Hyland, I., 2015. 'Meet the Ukippers Reveals a Circus Full of the Freaks of Casual Racism', *Mirror*, 23 February, available at: https://www.mirror.co.uk/tv/tv-news/meet-ukippers-reveals-circus-full-5218695, last accessed 1 July 2017.

Hyvönen, A-E., 2016. 'Political Action beyond Resistance: Arendt and "Revolutionary Spirit" in Egypt', *Redescriptions* 19(2), pp. 191–213.

Illouz, E., 2007. *Cold Intimacies*. Cambridge: Polity.

Ipsos MORI, 2006. *Issues Index: 1997–2006*, available at: https://www.ipsos.com/ipsos-mori/en-uk/issues-index-1997-2006, last accessed 7 July 2017.

Isaac, J., 2006. 'Oases in the Desert: Hannah Arendt on Democratic Politics', in G. Williams (ed.), *Hannah Arendt: Critical Assessments*, vol. II. London: Routledge, pp. 130–54.

Jackson, C., 2008. 'Mad Pride and Prejudices', *The Guardian*, 3 September, p. 7.

Jackson, J., 2017. 'Patronizing Depression: Epistemic Injustice, Stigmatizing Attitudes, and the Need for Empathy', *Journal of Social Philosophy* 48(3), pp. 359–76.

Jacobs, E., 2016. 'Brexit Anxiety Spreads from the City to Homes and Schools', *Financial Times*, 22 June, available at: https://www.ft.com/content/ba3aa5f2-386b-11e6-a780-b48ed7b6126f, last accessed 9 December 2016.

Jaggar, A. M., 1989. 'Love and Knowledge: Emotion in Feminist Epistemology', *Inquiry* 32(2), pp. 151–76.

James, W., 1884. 'What is an Emotion?' *Mind* 9, pp. 188–205.

Jenkins, S., 2016. 'On Brexit, Gender, Age and Political Party Are No Guide as to How We'll Vote', *The Guardian*, 31 March, p. 33.

Johnson, B., 2016. 'Don't be Taken in by Project Fear: Staying in the EU is the Risky Choice', *Daily Telegraph*, 29 February, p. 16.

Johnson, M. J., Flinders, M. and Degerman, D., 2021. 'What Makes for Successful Deployment of Fear during a Crisis?' *Global Discourse* 11(3), pp. 317–28.

Jost, J., Glaser, J., Kruglanski, A. and Sullaway, F., 2003. 'Political Conservatism as Motivated Social Cognition', *Psychological Bulletin* 129(3), pp. 339–75.

Kateb, G., 1984. *Hannah Arendt: Politics, Conscience, Evil*. Totowa, NJ: Rowman & Allanheld.

Kellner, P., 2013. 'How UKIP Voters Compare', *YouGov*, available at: https://yougov.co.uk/topics/politics/articles-reports/2013/03/05/analysis-ukip-voters, last accessed 6 December 2018.

Kelly, T., 2011. 'Cathedral Camp "is a Magnet for Criminals"', *Daily Mail*, 19 December.

Kemp, J., Parascandola, R. and Burke, K., 2011. 'Zuccotti Park Protester Nkrumah Tinsley Arrested after Threatening to Burn Down City', *Daily News*, 16 November, available at: http://www.nydailynews.com/new-york/zuccotti-park-protester-nkrumah-tinsley-arrested-threatening-burn-city-article-1.978770, last accessed 10 January 2017.

Kidd, I. J. and Carel, H., 2017. 'Epistemic Injustice and Illness', *Journal of Applied Philosophy* 34, pp. 172–90.

King, M. L., [1956] 1997. 'The "New Negro" of the South: Behind the Montgomery Story', in C. Carson, S. Burns, S. Carson, D. Powell and P. Holloran (eds), *The Papers of Martin Luther King, Jr.*, vol. III. Berkeley: University of California Press, pp. 280–6.

King, M. L., [1960] 2005. 'Suffering and Faith', in C. Carson, T. Armstrong, S. Carson, A. Clay and K. Taylor (eds), *The Papers of Martin Luther King, Jr.*, vol. V. Los Angeles: University of California Press, pp. 443–4.

Kingston, R., 2011. *Public Passion*. London: McGill-Queen's University Press.

Kinvall, C., 2018. 'Ontological Insecurities and Postcolonial Imaginaries: The Emotional Appeal of Populism', *Humanity & Society* 42(4), pp. 523–43.

Kirsch, M., 2007. 'Voices in Your Head? You May Not be Crazy', *The Times*, 23 January, p. 6.

Klein, S., 2014. '"Fit to Enter the World": Hannah Arendt on Politics, Economics, and the Welfare State', *American Political Science Review* 108(4), pp. 856–9.

Kleres, J. and Wettergren, Å., 2017. 'Fear, Hope, Anger, and Guilt in Climate Activism', *Social Movement Studies* 16(5), pp. 507–19.

Kohn, M., 2013. 'Privatization and Protest: Occupy Wall Street, Occupy Toronto, and the Occupation of Public Space in a Democracy', *Perspectives on Politics* 11(1), pp. 99–110.

Konnoth, C., 2020. 'Medicalization and the New Civil Rights', *Ethics, Medicine & Public Health* 12, 100435.

Krause, S., 2008. *Civil Passions*. Princeton, NJ: Princeton University Press.

Krause, S., 2011. 'Bodies in Action: Corporeal Agency and Democratic Politics', *Political Theory* 39(3), pp. 299–324.

Krause, S., 2013. 'Beyond Non-domination', *Philosophy & Social Criticism* 39(2), pp. 187–208.

Krause, S., 2016. 'Agency', *Political Concepts* 3, available at: http://www.politicalconcepts.org/agency-sharon-krause, last accessed 28 October 2018.

Kristof, N., 2011a. 'America's "Primal Scream"', *The New York Times*, 15 October, available at: http://www.nytimes.com/2011/10/16/opinion/sunday/kristof-americas-primal-scream.html, last accessed 12 April 2017.

Kristof, N., 2011b. 'The Bankers and the Revolutionaries', *The New York Times*, 1 October, available at: http://www.nytimes.com/2011/10/02/opinion/sunday/kristof-the-bankers-and-the-revolutionaries.html, last accessed 12 April 2017.

Krystal, J. H., 2012. 'Dr Marcia Angell and the Illusions of anti-Psychiatry', *Psychiatric Times*, 13 August, available at: http://www.psychiatrictimes.com/articles/dr-marcia-angell-and-illusions-anti-psychiatry.

Kurs, R. and Grinshpoon, A., 2017. 'Vulnerability of Individuals with Mental Disorders to Epistemic Injustice in Both Clinical and Social Domains', *Ethics & Behavior* 28(4), 336–46.

Kurz, E., 2016. 'Will I Become an Outsider? Brexit Anxiety', *Welldoing*, 20 July, available at: https://welldoing.org/article/will-become-outsider-brexit-anxiety, lat accessed 12 December 2016.

Kymlicka, W. and Donaldson, S., 2017. 'Inclusive Citizenship Beyond the Capacity Contract', in A. Shachar, R. Baubock, I. Bloemraad and M. Vink (eds), *The Oxford Handbook of Citizenship*. Oxford: Oxford University Press, pp. 839–60.

Kyratsous, M., and Sanati, A., 2017. 'Epistemic Injustice and Responsibility in Borderline Personality Disorder', *Journal of Evaluation in Clinical Practice* 23(5), pp. 974–80.

LaFollette, H., and Woodruff, M. L., 2015. 'The Righteous Mind: Why Good People are Divided by Politics and Religion', *Philosophical Psychology* 28(3) pp. 452–65.

Lakeman, R., 2010. 'Epistemic Injustice and the Mental Health Service User', *International Journal of Mental Health Nursing* 19(3), 151–3.

Lasch, C., 1991. *The True and Only Heaven*. New York: W. W. Norton.

LeBon, T., 2016. 'Brexit: 5 Stoic Strategies to Help You Cope. Socrates Satisfied', *Wise living with Tim LeBon, London CBT psychotherapist and life coach*, 26 June, available at: http://blog.timlebon.com/2016/06/brexit-5-stoic-strategies-to-help-you.html.

Lee, B. X. (ed.). 2017. *The Dangerous Case of Donald Trump*. New York: St. Martin's Press.

Leeb, C., 2020. 'The Hysteric Rebels: Rethinking Radical Socio-Political Transformation with Foucault and Lacan', *Theory & Event* 23(3), pp. 607–40.

Lepoutre, M., 2018. 'Rage Inside the Machine: Defending the Place of Anger in Democratic Speech', *Politics, Philosophy & Economics* 17(4), pp. 398–426.

Lewis, B., 2006. 'A Mad Fight: Psychiatry and Disability Activism', in L. J. Davis (ed.), *The Disability Studies Reader*. New York: Routledge, pp. 339–52.

Lewis, E., 2008. 'Weary Resignation', *The Guardian,* 12 March, p. 4.

Leys, R., 2017. *The Ascent of Affect.* Chicago: University of Chicago Press.

Lieberman, J. A., 2013. 'DSM-5: Caught between Mental Illness Stigma and Anti-Psychiatry Prejudice', *Scientific American*, 20 May, available at: https://blogs.scientificamerican.com/mind-guest-blog/dsm-5-caught-between-mental-illness-stigma-and-anti-psychiatry-prejudice.

Linklater, A., 2007. 'The Woman Who Ignores Her Voices', *The Guardian*, 8 September, p. 85.

Lock, M., 2004. 'Medicalization and the Naturalization Of Social Control', in C. R. Ember and M. Ember (eds), *Encyclopedia of Medical Anthropology*, vol. 1. New York: Springer Science+Business, pp. 116–24.

Lockett, J., 2016. 'Psychiatrists Reveal Alarming Rise in Number of Patients Seeking Help for "Brexit Anxiety"', *The Sun*, 11 July, available at: https://www.thesun.co.uk/news/1426878/psychiatrists-reveal-alarming-rise-in-number-of-patients-seeking-help-for-brexit-anxiety, last accessed 12 December 2016.

Loidolt, S., 2015. 'Hannah Arendt's Conception of Actualized Plurality', in T. Szanto and D. Moran (eds), *Phenomenology of Sociality*. London: Routledge, pp. 42–55.

Loidolt, S., 2018. *Phenomenology of Plurality.* London: Routledge.

Lorde, A., 2007. *Sister Outsider.* Berkeley, CA: Crossing Press.

Lozada, C., 2020. *What Were We Thinking.* New York: Simon & Schuster.

Lulle, A., Moroşanu, L. and King, R., 2018. 'And Then Came Brexit: Experiences and Future Plans of Young EU Migrants in the London Region', *Population, Space and Place* 24(1), e2122.

Lulle, A., King, R., Dvorakova, V. and Szkudlarek, A., 2019. 'Between Disruptions and Connections: "New" European Union Migrants in the United Kingdom Before and After the Brexit', *Population, Space and Place* 25(1), e2200.

Lupton, D., 1997. 'Foucault and the Medicalisation Critique', in A. Petersen and R. Bunton (eds), *Foucault, Health and Medicine*. London: Routledge, pp. 94–110.

Luxon, N., 2016. 'Beyond Mourning and Melancholia: Nostalgia, Anger and the Challenges of Political Action', *Contemporary Political Theory* 15, 139–59.

Mackay, K., 2011. 'Compounding Conditional Citizenship: To What Extent does Scottish and English Mental Health Law Increase or Diminish Citizenship?. *British Journal of Social Work* 41(5), pp. 931–48.

Mackenzie, M. 2016. 'Switching to Equities Offers Rewards in Face of Summer Shocks', *Financial Times*, 4 June, p. 18.

Maddock, J., 2012. 'Ban Cruel 'Cure' that Damages the Brain', *Sunday Times*, 15 April, p. 16.

Magee, D. 2016. 'How to Recover from Brexit Anxiety', *Welldoing*, 1 July, aailable at: https://welldoing.org/article/how-recover-brexit-anxiety, last accessed 12 December 2016.

Maharawal, M., 2011. 'Standing Up', in A. Taylor et al. (eds), *Occupy!* London: Verso, pp. 34–41.

Mahdawi, A., 2016. 'Disgust: How Donald Trump and Brexit Campaigners Win Votes', *The Guardian*, 21 June, available at: https://www.theguardian.com/politics/commentisfree/2016/jun/21/donald-trump-politics-of-disgust.

Mail on Sunday, 2016. 'If Brexit does Happen, EU is to Blame Too', *Mail on Sunday*, 19 June, p. 21.

Mansbridge, J., 1996. 'Using Power/Fighting Power', in S. Benhabib (ed.), *Democracy and Difference*. Princeton, NJ: Princeton University Press, pp. 46–66.

Mansbridge, J., 2002. 'The Making of Oppositional Consciousness', in J. Mansbridge and A. Morris (eds), *Oppositional Consciousness*. Chicago: University of Chicago Press, pp. 1–19.

Marcus, G. E., 2002. *The Sentimental Citizen*. University Park, PA: Pennsylvania State University Press.

Marcus, G. E., 2021. 'The Rise of Populism: The Politics of Justice, Anger, and Grievance', in J. P. Forgas, W. D. Crano and K. Fiedler (eds), *The Psychology of Populism*. London: Routledge, pp. 81–105.

Marcus, G. E. and Mackuen, M. B., 1993. 'Anxiety, Enthusiasm, and the Vote: The Emotional Underpinnings of Learning and Involvement During Presidential Campaigns', *American Political Science Review* 87(3), pp. 672–85.

Marcus, G., E., Valentino, N. A.,Vasilopoulos, P. and Foucault, M., 2019. 'Applying the Theory of Affective Intelligence to Support for Authoritarian Policies and Parties', *Political Psychology* 40(S1), pp. 109–39.

Mars, B., Heron, J., Kessler, D., Davies, N. M., Martin, R. M., Thomas, K. H. and Gunnell, D., 2017. 'Influences on Antidepressant Prescribing Trends in the UK: 1995–2011', *Social Psychiatry and Psychiatric Epidemiology* 52(2), pp. 193–200.

Markell, P., 2012. 'The Rule of the People: Arendt, *archê*, and Democracy', in S. Benhabib (ed.), *Politics in Dark Times*. Cambridge: Cambridge University Press, pp. 58–82.

Markell, P., 2014. 'The Moment has Passed: Power after Arendt', in R. Coles, M. Reinhardt and G. Shulman (eds), *Radical Future Pasts*. Louisville: University Press of Kentucky, pp. 113–43.

Massumi, B., 1995. 'The Autonomy of Affect', *Cultural Critique* 31(2), pp. 83–109.

Mayes, R. and Horwitz, A. V., 2005. 'DSM-III and the Revolution in the Classification of Mental Illness', *Journal of the History of the Behavioral Sciences* 41(3), pp. 249–67.

McAfee, N., 2015. 'Acting Politically in a Digital Age', in D. Allen and J. S. Light (eds), *From Voice to Influence*. London: University of Chicago Press, pp. 273–92.

McDaid, S., 2010. 'Redefining Empowerment in Mental Health: An Analysis using Hannah Arendt's Power Concept', *Journal of Power* 3(2), pp. 209–25.

McIntosh, L., 2015. 'Cameron will Appeal to "Hearts and Minds" on EU', *The Times*, 30 May, available at: https://www.thetimes.co.uk/article/cameron-will-appeal-to-hearts-and-minds-on-eu-065jrklbwnr, last accessed 29 October 2018.

McIvor, D., 2016. *Mourning in America*. Ithaca, NY: Cornell University Press.

MvIvor, D. W., Hooker, J., Atkins, A., Athanasiou, A. and Shulman, G., 2020. 'Mourning Work: Death and Democracy during a Pandemic', *Contemporary Political Theory*, available at: https://doi.org/10.1057/s41296-020-00421-5.

McManus, S., Bebbington, P., Jenkins, R. and Brugha, T. (eds)., 2016. *Mental Health and Wellbeing in England: Adult Psychiatric Morbidity Survey 2014*. Leeds: NHS Digital.

McNay, L., 2009. 'Self as Enterprise: Dilemmas of Control and Resistance in Foucault's *The Birth of Biopolitics*', *Theory, Culture & Society* 26(6), pp. 55–77.

McNay, L., 2014. *The Misguided Search for the Political*. Cambridge: Polity.

McNay, L., 2016. 'Agency', in L. Disch and M. Hawkesworth (eds), *The Oxford Handbook of Feminist Theory*. Oxford: Oxford University Press, pp. 39–60.

McNerthney, C., 2011. 'Occupy Protester with Miscarriage Claim Investigated Earlier', *Seattle Post Intelligencer*, 25 November, available at: http://www.seattlepi.com/local/article/Occupy-protester-with-miscarriage-claim-2293379.php, last accessed 6 January 2017.

McTague, T., 2018. 'Britain's Middle-class Brexit Anxiety Disorder', *Politico.eu*, 17 August, available at: https://www.politico.eu/article/brexit-anxiety-disorder-britain-middle-class.

McWade, B., 2016. 'Recovery-as-Policy as a Form of Neoliberal State-Making', *Intersectionalities* 5(3), pp. 62–81.

Meet the Ukippers, 2015. [TV documentary], directed by K. Hull, BBC 2, 21 February.

Meijnders, A. L., Midden, C. J. H. and Wilke, H. A. M., 2001. 'Communications about Environmental Risks and Risk-Reducing Behavior: The Impact of Fear on Information Processing', *Journal of Applied Social Psychology* 31, pp. 754–77.

Meltzer, T., 2013. '20 Online Talks to Change Your Life', *The Guardian*, 28 August, p. 6.

Mental Health Foundation, 2017. *Surviving or Thriving?* London: Mental Health Foundation.

Mental Health Foundation, 2020. *How to. . . Support Mental Health at Work*. London: Mental Health Foundation.

Metzl, J., 2009. *The Protest Psychosis*. Boston, MA: Beacon Press.

Mihai, M., 2016. *Negative Emotions and Transitional Justice*. New York: Columbia University Press.

Mikelionis, L., 2016. 'NHS Trust Offers Crybaby Staff post-Brexit Counselling', *Heatstreet*, 29 June, available at: http://heatst.com/world/nhs-trust-offers-crybaby-staff-post-brexit-counseling, last accessed 12 December 2016.

Mills, C. W., 1959. *The Sociological Imagination*. New York: Oxford University Press.

MindFreedom International, 2011. 'Mad Culture, Mad Community, Mad Life', *Asylum* 18(1), pp. 20–1.

Minton, A., 2012. *Ground Control*. London: Penguin.

Mitchell, W. J. T., 2013. Image, space, revolution. *In: Occupy: Three inquiries in disobedience*. Chicago: University of Chicago Press, pp. 93–130.

Mobbs, D., Hagan, C. C., Dalgleish, T., Silston, B. and Prévost, C., 2015. 'The Ecology of Human Fear: Survival Optimization and the Nervous System', *Frontiers in Neuroscience* 9, p. 55.

Moffitt, T. E., Caspi, A., Taylor, A., Kokaua, J., Milne, B. J., Polanczyk, G. and Poulton, R. 2009. 'How Common are Common Mental Disorders? Evidence that Lifetime Prevalence Rates are Doubled by Prospective Versus Retrospective Ascertainment', *Psychological Medicine* 40, pp. 899–909.

Monbiot, G., 2016. 'Neoliberalism is Creating Loneliness;, *The Guardian*, 12 October, available at: https://www.theguardian.com/commentisfree/2016/oct/12/neoliberalism-creating-loneliness-wrenching-society-apart.

Moncrieff, J., 2008. 'Neoliberalism and Biopsychiatry: A Marriage of Convenience', in C. I. Cohen and S Timimi (eds), *Liberatory Psychiatry*. Cambridge: Cambridge University Press, pp. 235–55.

Moncrieff, J., 2010. 'Psychiatric Diagnosis as a Political Device', *Social Theory & Health* 8(4), pp. 370–82.

Montague, M. 2009. 'The Logic, Intentionality, and Phenomenology of Emotion', *Philosophical Studies* 145, pp. 171–92.

Montgomerie, T., 2012. 'UKIP is a Magnet for Unhappy Tory Voters but it's Much, Much More than Europe that's Driving the Dissatisfaction', *Conservative Home*, 18 December, available at: https://www.conservativehome.com/thetorydiary/2012/12/ukipmagnet.html, last accessed 30 January 2017.

Moon, C., 2009. 'Healing Past Violence: Traumatic Assumptions and Therapeutic Interventions in War and Reconciliation', *Journal of Human Rights* 8(1), pp. 71–9.

Mooney, C., 2012. *The Republican Brain*. New York: Wiley.

Moore-Bridger, B. 2016. 'More City Staff Seek Help Since EU Vote', *London Evening Standard*, 29 September, p. 4.

Moran, R., 2011. 'Canadian at OWS Scales 70-foot Sculpture; Calls for Bloomberg Resignation', *American Thinker*, 23 October, available at: http://www.americanthinker.com/blog/2011/10/canadian_at_ows_scales_70_foot_sculpture_calls_for_bloomberg_resignation.html, last accessed 12 January 2017.

Morrow, M., 2013. 'Recovery: Progressive Paradigm or Neoliberal Smoke Screen', in B. A. LeFrancois, R. Menzies and G. Reaume (eds), *Mad Matters*. Toronto: Canadian Scholars' Press, pp. 323–33.

Morrow, M. and Weisser, J., 2012. 'Towards a Social Justice Framework of Mental Health Recovery', *Studies in Social Justice* 6(1), pp. 27–43.

Moss, J., Robinson, E. and Watts, J., 2020. 'Brexit and the Everyday Politics of Emotion: Methodological Lessons from History', *Political Studies* 68(4), pp. 837–56.

Mountain, D. and Shah, P. J., 2008. 'Recovery and the Medical Model', *Advances in Psychiatric Treatment* 14(4), pp. 241–44.

Myers, E., 2008. 'Resisting Foucauldian Ethics: Associative Politics and the Limits of the Care of the Self', *Contemporary Political Theory* 7(2), pp. 125–46.

Nadeau, R., Bélanger, É. and Atikan, E. Ö., 2021. 'Emotions, Cognitions and Moderation: Understanding Losers' Consent in the 2016 Brexit Referendum', *Journal of Elections, Public Opinion and Parties* 31(1), pp. 77–96.

National Survivor User Network, 2019. *NSUN Strategy 2016–2021*, available at: https://www.nsun.org.uk/Handlers/Download.ashx?IDMF=35ab8f55-a028-4b29-827f2701dd1bcb21, last accessed 24 November 2019.

Nelson, D., 2006. 'The Virtues of Heartlessness: Mary McCarthy, Hannah Arendt, and the Anesthetics of Empathy', *American Literary History* 18(1), pp. 86–101.

New York Post, 2011. 'Occupy Wall Street Protester Scales Statue, Says He Won't Come Down until Bloomberg Quits', *Fox News*, 22 October, available at: http://www.foxnews.com/us/2011/10/22/occupy-wall-street-protester-scales-statue-says-wont-come-down-until-bloomberg.html, last accessed 10 January 2017.

New York Times, The, 2011. 'Man Arrested after Video Surfaces of Macy's Bomb Threat', *The New York Times*, 16 November, available at: http://www.nytimes.com/2011/11/17/nyregion/man-arrested-after-video-surfaces-of-macys-bomb-threat.html, last accessed 10 January 2017.

Newbigging, K. and Ridley, J., 2018. 'Epistemic Struggles: The Role of Advocacy in Promoting Epistemic Justice and Rights in Mental Health', *Social Science & Medicine* 219, pp. 36–44.

Newcomb, A., 2011. 'Occupy Wall Street Protester Scales 70-foot Statue', *ABC News*, 22 October, available at: http://abcnews.go.com/Business/protester-scales-sculpture-occupy-wall-street-york/story?id=14792961, last accessed 10 January 2017.

Newcomb, M. J., 2007. 'Totalized Compassion: The (im)Possibilities for Acting Out of Compassion in the Rhetoric of Hannah Arendt', *JAC* 27, pp. 105–33.

Newsweek Staff, 2009. 'The Growing Push for "Mad Pride"', *Newsweek*, 1 May, available at: https://www.newsweek.com/growing-push-mad-pride-79919, last accessed 7 May 2017.

NHS Digital, 2021. 'Detentions under the Mental Health Act', *Gov. uk: Ethnicity Facts and Figures* 11 March, available at: https://www.ethnicity-facts-figures.service.gov.uk/health/mental-health/detentions-under-the-mental-health-act/latest.

Noorani, T., 2013. 'Service User Involvement, Authority and the 'Expert-by-Experience' in Mental Health', *Journal of Political Power* 6(1), pp. 49–68.

Norberg, J., 2010. 'The Political Theory of the Cliché: Hannah Arendt Reading Adolf Eichmann', *Cultural Critique* 76, pp. 74–97.

Nussbaum, M., 2001a. *Women and Human Development*. Cambridge: Cambridge University Press.

Nussbaum, M., 2001b. *Upheavals of Thought*. Cambridge: Cambridge University Press.

Nussbaum, M., 2010. *From Disgust to Humanity*. Oxford: Oxford University Press.

Nussbaum, M., 2014. *Political Emotions*. Cambridge, MA: Harvard University Press.

Nussbaum, M., 2016. *Anger and Forgiveness*. Oxford: Oxford University Press.

Nussbaum, M., 2018. *The Monarchy of Fear*. Oxford: Oxford University Press.

Occupy London, 2011. 'Initial Statement', *Occupy London*, 19 November, available at: https://occupylondon.org.uk/about/statements/initial-statement, last accessed 28 September 2018.

Office for National Statistics [ONS], 2017. *Changes in the Value and Division of Unpaid Volunteering in the UK: 2000 to 2015*. London: Office for National Statistics.

O'Hara, M., 2009. 'Out of the Cuckoo's Nest', *The Guardian*, 18 November, p. 1.

O'Hara, M., 2011. 'Opening the Box on Schizophrenia', *The Guardian*, 6 July, p. 2.

O'Neill, B., 2012. 'Occupy London is now Basically a Holding Camp for the Mentally Ill. It's Time to Call it a Day', *Daily Telegraph: Blogs*, 23 February.

Orbach, S. 2016. 'In Therapy, Everyone Wants to Talk about Brexit', *The Guardian*, 1 July, available at: https://www.theguardian.com/global/2016/jul/01/susie-orbach-in-therapy-everyone-wants-to-talk-about-brexit, last accessed 12 December 2016.

O'Reilly, B., 2011. 'Psychological Makeup of Occupy Wall Street Protestors', *The O'Reilly Factor*, Fox News, 18 October, available at: https://www.youtube.com/watch?v=e4wUKu2G8w0, last accessed 10 January 2017.

Parens, E., 2011. 'On Good and Bad Forms of Medicalization', *Bioethics* 27(1), pp. 28–35.

Parker, 2007. *Revolution in Psychology*. London: Pluto Press.

Parker, I., Harper, D. and Webster, G., 2008. 'Obituary: Other Lives: Terence McLaughlin: Norman Webster', *The Guardian*, 25 January, p. 42.

Parris, M., 2014. 'The Voters are Angry. But They're Also Wrong', *Daily Telegraph*, 24 May, p. 17.

Patterson, O., 1982. *Slavery and Social Death*. Cambridge, MA: Harvard University Press.

Perlin, M. L., 2006. 'International Human Rights and Comparative Mental Disability Law: The Role of Institutional Psychiatry in the Suppression of Political Dissent', *Israel Law Review* 39(3), pp. 69–97.

Peretti-Watel, P. and Moatti, J-P., 2009. *Le principe de prévention*. Paris: Seuil/La république des idées, 2009).

Pettigrove, P., 2012. 'Meekness and "Moral" Anger', *Ethics* 122(2), pp. 341–70.

Pickerill, J. and Krinsky, J., 2012. 'Why does Occupy Matter?' *Social Movement Studies* 11(3/4), pp. 279–87.

Pies, R., 2015. 'The War on Psychiatric Diagnosis', *Psychiatric Times* 32(4), available at: http://www.psychiatrictimes.com/couch-crisis/war-psychiatric-diagnosis.

Pies, R., 2019. 'Debunking the Two Chemical Imbalance Myths, Again', *Psychiatric Times* 36(8), available at: https://www.psychiatrictimes.com/view/debunking-two-chemical-imbalance-myths-again.

Pilgrim, D., 2005. 'Protest and Co-option: The Voice of Mental Health Service Users', in A. Bell and P. Lindley (eds), *Beyond the Water Towers: The Unfinished Revolution in Mental Health Services 1985–2005*. London: Sainsbury Centre for Mental Health.

Pilgrim, D., 2008. '"Recovery" and Current Mental Health Policy', *Chronic Illness* 4(4), pp. 295–304.

Pitkin, H. F., 1998. *The Attack of the Blob*. Chicago: University of Chicago Press.

Pitkin, H. F., 2006. 'Justice: On Relating Private and Public', in G. Williams (ed.), *Hannah Arendt: Critical Assessments*, vol. III. London: Routledge, pp. 214–36.

Piven, F. F. and Minnite, L. C., 2016. 'Poor People's Politics', in D. Brady and L. M. Burton (eds), *The Oxford Handbook of the Social Science of Poverty*. Oxford: Oxford University Press, 751–73.

Plato, 2004. *Republic*, trans. C. D. C. Reeve. Cambridge: Hackett.

PM, 2019. [Radio programme] *BBC Radio 4*, 28 April, available at: https://www.bbc.co.uk/sounds/play/m0003jrh, last accessed on 29 April.

Pool, H., 2015. 'Mourning Emmett Till', *Law, Culture and the Humanities* 11(3), pp. 414–44.

Potter, N., 2004. 'Gender', in J. Radden (ed.), *The Philosophy of Psychiatry: A Companion*. Oxford: Oxford University Press, pp. 237–44.

Potter, N., 2009. *Mapping the Edges and the In-between*. Oxford: Oxford University Press.

Potter, N., 2016. *The Virtue of Defiance and Psychiatric Engagement*. Oxford: Oxford University Press.

Price, C., 2015. *Emotion*. Cambridge: Polity.

Prinz, J., 2004. *Gut Reactions*. Oxford: Oxford University Press.

Private Psychiatry, 2016. 'Brexit and Your Mental Health', *Private Psychiatry*, 23 August, available at: http://www.privatepsychiatry.co.uk/news/brexit-and-your-mental-health, last accessed 16 December 2016.

Protevi, J., 2018. 'The Berserker Rage', in M. Cherry and O. Flanagan (eds), *Moral Psychology of Anger*. New York: Rowman & Littlefield, pp. 139–56.

Prynn, J. 2016. '"Brexit Anxiety" Brings Queue of Patients for Psychiatrists', *London Evening Standard*, pp. 8–9.

Public Health England, 2019. *Guidance: Health Matters: Health and Work*, available at: https://www.gov.uk/government/publications/health-matters-health-and-work/health-matters-health-and-work.

Pupavac, V., 2002. 'Pathologizing Populations and Colonizing Minds: International Psychosocial Programs in Kosovo', *Alternatives* 27(4), pp. 489–511

Rahtz, M., 2014. 'It's Not Just Adult Mental Health Services that are Hurting from Cuts', *The Guardian*, 28 January, p. 29.

Rancière, J., 1999. *Disagreement and Philosophy*, trans. J. Rose. London: University of Minnesota Press.

Rashed, M. A., 2019. *Madness and the Demand for Recognition*. Oxford: Oxford University Press.

Ratcliffe, M., 2015. *Experiences of Depression*. Oxford: Oxford University Press.

Ratcliffe, M., 2016. 'Relating to the Dead: Social Cognition and the Phenomenology of Grief', in T. Szanto and D. Moran (eds), *Phenomenology of Sociality*. London: Routledge.

Ratcliffe, M., 2017. 'Grief and the Unity of Emotion', *Midwest Studies in Philosophy* 41(1), pp. 154–74.

Rawnsley, A., 2014. 'All Three Main Parties are Jittery', *The Observer*, 26 January, p. 41.

Read, C., 2018. Brexit Anxiety Disorder. *The Express*, 20 August. Accessed 3 October 2018. Available at: https://www.express.co.uk/news/politics/1005949/brexit-news-remain-EU-anxiety-disorder-philip-corr-simon-stuart.

Reade, B. 2016. 'Don't Let Shower of Con Artists Win', *Daily Mirror*, 18 June, p. 17.

Recovery in the Bin, 2019. 'About', *Recovery in the Bin*, available at: https:// recoveryinthebin.org, last accessed 24 November 2019.

Reddy, W. M., 2001. *The Navigation of Feeling*. Cambridge: Cambridge University Press.

Reid, S., Hinchliffe, S. and Waterton, J., 2014. *Attitudes to Mental Health in Scotland: Scottish Social Attitudes Survey 2013*. Edinburgh: Scottish Government Social Research.

Richards, B., 2008. 'The Emotional Deficit in Political Communication', in M. Greco and P. Stenner (eds), *Emotions*. Abingdon: Routledge, pp. 361–7.

Richardson, L., Ratcliffe, M., Millar, B. and Byrne, E., 2021. 'The COVID-19 Pandemic and the Bounds of Grief', *Think* 20(57), pp. 89–101.

Rimke, H., 2016. 'Mental and Emotional Distress as a Social Justice Issue', *Studies in Social Justice* 10(1), 4–17.

Robin, C., 2004. *Fear: The History of a Political Idea*. New York: Oxford University Press.

Rose, D., 2014. 'The Mainstreaming of Recovery', *Journal of Mental Health* 23(5), pp. 217–18.

Rose, D., 2015. 'The Contemporary State of Service-user-led Research', *The Lancet Psychiatry* 2, pp. 959–60.

Rose, N., 1996. 'Psychiatry as a Political Science: Advanced Liberalism and the Administration of Risk', *History of the Human Sciences* 9(2), pp. 1–23.

Rose, N., 1998. 'Governing Risky Individuals: The Role of Psychiatry in New Regimes of Control', *Psychiatry, Psychology and Law* 5(2), pp. 177–95.

Rose, N., [1989] 1999a. *Governing the Soul*, 2nd edn. London: Free Association Books.

Rose, N., 1999b. *Powers of Freedom*. Cambridge: Cambridge University Press.

Rose, N., 2006. *The Politics of Life Itself*. Princeton, NJ: Princeton University Press.

Rose, N., 2007. 'Beyond Medicalisation', *The Lancet*, 369 (9562), pp. 700–2.

Rose, N., 2019. *Our Psychiatric Future*. Cambridge: Polity

Rose, N. and Abi-Rached, J., 2013. *Neuro*. Oxford: Princeton University Press.

Rose, N. and Miller, P., 1992. 'Political Power Beyond the State: Problematics of Government', *British Journal of Sociology* 43(2), pp. 173–205.

Rowland, M. 2016. 'Coping with post-Brexit Anxiety', *Mental Health Foundation*, 29 June, available at: https://www.mentalhealth.org.uk/blog/coping-post-brexit-anxiety, last accessed 16 December 2016.

Rowson, J., 2014. 'The UKIP Paradox: Why the Party that Needs to get Serious will Suffer When it Does', *The RSA*, available at: https://www.thersa.org/discover/publications-and-articles/rsa-blogs/2014/03/the-ukip-paradox-why-the-party-that-needs-to-get-serious-will-suffer-when-it-does, last accessed 30 January 2017.

Samnotra, M., 2020. *Worldy Shame*. London: Lexington.

Sanders, D., 2016. 'Dear Deidre I think my . . .', *The Sun*, 7 January, p. 38.

Sanderson, R., 2016. 'Brexit Anxiety: How to Stop Feeling Anxious', *The Mindset Clinic*, 27 June, available at: http://themindsetclinic.co.uk/brexit-anxiety, last accessed 12 December 2016.

Sansone, R. A. and Sansone, L. A. 2011. 'Gender Patterns in Borderline Personality Disorder', *Innovations in Clinical Neuroscience* 8(5), pp. 16–20.

Saxonberg, S., 2013. 'Revolutionary Potential under Soviet-Type Regimes: The Role of Emotions in Explaining Transitions and Non-Transitions', in N. Demertzis (ed.), *Emotions in Politics*. New York: Palgrave, pp. 204–27.

Scarantino, A. and de Sousa, R., 2018. 'Emotion', in E. N. Zalta (ed.), *Stanford Encyclopedia of Philosophy*, available at: https://plato.stanford.edu/entries/emotion.

Schaap, A., 2021. 'Democracy', in P. Gratton and Y. Sari (eds.), *The Bloomsbury Companion to Hannah Arendt*. London: Bloomsbury, pp. 481–92.

Schachter, S. and Singer, I. E., 1962. 'Cognitive, Social, and Physiological Determinants of Emotional State', *Psychological Review* 69, pp. 379–99.

Schama, S. 2016. 'Let Us Write Our Own History and Vote to Remain a Beacon of Tolerance', *Financial Times*, 18 June, p. 11.

Scheff, T., 2013. 'Repression of Emotion: A Danger to Modern Societies?' in N. Demertzis (ed.), *Emotions in Politics*. New York: Palgrave, pp. 84–92.

Schein, R., 2012. 'Whose Occupation? Homelessness and the Politics of Park Encampments', *Social Movement Studies* 11(3/4), pp. 335–41.

Schlesinger, F., 2011. 'Protest Camp is Harming the Homeless, say Charities', *The Times*, 11 November, available at: http://www.thetimes.co.uk/tto/news/uk/article3223150.ece, last accessed 10 January 2017.

Schmitt, E. and Taylor, A., 2011. 'Scenes from an Occupation', in A. Taylor et al. (eds), *Occupy!* London: Verso, pp. 83–6.

Scott, W., 1990. 'PTSD in DSM-III: A Case in the Politics of Diagnosis and Disease', *Social Problems* 37(3), pp. 294–310.

Scull, A., 1991. 'Psychiatry and Social Control in the Nineteenth and Twentieth Centuries', *History of Psychiatry* 2(6), pp. 149–69.

Scull, A., 1992. 'A Failure to Communicate? On the Reception of Foucault's *Histoire de la folie* by Anglo-American Historians', in A. Still and I. Velody (eds), *Rewriting the History of Madness: Studies in Foucault's Histoire de la folie*. London: Routledge, pp. 150–63.

Scull, A., 2009. *Hysteria*. Oxford: Oxford University Press.

Sedgwick, P., 1982. *Psycho Politics*. London: Pluto Press.

Segalov, M., 2015. 'We Went to the UKIP Spring Conference and it was Even More Insane than You'd Imagine', *Vice*, available at: https://www.vice.com/en_uk/article/the-ukip-conference-was-more-insane-than-we-imagined-189, last accessed 3 February 2017.

Seneca, 2010. 'On Anger', trans. R. A. Kaster, in R. A. Kaster and M. C. Nussbaum (eds), *Anger, Mercy, Revenge*. Chicago: University of Chicago Press, pp. 14–96.

Shah, A., 2009. 'Eight Years of Controversy: Has it Made any Difference?' *Psychiatry, Psychology and Law* 16(1), pp. 60–8.

Shaw, C. and Proctor G. I., 2005. 'Women at the Margins: A Critique of the Diagnosis of Borderline Personality Disorder', *Feminism & Psychology* 15(4), pp. 483–90.

Shipman, T., 2014. 'Ukip Chief: I'm Always Sifting out "Lunatics"', *The Sunday Times*, 14 December, available at: http://www.thesundaytimes.co.uk/sto/news/Politics/article1496047.ece, last accessed 3 February 2017.

Shklar, J. N., 1989. 'The Liberalism of Fear', in N. L. Rosenblum (ed.), *Liberalism and the Moral Life*. Cambridge, MA: Harvard University Press, pp. 21–38.

Sholl, J., 2017. 'The Muddle of Medicalization: Pathologizing or Medicalizing?' *Theoretical Medicine and Bioethics* 38(4), pp. 265–78.

Shortall, E., 2009. 'Angry Undercurrent', *Sunday Times*, 13 December, p. 16.

Sieger, K. 2016. 'Coping with Brexit Anxiety', *Between Self and Doubt*, 24 June, available at: https://betweenselfanddoubt.com/brexit-anxiety, last accessed 9 December 2016.

Silva, L. L., 2021. 'Anger and its Desires', *European Journal of Philosophy*, available at: https://doi.org/10.1111/ejop.12628.

Simon, L., 2008. 'Letters to the Editor – Mad Pride', *The New York Times*, 18 May, p. ST10.

Singh, A., 2015. 'Meet the Ukippers: 9 Slightly Terrifying Things We Learned. *Daily Telegraph*, 23 February, available at: https://www.telegraph.co.uk/news/politics/ukip/11429785/Meet-the-Ukippers-9-slightly-terrifying-things-we-learned.html.

Skey, M., 2014. '"How Do You Think I Feel? It's My Country": Belonging, Entitlement and the Politics of Immigration', *Political Quarterly* 85(3), pp. 326–32.

Slack, J. and Peev, G., 2016. 'Now Cameron Warns Brexit would Lead to War and Genocide', *Daily Mail*, 10 May, available at: http://www.dailymail.co.uk/news/article-3580060/Now-Cameron-warns-Brexit-lead-war-genocide-PM-s-extraordinary-intervention-leads-campaigners-accuse-Downing-Street-desperation.html, last accessed 24 January 2022.

Slovenko, R., 2011. 'The DSM in Litigation and Legislation', *Journal of the American Academy of Psychiatry and the Law* 39(6), pp. 6–11.

Smith, D., 2009. 'I Talk Back to the Voices in My Head', *The Guardian*, 4 April, available at: https://www.theguardian.com/lifeandstyle/2009/apr/04/mental-health-health-and-wellbeing, last accessed 26 September 2018.

Smith, V., 2010. 'Dissent in Dark Times: Hannah Arendt on Civil Disobedience and Constitutional Patriotism', in R. Berkowitz, T. Keenan and J. Katz (eds.), *Thinking in Dark Times*. New York: Fordham University Press, pp. 105–14.

Smyth, S., 2016. 'The Fear Factor Fuelling Trump and Brexiteers', *Mail on Sunday*, 12 June, p. 20.

Sokolon, M., 2006. *Political Emotions*. Ithaca, NY: Cornell University Press.

Solnit, R., 2016. *Hope in the Dark*. Canons edn. Edinburgh: Canongate.

Solomon, R. C., [1990] 1995. *A Passion for Justice*. Lanham, MD: Rowman & Littlefield.

Solomon, R. C., [1998] 2003a. 'The Politics of Emotion', in *Not Passion's Slave*. Oxford: Oxford University Press, pp. 143–61.

Solomon, R. C., [2001] 2003b. 'Against Valence ("Positive" and "Negative" Emotions)', in *Not Passion's Slave*. Oxford: Oxford University Press, pp. 162–77.

Solomon, R., 2008. *True to Our feelings: What Our Emotions are Really Telling Us*. Oxford: Oxford University Press.

Srinivasan, A., 2018. 'The Aptness of Anger', *Journal of Political Philosophy* 26(2), pp. 123– 44.

Speakmans, The, 2016. 'Brexit Anxiety', *The Speakmans*, 25 June., available at: http://www.speakman.tv/brexit-anxiety, last accessed 14 December 2016.

Staff Counselling and Psychological Support Service, 2016. *Strategies and Tools to Help Work with Change and Uncertainty*. Leeds: University of Leeds, available at: http://www.leeds.ac.uk/forstaff/download/downloads/id/1373/coping_with_change_and_uncertainty, last accessed 13 April 2017.

Staiger, J., Cvetkovich, A. and Reynolds, A. (eds). 2010. *Political Emotions*. London: Routledge.

Stalley, R. F., 1980. 'The Role of the Doctor: Technician or Statesman?' *Journal of Medical Ethics* 6(1), pp. 19–22.

Standing, G., 2011. *The Precariat*. London: Bloomsbury.

Stearns, P. N., 2006. *American Fear*. London: Routledge.

Stephens, E., 2016. 'Bad Feelings: An Affective Genealogy of Feminism', *Australian Feminist Studies* 30(85), pp. 273–82.

Stephens, P. 2016. 'Brexit: Hard Interests Battle Potent Emotion', *Financial Times*, 22 January, p. 9.

Stevens, J., 2011. 'Occupy Wall Street Protester Scales 70ft Art Sculpture demanding Mayor Bloomberg's Resignation . . . and a Pack of Cigarettes, *Daily Mail*, 23 October, available at: http://www.dailymail.co.uk/news/article-2052387/Occupy-Wall-Street-protester-scales-sculpture-demanding-Mayor-Bloombergs-resignation.html, last accessed 6 January 2017.

Stevens, J. 2016. 'NHS Trust Offers Nurses and Mental Health Carers Free Counselling to Get Over the Referendum Vote', *Daily Mail*, 28 June, available at: http://www.dailymail.co.uk/news/article-3664762/NHS-trust-offers-nurses-mental-health-carers-free-counselling-referendum-vote.html, last accessed 17 December 2016.

Sunday Times, 2012a. 'John McCarthy', *Sunday Times*, 15 January, p. 10.

Sunday Times, 2012b. 'Shock Therapy', *Sunday Times*, 8 April, p. 12.

Sunderland, R. 2016. 'After the Pantomime over Moving their HQ to Hong Kong, HSBC Now Say Brexit would Force Them to Quit for Paris', *Daily Mail*, 19 February, available at: http://www.dailymail.co.uk/money/comment/article-3455127/RUTH-SUNDERLAND-pantomime-moving-HQ-Hong-Kong-HSBC-say-Brexit-force-quit-Paris-cue-world-s-smallest-violin.html, last accessed 13 April 2017.

Swift, S., 2011. 'Hannah Arendt's Tactlessness: Reading Eichmann in Jerusalem', *New Formations* 71, pp. 79–94.

Sylvester, R., 2007. 'Clever, Detailed and Confident, but Where was the Sparkle?' *Daily Telegraph*, 25 September, p. 22.

Sylvester, R., 2013. 'Governments Manage Change. UKIP Fears It', *The Times*, 7 May, p. 23.

Szanto, T. and Slaby, J., 2020. 'Political Emotions', in T. Szanto and H. Landweer (eds), *The Routledge Handbook of Phenomenology of Emotions*. London: Routledge, pp. 478–94.

Szasz, T., [1965] 1984. 'Toward the Therapeutic State', in *The Therapeutic State*. Buffalo, NY: Prometheus Books.

Tappolet, C., 2018. 'Nasty Emotions and the Perception of Values', in C. Tappolet, F. Teroni and A. Konzelmann Ziv (eds), *Shadows of the Soul: Philosophical Perspectives on Negative Emotions*. London: Routledge, pp. 20–9.

Tappolet, C., Teroni, F. and Konzelmann Ziv, A. (eds), 2018. *Shadows of the Soul: Philosophical Perspectives on Negative Emotions*. London: Routledge.

Taussig, M., 2013. 'I'm So Angry I Made a Sign', in *Occupy: Three Inquiries in Disobedience*. Chicago: University of Chicago Press, pp. 3–44.

Taylor, C., 2010. 'Fanon, Foucault, and the Politics of Psychiatry', in E. A. Hoppe and T. Nicholls (eds), *Fanon and the Decolonization of Philosophy*. Lanham, MD: Lexington Books.

von Tevenar, G., 2014. 'Invisibility in Arendt's Public Space', in M. Ure and M. Frost (eds), *The Politics of Compassion*. London: Routledge, pp. 37–50.

Theodossopoulos, D., 2014. 'On De-pathologizing Resistance', *History and Anthropology* 25(4), pp. 415–30.

Thomas, S., 2014. 'Our Political Masters are Horrified by Ukip. Trouble is, the Voters Aren't', *Daily Telegraph*, 17 May, available at: https://search. proquest.com/docview/1525546983?accountid=11979, last accessed 30 January 2017.

Thompson, S. and Hoggett, P. (eds), 2012. *Politics and the Emotions*. London: Bloomsbury.

TNS BRMB, 2015. *Attitudes to Mental Illness 2014*. London: TNS BRMB.

Trivedi, P., 2010. 'A Recovery Approach in Mental Health Services: Transformation, Tokenism or Tyranny?' in T. Basset and T. Stickley (eds), *Voices of Experience: Narratives of Mental Health Survivors*. London: John Wiley, pp. 152–64.

Tyrer, P., 2014. A Comparison of DSM and ICD Classifications of Mental Disorder, *Advances in Psychiatric Treatment* 20(4), pp. 280–5.

University of Nottingham, 2016. 'Responding to Uncertainty: Skills for Well-being', *Nottingham.ac.uk.*, available at: https://training.nottingham.ac.uk/cbs-notts/Guests/GuestCourse.aspx?CourseRef=RESPUNC, last accessed 13 April 2017.

Ure, M. and Frost, M., 2014. 'Introduction', in M. Ure and M. Frost (eds), *The Politics of Compassion*. London: Routledge, pp. 1–17.

Van Voren, R. and Keukens, R., 2015. 'Political Abuse of Psychiatry', in J. Z. Sadler K. W. M. Fulford and W. C. W. van Staden (eds), *The Oxford Handbook of Psychiatric Ethics*. Oxford: Oxford University Press.

Varga, S. and Gallagher, S., 2020. 'Anticipatory-Vicarious Grief: The Anatomy of a Moral Emotion', *The Monist* 103(2), pp. 176–89.

Vasilopoulou, S. and Wagner, S., 2016. 'Emotions to Shape Debates and Decisions in the Upcoming Referendum', *LSE BrexitVote Blog*, 25 February, available at: http://blogs.lse.ac.uk/brexit/2016/02/25/emotions-to-shape-debates-and-decisions-in-the-upcoming-referendum, last accessed 7 December 2016.

Vasilopoulou, S. and Wagner, S., 2020. 'Emotions and Domestic Vote Choice', *Journal of Elections, Public Opinion and Parties*, available at: https://doi.org/10.1080/17457289.2020.1857388.

Vatel, B., Goodfellow, W., Smith, A. L. and Pies, R., 2019. 'Chemical Imbalance? Readers Respond', *Psychiatric Times* 11 September, available at:

https://www.psychiatrictimes.com/view/chemical-imbalance-reader-responds.

Vathi, Z. and Trandafoiu, R., 2020. 'EU Nationals in the UK after BREXIT: Political Engagement through Discursive Awareness, Reflexivity and (In) Action', *Journal of Language and Politics* 19(3), pp. 479–97.

von Hirsch, A. and Shearing, C., 2001. 'Exclusion from Public Space', in A.Von Hirsch, D. Garland and A. Wakefield (eds), *Ethical Perspectives in Situational Crime Prevention*. Oxford: Hart, pp. 77–96.

Villa, D., 1995. *Arendt and Heidegger*. Princeton, NJ: Princeton University Press.

Villa, D., 2008. *Public Freedom*. Princeton, NJ: Princeton University Press.

Vries, C. de and Hoffman, I., 2016. *Fear not Values*. Gütersloh: Bertelsmann Stiftung.

Waldron, J., 2000. 'Arendt's Constitutional Politics', in D. Villa (ed.), *The Cambridge Companion to Hannah Arendt*. Cambridge: Cambridge University Press, pp. 201–19.

Wall Street Journal, 2011. 'Revolting the Masses', *Wall Street Journal*, 21 November, available at: https://www.wsj.com/articles/SB1000142405 2970203699404577044583038468266, last accessed 5 January 2017.

Wall Street Journal, 2014. 'The Definition of Insanity', *Wall Street Journal*, 1 April, p. 14.

Walker, P., 2012. 'Occupy Protesters at London's Finsbury Square Site Face Eviction', *The Guardian*, 11 May, available at: https://www.theguardian.com/uk/2012/may/11/occupy-london-finsbury-square-eviction, last accessed 5 January 2017.

Walters, J., 2011. 'Occupy London: Eviction Bid Cites Desecration, Defecation and Drugs', *The Guardian*, 21 November, available at: https://www.theguardian.com/uk/2011/nov/21/occupy-london-camp-eviction-bid, last accessed 18 January 2017.

Ward, V., 2011. 'St Paul's Cathedral to Reopen on Friday Despite Occupy London Protest Camp', *Daily Telegraph*, 26 October, available at: http://www.telegraph.co.uk/news/religion/8851415/St-Pauls-Cathedral-to-reopen-on-Friday-despite-Occupy-London-protest-camp.html, last accessed 7 January 2017.

Wardrope, A., 2015. 'Medicalization and Epistemic Injustice', *Medicine, Health Care and Philosophy* 18(3), pp. 341–52.

Wardrope, A., 2017. 'Mistaking the Map for the Territory: What Society Does with Medicine', *International Journal of Health Policy and Management* 6(10), pp. 605–7.

Watts, J., 2016. 'The EU Referendum has Caused a Mental Health Crisis', *The Guardian*, 29 June, available at: https://www.theguardian.com/commentisfree/2016/jun/29/eu-referendum-mental-health-vote, last accessed 7 December 2016.

Watts, J., 2017. 'As a Psychologist I See the Fantasy of Neoliberal Values Having a Devastating Effect on Mental Health Treatment', *The Independent*, 4 November, available at: https://www.independent.co.uk/voices/mental-health-treatment-tory-government-nhs-funding-access-work-benefits-a8037331.html.

Westen, D., 2008. *The Political Brain*. New York: PublicAffairs.

Wheatley, E. E., 2005. 'Disciplining Bodies at Risk', *Journal of Sport & Social Issues* 29(2), pp. 198–22.

Whitney, S., 2018, 'Affective Intentionality and Affective Injustice: Merleau-Ponty and Fanon on the Body Schema as a Theory of Affect', *Southern Journal of Philosophy* 56(4), pp. 488–515.

Wilkinson, I. and Kleinman, A., 2016. *A Passion for Society*. Oakland, CA: University of California Press.

Williams, G., 1998. 'Love and Responsibility: A Political Ethic for Hannah Arendt', *Political Studies* 45(5), pp. 937–50.

Williams, R., 2011. 'Rioting is the Choice of Young People with Nothing to Lose', *The Guardian*, 5 December, available at: https://www.theguardian.com/commentisfree/2011/dec/05/reading-riots-nothing-to-lose, last accessed 16 January 2017.

Wodak, R., 2015. *The Politics of Fear*. London: Sage.

Woods, A., Hart, A. and Spandler, H., 2019. 'The Recovery Narrative: Politics and Possibilities of a Genre', *Culture, Medicine, and Psychiatry*, available at: https://doi.org/10.1007/s11013-019-09623-y.

Wouters, C., 2012. 'The Slippery Slope and the Emancipation of Emotions', in S. Thompson and P. Hoggett (eds), *Politics and the Emotions*. New York: Bloomsbury, pp. 199–216.

WPF Therapy, 2016. 'Brexit: Depression in More Ways than One', *WPF Therapy*, 28 June, available at: http://wpf.org.uk/4406-2, last accessed 8 December 2016.

Wright, A. L., 2012. 'Counterpublic Protest and the Purpose of Occupy: Reframing the Discourse of Occupy Wall Street', *Plaza* 2(2), pp. 138–46.

Ussher, J. M., 2013. 'Diagnosing Difficult Women and Pathologising Femininity: Gender Bias in Psychiatric Nosology', *Feminism & Psychology* 23(1), pp. 63–9.

Yates, C., 2019. '"Show Us You Care!" The Gendered Psycho-Politics of Emotion and Women as Political Leaders', *European Journal of Politics and Gender* 2(3), pp. 345–61.

Young, I. M., 2000. *Inclusion and Democracy*. Oxford: Oxford University Press.

Young, I. M., 2001. 'Activist Challenges to Deliberative Democracy', *Political Theory* 29(5), pp. 670–90.

Young-Bruehl, E., 1982. *Hannah Arendt: For the Love of the World*. New Haven, CT: Yale University Press.

Zachar, P., 2014. *A Metaphysics of Psychopathology*. Cambridge, MA: MIT Press.

Zanarini, M. C., Frankenburg, F. R., Reich, D. B., Marino, M. F., Haynes, M. C. and Gunderson, J. G., 1999. 'Violence in the Lives of Adult Borderline Patients', *Journal of Nervous & Mental Disease* 187(2), pp. 65–71.

Zerilli, L., 2005. *Feminism and the Abyss of Freedom*, new edn. Chicago: University of Chicago Press.

Zerilli, L., 2015. 'The Turn to Affect and the Problem of Judgment', *New Literary History* 46(2), pp. 261–86.

Tufekci, Z., 2017. *Twitter and Tear Gas*. New Haven, CT: Yale University Press.

Zola, I., 1972. 'Medicine as an Institution of Social Control', *Sociological Review* 20(4), pp. 487–504.

Index

EU representative:
Easy Access System Europe
Mustamäe tee 50, 10621 Tallinn, Estonia
Gpsr.requests@easproject.com

www.ingramcontent.com/pod-product-compliance
Lightning Source LLC
Chambersburg PA
CBHW071103280326
41928CB00051B/2777